Nationalism in Europe & America

University of North Carolina Press   Chapel Hill

Nationalism in Europe & America

Politics, Cultures, and Identities since 1775

LLOYD KRAMER

© 2011 The University of North Carolina Press

All rights reserved. Designed by Courtney Leigh Baker and set in Arno Pro by IBT. Manufactured in the United States of America. The paper in this book meets the guidelines for permanence and durability of the Committee on Production Guidelines for Book Longevity of the Council on Library Resources. The University of North Carolina Press has been a member of the Green Press Initiative since 2003.

Library of Congress Cataloging-in-Publication Data
Kramer, Lloyd S.
Nationalism in Europe and America : politics, cultures, and identities
since 1775 / Lloyd Kramer.
p. cm.
Includes bibliographical references and index.
ISBN 978-0-8078-3484-8 (cloth : alk. paper)— ISBN 978-0-8078-7200-0
(pbk. : alk. paper)
1. Nationalism—United States—History.
2. Nationalism—Europe—History. 3. Political culture—
United States—History. 4. Political culture—Europe—History.
5. Group identity—United States—History. 6. Group identity
—Europe—History. I. Title.

E169.1.K685 2011
305.800973—dc22
2010052564

cloth   15 14 13 12 11   5 4 3 2 1
paper   15 14 13 12 11   5 4 3 2 1

MIX
Paper from
responsible sources
FSC
www.fsc.org   FSC® C013483

For Kyle Pomeroy Kramer and Renee Pomeroy Kramer

Contents

Illustrations & Maps

Acknowledgments

This book is a much-revised version of a work that originally appeared in 1998. Twayne Publishers produced that book as part of a series entitled Studies in Intellectual and Cultural History (edited by Michael Roth). The earlier edition carried a different title and included only six chapters; the final two chapters of this book are therefore completely new. All other chapters, as well as the introduction and conclusion, have been significantly revised and updated. The bibliography and notes have also been extensively revised to include new scholarship that has emerged over the last fifteen years. There are new maps and numerous new images, and the title has been changed to reflect more accurately the book's expanded contents. I would like to thank Charles Scribner's Sons for releasing all obligations from the former edition.

I would also like to acknowledge the assistance and support of others who helped to make this book possible. Thoughtful, critical-minded students have pushed me to rethink the evolving history of nationalism as we have discussed transnational historical questions in various classes at the University of North Carolina at Chapel Hill (UNC). I particularly remember the emotionally charged discussions in a UNC undergraduate course on nationalism during the fall semester of 2001—a time in which contemporary events gave students a new sense of personal engagement with the historical meaning of nationalism in the United States. Unexpected, complex events provoke each generation to bring new perspectives and questions to the study of the past, which helps to explain why the "teaching" of history is really a process of lifelong learning.

I have benefited greatly from the astute comments of faculty colleagues in UNC's History Department, in the Triangle Area Intellectual History Seminar, and in the Triangle Area French Studies Seminar. The seminars meet regularly at the National Humanities Center in North Carolina's Research Triangle Park, and they provide exceptional opportunities for exchanging ideas and responding to new research. Regular participants in these various seminars—including Don Reid, Jay Smith, Jim Winders, Steven Vincent, Linda Orr, Bill Reddy, Keith Luria, Mary Sheriff, Dan Sherman, Anoush Terjanian, Melissa Bullard, Malachai Hacohen, Anthony LaVopa, Martin Miller, and others too numerous to name— have enriched my understanding of modern history in more ways than I can acknowledge here. I am grateful to all of these colleagues and friends for their encouragement and insights.

I thank Chuck Grench, Jay Mazzocchi, and their talented colleagues at UNC Press who have helped to produce this book. I have also relied on numerous librarians and archivists for assistance in collecting illustrations for this volume (specific institutions are acknowledged in credits for the images); and I thank Bill Nelson for designing the maps. I began to plan a new version of this book when I was a fellow at the National Humanities Center (NHC) in 2002–3. I gained a great deal from the conversations with other NHC fellows and from the extraordinary support of the center's outstanding staff. I have also benefited more recently from the generous support of a Kenan Research Fellowship at UNC and a Chapman Family Fellowship at UNC's Institute for the Arts and Humanities (IAH), both of which made it possible for me to complete this book. The IAH is an active, creative center for interdisciplinary seminars and conferences that have often carried me into new intellectual territories and imaginative communities.

Finally, I thank my wife, Gwynne Pomeroy; my son, Kyle Kramer; and my daughter, Renee Kramer, for the diverse, enriching experiences that I share with each of these special people. I deeply value the knowledge and insights they bring to our unpredictable, ongoing conversations. This book is dedicated to Kyle and Renee, who live with curiosity and imagination amid the transnational cultures of the twenty-first century.

Nationalism & Modern World History

Nationalism has decisively influenced world history for more than two centuries. Although it first developed its distinctive modern characteristics in late eighteenth-century America and Europe, it has spread rapidly across every part of the world, absorbing or intersecting with other ideologies such as romanticism, liberalism, conservatism, socialism, and ancient religions. Nationalist movements and ideologies have helped to reshape modern descriptions of human identity, and they have arguably contributed to more violent conflicts than any other political or ideological force in the contemporary world. Despite frequent predictions of nationalism's impending decline, people everywhere continue to describe their personal lives and social communities in the context of national cultures. There are numerous definitions for the meaning of nationalism, and, as the following chapters will argue, there are multiple layers of nationalist cultures. In the most general terms, however, nationalism can be defined as the widely held belief that people living in particular geographical spaces share distinctive cultural and historical traditions and have the right to live in an independent political state.

This book examines the history of nationalism since the late eighteenth century, focusing on political and cultural themes that constantly reappear in modern nationalist thought. The overall argument therefore emphasizes similarities in the nationalisms of various societies and historical eras. Although the specific claims about national identities or histories differ in each society, the underlying structures of nationalist thought show remarkable continuities across time. All national identities, for example, emerge through repeated descriptions of national cultural differences, national geographical spaces, and the history of famous national events. There are also historical continuities in the inextricable nationalist connections between politics and culture, in the overlap of American and European nationalist themes, in the linkage of national "rights" with individual human rights, in the interplay of "ethnic" and "civic" identities, in the fusion of the "personal" with the "national" in modern families, and in the nationalist opposition to empires from the American Revolution to the anticolonial revolutions after 1945.

The following chapters stress that nationalism has had exceptional historical influence because it has always offered people the emotionally important sense of safely belonging to supportive social groups; this key theme of nationalist thought has been reiterated constantly in many different places around the modern world. Nationalism has entered deeply into the lives of modern people who believe that their personal well-being depends on the well-being of their national state and society. Nobody is born with an innate national identity, however, so the belief in a national selfhood must develop through specific cultural experiences. Children learn their national identities as they grow up in families and other institutions that convey a shared nationality. The history of nationalism therefore becomes also the history of cultural processes that teach people how they are connected to their nations. A collective national identity is linked to each personal identity, and the long lives of nations provide consolation or meaning for the short lives of its individual citizens.

The power of modern nationalist movements has attracted the wide-ranging scholarly attention of social scientists as well as the commentaries of journalists and official policy makers. The vast literature on nationalism can thus overwhelm anyone who sets out to study its history or understand its influence in the contemporary world. Much of this endless writing seeks to explain recent political and economic conflicts, but most accounts of contemporary issues provide little historical or theoretical perspective on the cultural traditions that shape modern nationalist identities. Meanwhile, other analysts in the popular scholarly field of "cultural studies" have produced an extensive theoretical literature on the cultural construction of modern identities. This innovative cultural approach to nationalism emphasizes the importance of languages and symbols in nationalist thought, but, as with the social scientists and journalists, the analysis usually focuses on contemporary issues or drifts into difficult theoretical jargon.

In contrast to most books on contemporary national identities and conflicts, my approach to nationalism focuses especially on the historical emergence of American and European nationalisms in the century after 1775. Although historians have long recognized the importance of this era for the development of nationalist ideas and institutions, the recent scholarly emphasis on the cultural history of collective memories and identities has opened new paths for the study of early nationalist thought. I therefore draw on the methods of cultural history to discuss specific nationalist ideas, writers, and political leaders who helped create the modern meaning of nationalism in the late eighteenth and nineteenth centuries.

The first five chapters of this book examine the common political and cultural themes that have shaped most modern nationalisms—what might be called the deep continuities of nationalist thought. (Chapter 1 also includes sections that summarize various scholarly interpretations and debates about the history of nationalism.) The last three chapters look at some specific examples of how nationalist ideas entered into early American history and influenced the twentieth-century history of global wars, anticolonialism, and powerful national states. Neither the thematic sections nor the overview of modern events can provide comprehensive accounts of all nationalist ideas and conflicts; but each chapter offers a concise introduction to historical issues that still influence national identities, cultures, and conflicts in our own time. Anyone who seeks to understand the history of the modern world must eventually examine the historical development of nationalism because nationalist ideas and aspirations have helped to shape almost all modern cultures, economies, political systems, and wars. Although this book inevitably excludes certain aspects of nationalist thought and important regions of the world, it is designed to give readers a manageable, historical starting point for a wider or more detailed analysis of nationalism's most enduring themes.

Despite the limits of my geographical and chronological framework, I argue that nationalisms in other places and eras tend to replicate, extend, or reshape themes that first emerged in American and European nationalisms. This tendency of all nationalisms to replicate similar cultural assumptions and practices suggests why, as noted earlier, this book emphasizes continuities that reappear in even the most diverse modern societies. All nationalist cultures have asserted a distinctive collective identity through accounts of national difference, and all have claimed to represent the political sovereignty of a specific "people." Nationalists have always created narratives about a shared national history. They have also tried to link their views of the nation to religious traditions, gender identities, and the meanings of family, race, or land. The following chapters explore all of these themes, with particular reference to European and American examples. The history of nationalism suggests important similarities in the transatlantic history of politics and cultures, thereby challenging the once-popular belief in American "exceptionalism." A thematic, Atlantic history of nationalism shows the overlapping arguments for national sovereignty and the shared, quasi-religious conceptions of national sacrifice. The early history of American nationalism encompasses almost all of the important cultural patterns of nationalist identities (including pervasive beliefs in a unique national "mission"), so the American example can tell us a great deal about modern nationalism's emotional messages and political power. The responses to the terrorist attacks of September 11, 2001, provide a notable recent example of nationalism's emotional significance in the United States; and the final chapter of this book suggests how America's "post-9/11" political culture returned to the most enduring components of a long-existing national identity.

America has also become one of the most self-consciously "multicultural" nations, and this theme provides yet another connection between the evolving nationalisms on both sides of the Atlantic. I have noted my interest in the continuities of nationalism, but there are also variations that show how nationalist thought never stays exactly the same. Twentieth-century nationalisms led to the catastrophic human costs of the two world wars and to the unexpected consequences of "national self-determination." Nationalism's history is always open-ended, however, which suggests why the European nation-states could evolve after 1945 into a new, collaborative European Union and the United Nations could provide a new framework for transnational cooperation among post-colonial societies. These examples point to the ways in which nationalism has begun to change in the contemporary world. The modern history of nationalism therefore raises analytical questions that this book invites you to ask about every theme and event it discusses: what has changed and what has stayed the same as nationalist ideas have evolved over the last two centuries?

It is much easier to recognize the nationalist beliefs of other cultures than to see the nationalism in one's own society. We all absorb nationalist ideas through the activities and social networks of our daily lives, though we can rarely recognize the nationalism in these ideas unless they are placed in broader historical frameworks. The historical study of nationalism thus becomes important for a critical understanding of one's own life as well as the lives of others around the world. In this respect, exploring the history of nationalism is like foreign travel because the distancing perspectives offer a new view of the nationalism in our own culture and the nationalist components of our own personal identities.

I have referred to numerous themes that reappear often in the following chapters. These themes can be concisely summarized here as the key points of the book's overall argument: (1) modern nationalism emerged in the late eighteenth-century American and French Revolutions; (2) American and European nationalisms have far more similarities than differences; (3) "civic" (or political) and "ethnic" (or racial) nationalisms often overlap, so these analytical categories should not be viewed as sharp dichotomies; (4) nationalist thought shows remarkable continuities across time; (5) nationalists always make strong claims to defend specific geographical territories, specific historical memories, and the specific right to a sovereign political state; (6) all nationalisms require a constant "cultural education" that teaches people the meaning of their nationality; (7) nationalism connects with deep human emotions (much like religions), expresses strong emotional desires to belong to social groups, and gives emotional meaning to personal sacrifices and death; (8) modern categories of personal identity such as gender, family, and race are connected to collective national identities; (9) all nationalisms construct collective identities by stressing their *differences* from other nations and peoples; (10) nationalist ideas and aspirations have shaped or influenced all of the major wars of modern history; (11) newer forms of multicultural nationalism and transnational institutions have emerged in recent decades to challenge older, more exclusionary aspects of nationalist thought; and (12) despite these transnational tendencies (for example, the European Union), nationalism and nationalist thought retain enormous influence almost everywhere in the modern world.

Each theme in this twelve-point summary raises multiple questions and suggests wider issues in the continuing historical conversation that this book invites you to join. Although all of my themes are therefore debatable, I will argue that historical evidence supports the claims I have enumerated and that these themes explain why nationalism remains the most pervasive political and cultural "ism" in the modern world. Historical study provides one of the essential methods for understanding how nationalism gained this influence, and an analysis of the most powerful, enduring themes in contemporary national cultures shows how many of these nationalist ideas had already emerged in America and Europe by the early nineteenth century.

CHAPTER ONE

The Cultural Meaning of Nationalism

Nationalism became one of the most influential political and cultural forces in the modern world because it gives people deep emotional attachments to large human communities and provides powerful stories to explain the meaning of public and personal lives. Modern people encounter stories about their nations in almost every sphere of their political, social, and economic activities—from election campaigns and tax payments to professional training, military service, and family relationships. Children learn their nationality almost as soon as they learn to talk, and virtually everyone refers to national cultures when they describe personal or group identities: "He is French, she is Russian, they are Japanese, we are Egyptians, I am American," and so on through every part of the world. Nationalism expresses the deep and apparently universal human desire to participate in and identify with social communities, but these identities have only acquired their distinctive nationalist meanings over the last two or three centuries. The history of nationalism thus leads everywhere to the history of modern politics, cultures, and personal identities.

Three stories from the early history of modern nations can introduce us to the cultural influence of nationalism. In September 1776 a twenty-one-year-old man named Nathan Hale was executed by the British army in New York on charges of spying for America's new Continental army. Hale therefore became an early symbol of national sacrifice in the new American nationalism that was emerging in a war for political independence from Britain, and his famous last words—"I only regret that I have but one life to lose for my country"—became a moral lesson for every subsequent American generation.

In April 1792 a soldier in the French army named Claude Joseph Rouget de Lisle sat down near the Rhine River in Strasbourg to write a song about France's just-declared war with Prussia and Austria. Rouget de Lisle completed the song in a day, but its revolutionary call to arms became a permanent expression of French nationalism. "La Marseillaise" (as the song was soon called) resembles Hale's last words in stressing the virtues of sacrifice, and it describes the nation's cause as the highest duty for every citizen:

> Let us go, children of the Fatherland
> Our day of glory has arrived.
> Against us stands tyranny
> The bloody flag is raised;
> the bloody flag is raised.

In the winter of 1807–8, the German philosopher Johann Gottlieb Fichte delivered a series of popular "Addresses to the German Nation" to large audiences in Berlin. Speaking shortly after the French army had taken control of the city, Fichte predicted that a new Germany would arise from this national humiliation. He conceded that the French dominated Europe in 1807, but he offered his audiences the philosophical assurance that decisive German actions would create a different future in which "you will see the German name exalted . . . to the most illustrious among all the peoples, you will see in this nation the regenerator and restorer of the world."[1]

The American spy, French soldier-songwriter, and German philosopher lived in different places, spoke different languages, and advocated different national causes, yet they all contributed the words and exemplary actions for new nationalisms. Representing three social roles that every nationalism requires (martyr, lyricist, prophet), each man stressed the danger of enemies, the need for sacrifice, and the national ideal as an essential component of human identity. Their stories were connected with the revolutions and wars that first produced and expressed the modern ideas of nations and nationalism, and their lives point to the overlapping personal and public identities that have made nationalism so pervasive and powerful in modern world history. More generally, the actions and cultural memories of Hale, Rouget de Lisle, and Fichte exemplify the cultural construction of nationalism—the ubiquitous historical process that is the subject of this book. Nationalism has evolved in very different places, political systems, and historical contexts, but all nationalists assume that each person's life is inextricably connected to the history, culture, land, language, and traditions that (theoretically) form a coherent national society and state.

Unknown artist, *The Execution of Captain Hale*, photo engraving. The weeping woman and the two children suggest how Nathan Hale's death was portrayed in history books as an exemplary sacrifice for the American nation and a patriotic model for later generations. (In Benson J. Lossing's popular illustrated book, *Lossing's History of the United States* 3:887 [New York, 1909])

Nationalism and Modernity

Although nationalist movements frequently claim to represent long-existing cultural or ethnic groups, most historians argue that modern nationalist ideas and political campaigns did not develop before the late eighteenth century. This historical argument therefore challenges the typical nationalist's belief in the very old or even primordial existence of national identities. In contrast to the nationalists' emphasis on an enduring national spirit or essence that reappears constantly in the nation's history, most historians stress the influential cultural work of intellectuals and political activists who created the modern stories of national heroes, popular folklore, and shared traditions. To be sure, this historical approach to nationalism recognizes that people have always shared collective identities in their towns, families, religions, and geographical regions, but the nationalisms that spread in modern texts and state institutions promoted new personal identifications with much larger territories and more diverse populations.

Despite their general agreement on the historical influence and modernity of nationalist politics and ideas, historians frequently disagree about the premodern origins of national communities and identities. The resurgence of nationalist and ethnic violence in the 1990s contributed to new historical interest in the earliest emergence of nationalist thought, which some writers have traced back to ancient Israel or other ancient Mediterranean cultures.[2] Most historians, however, continue to describe nationalism as a distinctive form of modern thought and political culture. They assume that nationalism has grown out of and shaped specific social and political systems in modern cultures and has no essential origin in ancient or premodern societies. As the historian Hans Kohn noted in a classic study of the "idea" of nationalism, it "is first and foremost a state of mind, an act of consciousness," which is constructed like other ideas through constantly evolving historical conflicts, social relations, and political movements.[3] A more recent historian of nationalism, Liah Greenfeld, argues that nationalism is not simply the outcome of modernizing social and political institutions (for example, capitalism and nation-states); it is instead a key source of modernity. "Historically," Greenfeld explains, "the emergence of nationalism predated the development of every significant component of modernization." Although other historians differ from Greenfeld by exploring the constant interplay of modern and premodern ideas or by inverting her account to argue that modern social institutions actually produced nationalist ideologies, the linkage between nationalism and modernity has become a widely accepted truism of historical explanation.[4]

My own account of nationalism draws on recent historical and theoretical perspectives to argue that national identities are historically constructed and began to develop their modern forms in late eighteenth-century Europe and America. In contrast to many histories of Western nationalism, the following chapters show how the themes of European nationalism appeared also in the nationalism of the emerging United States, where the construction of a new national identity against an imperial European power can be compared to subsequent nationalisms in other regions of the world. Nationalism has always developed overlapping political and cultural ideas, all of which share the central assumption that the well-being and identity of individuals depend on their participation in a national culture. This assumption shapes the cultural claims of nationalism and provides a starting point for the historical analysis of nationalist thought. If social groups and individuals define their identities with the language of national cultures, then the historical construction of those cultures becomes crucial for understanding a whole range of historical issues—from politics and public conflicts to the interpretation of family life, gender roles, education, and death.

The intersection of collective and personal identities suggests why the cultural history of nationalism (the influence of language, history, religion, literature, and public symbols) goes beyond what social or military or economic history can explain about the emergence of nationalist institutions. Nationalism develops in the convergence of modern political and cultural narratives that construct the shared history of people living in a specific geographical space; these narratives then typically claim a fundamental human right for such populations to have an independent, sovereign state. National narratives also affirm unique, collective identities by stressing that each national population differs from the people and cultures in all other nations. Nationalism is therefore a more coherent system of beliefs than patriotism, which, in my view, expresses emotional identifications with particular places, communities, or governments but lacks the self-conscious cultural themes of nationalist movements and institutions. My interest in the cultural construction of nationalism, however, does not ignore or negate other explanations for the popularity and power of modern nationalisms; in fact, the cultural approach to the multiple layers and political power of nationalism should also recognize the insights of alternative interpretations, including the ethnic and economic themes of recent social theorists.

I noted earlier that the violence of contemporary ethnic conflicts has prompted some analysts to question the modernity of nationalisms and examine the premodern origins of modern national identities. The English sociologist Anthony D. Smith, for example, complains that contemporary fascination with the "cultural invention" of nations leads too many historians to ignore the ways in which national identities depend on long-developing *"patterns of values, symbols, memories, myths, and traditions that form the distinctive heritage of the nation."* This "distinctive heritage" limits what intellectuals or politicians can actually claim for the cultural traditions of a nation, and cultural elites can never simply construct a new national culture. The modern language of nationalism must refer to realities or remembered experiences outside of writing, Smith argues, and these realities are evoked in the *"common myths and memories"* of ethnic groups and national populations who claim to *"constitute an actual or potential 'nation.'"*[5]

Smith therefore assumes that nationalism has deep roots, because the people in each specific ethnic or national community learn the stories of a shared past that are "handed down from generation to generation in the form of subjective 'ethnohistory,' [which] sets limits to current aspirations and perceptions." Smith assumes that this "ethnohistory" or "ethnosymbolic" memory sets the parameters of national cultures and forces the would-be creators of a national identity to reconstruct the "traditions, customs and institutions of the ethnic community or communities which form the basis of the nation."[6] The concept of ethnic identity for Smith and others who build on his theories refers to cultural traditions and a shared history rather than to specific racial or biological traits. As Walker Connor explains in a somewhat different analysis of "ethnonationalism," the "nation connotes a group of people who believe they are ancestrally related," though Connor insists that this "sense of unique descent . . . need not, and *in nearly all* cases *will not,* accord with factual history." It is the *belief* in a common "descent," however, that shapes nationalism and elicits emotional attachments to what the historian Steven Grosby calls a "community of kinship" among those who describe themselves as a nation.[7] Although the ethnohistorians tend to lose sight of how national languages, symbols, and memories constantly (and rapidly) evolve through new systems of communication, their insistence on the premodern origins of the belief in a shared ancestry offers important critical alternatives to the recent emphasis on the modern cultural construction of nationalisms.[8]

Another influential alternative to recent cultural histories of nationalism appears in the work of Ernest Gellner, who, unlike the ethnohistorians, argues that nationalism emerged as an ideological response to the far-reaching economic changes that spread across the Western world in the nineteenth century. Describing nationalism as a practical solution to the needs of industrializing modern societies, Gellner explains that new, complex economies required specialized divisions of labor, educated workers who could communicate across long distances, and mobile populations that could read the same language and follow the same laws. Nationalism thus provided the rationale and institutions for this educated, mobile workforce through the creation of the standardized languages, schools, and technical training that separated industrialized nations from traditional agrarian cultures. This pattern would reappear often in modernizing societies around the world. "The roots of nationalism in the distinctive structural requirements of industrial society are very deep indeed," Gellner argues, and nationalism develops whenever the social structures of a culture begin to evolve away from the relatively stable, hierarchical relations of peasant communities. "It is not the case . . . that nationalism imposes homogeneity; it is rather that a homogeneity imposed by objective, inescapable imperative eventually appears on the surface in the form of nationalism."[9]

Gellner's economic structuralism carries a valuable reminder that politics and culture always remain connected with economic life, yet his economic explanations fail to account for the complexity of national cultures or the emotional passions that such cultures regularly generate. The cultural meanings of nationalism go beyond economic modernization into nuances of language, history, and religion that have little or no value for standardized labor forces, though they create emotionally charged identities for which people are willing to kill and die. Indeed, Smith's search for continuities with premodern ethnic, cultural traditions may tell us more about the powerful emotional attraction of nationalism than we can learn from Gellner's account of economic modernization. But if neither premodern ethnic communities nor modernizing economic systems can adequately account for the political power and emotional meanings of modern national cultures, how do political nationalisms and national cultures come together in the overlapping personal and public spheres of individual lives?

Cultures and Identities

People always have multiple identities. They describe themselves (and are described by others) through references to their families, work and professional status, wealth, gender and race, education, religious affiliations, and political allegiances—not to mention their other identities such as loyalties to sports teams, club memberships, or hometowns. All of these identities depend on social relations and interactions with other people, and many have been integral to human experience since the beginning of civilization. Nationalism does not usually deny or displace other forms of personal identity, but it typically defines national identity as an essential identity that gives coherence to all other aspects of a person's life. The ascribed traits of nationality are used to define virtually every level of public and private life, so that we hear about "Italian" families, "German" workers, "American" Protestants, "Chinese" food, "English" gardens, or maybe a "French" kiss.

Nations are thus pervasive cultural categories that structure, regulate, and contribute meanings to most of the actions and relationships through which we understand our lives. Loyalty to the nation "flourishes," as the historian David Potter has explained, "not by challenging and overpowering all other loyalties, but by subsuming them all and keeping them in a reciprocally supportive relationship to one another."[10] This implicit nationalism in the relationships of everyday life becomes more explicit and coercive during wars, when national governments demand the lives of young people and the labor, wealth, or disciplined loyalty of entire societies. Nationalism provides the justification for the most wide-ranging military and political mobilizations of modern populations, but it can also be found, notes Peter Alter, "whenever individuals feel they belong primarily to the nation, and whenever affective attachment and loyalty to that nation override all other attachments and loyalties."[11] Indeed, nationalists believe that even the most private human activities and attachments acquire wider significance through their connections with a nation: "family values" and "religious morality," for example, may be celebrated as essential to the survival of a strong national culture, whereas a declining commitment to marriage or religion may be interpreted as the cause of national weakness and decline.

Modern nationalism provides more than reinforcement of traditional families or religions, however, because it can also compensate for the breakdown of traditional social, cultural, and religious hierarchies and attachments. Identifying with the power of a nation may become a consolation or replacement for losses and disappointments that accompany the growth of modern cities and economic institutions. Liah Greenfeld, for example, argues that a social and cultural "identity crisis" has preceded the embrace of nationalism in almost every modern society. Set free from the hierarchies and social categories of traditional cultures, individuals and groups in modernizing societies have regularly experienced what Greenfeld calls a sense of social "anomie" and disorientation. Fervent nationalists often emerge in such contexts, transforming deep resentments about the lack of recognition for their work, social status, or social group into passionate claims for national achievement and superiority. The most intense nationalist identities, as Greenfeld describes them, have often emerged among those who believe they are losing public influence

[handwritten margin note: Used as justification → connection to motivation of exiles]

or respect and also among unhappy intellectuals—many of whom have turned to nationalism as an empowering political and cultural solution for their own frustrations. "Wherever it [*ressentiment*] existed," Greenfeld writes, "it fostered particularistic pride and xenophobia, providing emotional nourishment for the nascent national sentiment and sustaining it whenever it faltered."[12]

National identities developed as cultural constructions that lacked the long history of traditional social hierarchies and religions, yet they enabled otherwise alienated persons to identify with a power beyond themselves and their own situation. "Nationality makes people feel good," Greenfeld explains, especially when it promotes a "collectivistic nationalism" that allows individuals "to partake in the dignity of a far greater, stronger, and more perfect being, the brilliance of whose virtues has the power to blind one to one's own failings."[13] Nationalist narratives thus stress the coherence and unity of the nation much like religious narratives describe the unity of God, thereby offering access to coherence and unity for individuals who might feel threatened by the fragmentation of modern social life. The much-desired coherence of national identities produces repression as well as consolation, however, because the belief in unified national cultures has often justified attacks on people who resist or stand outside the utopian aspiration for full coherence. When strong national identities become embedded within individual identities, every perceived threat to the nation can also become a threat to one's own selfhood or personal well-being—and a rationale for repression.

The history of nationalist violence and repressive ethnic "purifications" has provoked some critics to condemn all forms of nationalism, but the pervasive influence of national cultures and identities in the modern world calls for a more complex response and question: how can people positively affirm their personal and collective national identities without lapsing into the totalizing claims and repressions of the fervent nationalist? Seeking answers to this question, the recent study of national identities has increasingly turned away from the traditional nationalist aspiration for a fully coherent national identity or essence to emphasize the multiple identities that challenge the desire to create a completely unified nation (or individual). This "multicultural" view of nations produces a new history of nationalism and the construction of national identities. Where nationalists stress the deep reality and essential coherence of national identities, the multicultural analysis of nationalism stresses the differences and diversity within every national society. Personal and collective identities are still closely connected, but the connections are seen as ambiguous, unstable, and always evolving. Reduced to its most basic theme, the multicultural argument denies that fully unified national identities can ever exist because nations always contain diverse social groups and internal cultural differences that must be constantly mediated in personal and public life.

This emphasis on difference rather than essence in the construction of nationalist identities opens new historical approaches to the never-ending process of national identity formation. Nationalism comes to be understood as an ongoing political-cultural exchange and conflict among different people who develop contending accounts of the nation in which they live and the other nations with which they interact. As the cultural theorist Stuart Hall has explained in a concise account of this evolving cultural process, national identity "is not something which already exists, transcending place, time, history, and culture. Cultural identities come from somewhere, have histories." The history of nationalism in this view—and it is also a theme of this book—becomes a history of constant cultural reconstruction as each generation extends, debates, and redefines the meaning of the nation. A national cultural identity, to continue with Hall's themes, "is always constructed through memory, fantasy, narrative and myth. Cultural identities are . . . the unstable points of identification or suture, which are made within the discourses of history and culture. Not an essence but a *positioning*." Equally important, this continual "positioning" of national cultures carries the legacy of multiple cultural groups and produces a multicultural historical reality that exceeds and defies traditional nationalist narratives of pure national origins and simple beginnings. Hall's description of Afro-Caribbean people who descend from the African diaspora could also apply to virtually every modern national culture. "The diaspora experience," he writes, "is defined, not by essence or purity, but by the recognition of a necessary heterogeneity and diversity; by a conception of 'identity' which lives with and through, not despite difference; by *hybridity*."[14]

The search for "hybrid," diverse levels of culture that converge and diverge in national identities has generated new studies of the cultural and social exchanges that create identities for individuals and groups alike. Challenging the ethnohistorical emphasis on long-developing and relatively coherent "communities of descent," the recent cultural and multicultural approach to nations examines the interactions of different groups who share a common territorial space. All such interactions evolve through the languages, symbols, and narratives that define and spread emotionally charged ideas about the meaning of a nation. The last words of Nathan Hale, the song of Rouget de Lisle, and the lectures of J. G. Fichte, for example, would have no historical or cultural significance without the narratives, symbols, and conceptions of difference that carried each text into the cultural memory of a nation. Growing interest in these processes of cultural construction and diffusion has therefore brought the study of nationalism into a new cultural history of the languages and symbols that construct the meaning of all social realities.

Nationalism and Cultural History

Contemporary cultural historians have challenged an earlier historical assumption that social and economic realities have an objective existence outside of language and cultural interpretations—a kind of material base that language can describe but not construct. Although cultural historians definitely recognize the reality of material existence, they generally assume that language and cultural symbols actively shape all human encounters with nature, social life, and other material realities. In other words, most cultural historians argue that material objects and the social world can have no meaning for people without the words and cultural values that we use to organize, compare, describe, remember, and understand every object or person we encounter. Language does not merely reflect objective realities that are "out there" in the world; it actively creates connections among sensory experiences, establishes hierarchies of significance, and brings philosophical assumptions into the most mundane actions of daily life.[15] If human beings lost language, they would also lose their history, memory, and culture; and it is this dynamic linguistic component of all cultural life that leads some theorists to claim that the past history of the world *as we know it* is really a history of language.

Although even the most linguistically inclined historians would not describe the social world or state institutions as simply systems of words and texts, the recent emphasis on the dynamic, shaping force of language has pushed cultural historians to give close attention to the words and symbols that define and construct social relations, political movements, religions, wars, and the exercise of power. This search for linguistic meanings influences the study of historical transitions such as the growth of cities and the social consequences of modern warfare, but it has become especially prominent in the study of influential ideas such as nationalism.

Nations do not exist in nature. They are created by human cultures, and they provide a good example of how human realities that appear to be "natural" actually develop in history through specific institutions and the evolving use of languages, symbols, and imaginative narratives.

The cultural construction and meanings of nations enter daily life in both state-sponsored and unofficial cultural objects or experiences that we assimilate with little conscious reflection: maps, flags, money, stamps, public buildings and monuments, museums, passports, songs, history books, school examinations, religious services, uniforms, youth scout groups, sports events, political constitutions, election campaigns, military service, taxes, newspaper stories, weather reports, films, television shows, Internet websites, advertisements, and local cemeteries. This list by no means includes all of the places or activities where nationalism comes into daily life, but it is long enough to suggest why national identities are so important in modern societies and why cultural history has become so influential in the study of nationalism.

The search to understand modern nationalism's wide-ranging cultural history therefore uses theories and examples from all the scholarly disciplines that seek to explain human societies, cultures, and languages, including anthropology, sociology, and literary studies as well as social and political history. This interdisciplinary scholarship has generated a vast literature that can easily overwhelm the most indefatigable reader.[16] Among the countless publications on the history of nationalism, however, I will mention three influential works that have helped to shape the analysis of nationalism in recent decades and also contributed to the conceptual framework of this book.

The first is *Imagined Communities: Reflections on the Origin and Spread of Nationalism* (1983; revised editions in 1991 and 2006), an important work by Benedict Anderson that became the provocative starting point for a whole wave of new commentaries on cultural and national identities. Anderson describes nations as distinctive modern constructions that emerge when people imagine themselves to be closely affiliated, though they never meet and may differ widely in education, work, income, and personal beliefs. The nation brings these diverse populations to a shared identity, writes Anderson, in "an imagined political community" that is "imagined as both inherently limited and sovereign."

This national community is much larger than traditional families, villages, and geographical regions, but it becomes imaginable for people who read the stories of nations in the schools, newspapers, and novels of modern, centralizing states and colonies. Anderson's influential account of the modern nation is best summarized in his own well-known definitions.

> [The nation] is *imagined* because the members of even the smallest nation will never know most of their fellow-members, meet them, or even hear of them, yet in the minds of each lives the image of their communion.... In fact, all communities larger than primordial villages of face-to-face contact (and perhaps even these) are imagined....
>
> The nation is imagined as *limited* because even the largest of them ... has finite, if elastic boundaries, beyond which lie other nations....
>
> It is imagined as *sovereign* because the concept was born in an age in which Enlightenment and Revolution were destroying the legitimacy of the divinely-ordained, hierarchical dynastic realm....
>
> Finally, it is imagined as a *community*, because, regardless of the actual inequality and exploitation that may prevail in each, the nation is always conceived as a deep, horizontal comradeship.[17]

Anderson provides a paradigm for understanding how nations develop political and cultural unity for widely dispersed populations and how these imagined (but real) identifications produce emotional passions and consolations for the pains of life and death. Although he emphasizes the importance of language and writing in the formation of national identities, he also insists that narratives of national life carry a deeper emotional meaning than other political ideologies because they link the transience of individual lives to the ongoing existence of a national population. Anderson's account of modern imagined communities—constructed in language, emerging first in eighteenth-century revolutions, gaining coherence in the publications of "print capitalism," and generating both personal and collective identities—remains important for most historians of nationalism, though critics have increasingly questioned specific limitations in his work (for example, he gives little attention to the gendered themes in nationalist thought).[18]

A related cultural and conceptual approach to nationalism appeared in the essays that Eric Hobsbawm and Terence Ranger collected for publication in *The Invention of Tradition* (1983). Hobsbawm and Ranger resemble Anderson in assuming that nations are constructed through symbolic, imaginative processes, but the essays in their book often suggest a more self-conscious development of "invented traditions" that come to be seen as the continuing, modern expression of a national past. Rejecting both the nationalists' belief in the enduring, essential truth of the nation and the ethnohistorical account of premodern discourses that nationalists can refashion, Hobsbawm focuses on "the peculiarity of 'invented' traditions," whose much affirmed continuity with the historic past is "largely fictitious." He therefore sees almost all nationalists' claims for their nation's premodern heritage and traditions as cultural masks that hide the radical novelty of what was in fact invented by the public actions of specific people in a specific era, especially during the nineteenth century.[19] Hobsbawm, Ranger, and others tend to find too much coherence in these "invented traditions," and, as the ethnohistorical critics have repeatedly noted, they overlook the cultural continuities that give "new" traditions their social meaning and emotional appeal in changing historical contexts. The Hobsbawm-Ranger analysis of modern national rituals has nevertheless stimulated much innovative research on the symbols, monuments, and histories that sustain the nationalist account of "old" national traditions and the belief in a shared descent from national ancestors.

"Imagined communities" and "invented traditions" have thus given historians a thematic structure for numerous studies of nationalism, but the work of Anderson and Hobsbawm has been extended and redefined in the fields of literary and cultural studies. Some of the important early examples of this literary approach to nationalism can be found in Homi Bhabha's edited collection, *Nation and Narration* (1990), which showed the strong influence of the "linguistic turn" in cultural history. Where Anderson and Hobsbawm continued to express the traditional historian's desire to describe the coherence of past cultures, Bhabha and his colleagues sought to uncover the fragments, tensions, and incoherence of nationalist writings and cultural traditions. The essays in Bhabha's book thus draw on poststructuralist theories to argue that nations are like other imaginary texts inasmuch as they are "narrated" by authors who strive for a coherence and order that can never be fully achieved. Narratives about the nation cannot create the national purity and clarity that their authors desire because the inescapable differences within a nation's imagined cultural boundaries stymie the quest for national homogeneity. Bhabha argues, in short, that stories of national identity, like the narratives in other texts, cannot finally master what they seek to describe. "Counter-narratives of the nation that continually evoke and erase its totalizing boundaries . . . disturb those ideological manoeuvres through which 'imagined communities' are given essentialist identities." Although

Bhabha's theoretical prose is difficult to follow, his themes are important. Nationalism is a form of "writing" that seeks to transform the "cultural difference and the heterogeneous histories of contending peoples" into a unified cultural reality.[20] The inevitable obstacles to this project give nationalism an endless cultural campaign and a constant need to "rewrite" the nation in every generation; but nationalists can never reach the total national coherence and unity they imagine and seek.

Bhabha and the literary critics therefore expanded the cultural history of nationalism beyond Anderson, Hobsbawm, and the social scientists with two important themes: (1) narratives about the nation fail to achieve a much-desired literary and political coherence, in part because (2) the meaning of all such narratives depends on the presence of both internal and external differences that can never disappear. Definitions of the nation, like all other ideas and collective identities, develop through polarities that nationalists see as clear, distinct, and oppositional but whose meanings are always already entangled with the differences they theoretically oppose. The meaning of "German," for example, emerges through interactions with the "French"; and the often-invoked racial category "white" derives meaning from its relation to "black" or "brown."

Nationalism and Difference

The recent cultural history of national identities thus develops the "anti-essentialist" argument that identities are always relational. The meaning of a nation depends on definitions of difference and on interactive relations with people in other cultures, so that the nation's imaginary essence evolves as definitions of difference and cultural boundaries also evolve. "National identity," Peter Sahlins writes in a concise summary, "is a socially constructed and continuous process of defining 'friend' and 'enemy.'"[21] Campaigns for national unity or coherence thus achieve the greatest success when the majority of a national population agrees that they face dangerous enemies. Indeed, as Anthony W. Marx has argued in a wide-ranging study of early modern national monarchies, the consolidation of centralized states typically included the systematic scapegoating and removal of internal (religious) "enemies" who were portrayed as an extreme danger to unified, stable societies. The Spanish monarchs Ferdinand and Isabella, for example, expelled Jews and Moors; the French King Louis XIV persecuted and imprisoned Protestants; and English monarchs systematically excluded Catholics from the English "body politic"

François Georgin, *Napoleon at Arcis-Sur-Aube*, woodcut, 1836. A common military image of national difference appears in this portrayal of the last phases of the Napoleonic wars (1814); Napoleon leads French troops against the Prussian army, but the dark cloud and the stark confrontation with invading soldiers emphasize the acute danger of national enemies. (Burton Emmett Collection, Ackland Art Museum, University of North Carolina at Chapel Hill)

between the sixteenth and nineteenth centuries. The persecution of religious or ethnic minorities *within* national territories therefore accompanied modern state building long before the revolutionary upheavals of the eighteenth century.[22]

Modern national states continued to mobilize popular hostility for various internal minorities, but they increasingly stressed the threat from external enemies as the justification for internal unity. The Dutch historian Joep Leerssen, among others, has summarized this common historical pattern in an insightful history of nationalist thought. "A collective sense of identity," Leerssen explains, "derives . . . not from a group's pre-existing cohesion, but from the perception and articulation of external differences."[23] This evolving perception of enemies and difference suggests why a change in friends or international threats also changes the meaning of a nation's identity. The end of the Cold War, for example, affected America's national identity because the demise of the Soviet Union removed a clearly defined enemy that had long helped to sustain the unity of American nationalism; but radical Islamic groups soon emerged as a new external threat and thus a new unifying "other" for America's national identity in the early twenty-first century.

The influence of "difference" in the construction of national identities leads back to my earlier description of nationalism as a belief in the distinctive characteristics of people whose history, institutions, and ideals are said to differ in crucial respects from other cultures and national societies. This assertion of national differences typically justifies the expansive use of power in existing nation-states or long campaigns for statehood among peoples who seek a stronger collective identity and political independence through the establishment of new nation-states. In every case, however, the existence of an independent nation depends on cultural and political boundaries that define differences and separate insiders from outsiders.

Each chapter of this book refers to the use of "difference" as an organizing idea in nationalist thought and practice. This theme appears constantly in the rituals of national political cultures; in the praise for national languages, histories, and literatures; in the affirmation of national religions; in the nationalist definitions of gender, race, or ethnicity; in the arguments for modern wars; and in the anticolonial campaigns against twentieth-century empires. All nationalisms require identity-shaping cultural actions to show how a specific population differs from the people in other nations, but nationalist movements develop remarkably diverse accounts of their national achievements. Examining the evolution of these constantly redefined national differences, historians of nationalism often draw sharp contrasts between various forms of nationalist culture and political action. Such contrasts are needed for historical understanding, yet they should not distort the fact that the belief in national differences shapes the emergence and survival of all modern nationalisms.

Varieties of Nationalism

Historians have been categorizing nationalisms and national identities since the early twentieth century, striving to find broad historical patterns in political and cultural movements that regularly claim to be unique. Although the contributors to this debate disagree about the appropriate analytical categories, they have often characterized the historical diversity of nationalisms with dichotomies such as Western/Eastern, Political/Cultural, Old/New, Early/Late, Liberal/Conservative, and Civic/Ethnic. These oppositional categories help historians compare and identify various phases of nationalism, but they can also convey simplifying ethical distinctions between good and bad. Historians in western Europe and America have tended to argue that the "good side" of these oppositions (Western, political, old, liberal, early, and civic) appeared mostly in the nationalisms of countries such as England, France, and the United States; and they have frequently found the "bad side" of nationalist ideologies (Eastern, cultural, new, conservative, late, and ethnic) in countries such as Germany, in Slavic eastern Europe, or in anticolonial states in Asia and Africa. Historians need to make analytical distinctions, of course, and they have often provided insightful cross-cultural comparisons in their accounts of the differences among nationalist movements, but the analysts' own national identities have also carried exceptional influence in shaping some scholarly accounts of "good" and "bad" nationalisms.[24]

The analytical categories in many modern histories of nationalism, for example, have expressed (understandable) moral responses to the horrors of Nazism or the brutalities of colonial wars or the violence of "ethnic cleansing." Historical accounts of such horrific violence have generated repeated commentary on the differences between "Western" nationalisms and "Eastern" nationalisms, usually stressing the difference between beliefs in universal human rights and beliefs in a specific national culture. The first form of nationalism, which is often called liberal nationalism, typically includes individual rights in its definition of the nation's fundamental ideals. The second form of nationalism, often called integral nationalism, typically subsumes the individual into a national community and identifies the nation in terms of race, ethnicity, or culture rather than politics and individual rights.[25] The civic, political nation is theoretically open to newcomers because individuals can choose to join the civic nation, whereas the ethnic, linguistic nation is theoretically closed to outsiders because individuals are *born into* ethnic and linguistic communities. Although historians increasingly recognize the ethnic and cultural dimensions of "civic nationalisms" and the civic themes in most "ethnic nationalisms," the traditional dichotomies still provide a framework for explaining the differences among nationalist movements.

Schematic models of contrasting nationalisms have enabled historians to separate France from Germany or western Europe from eastern Europe, but the civic/ethnic distinction also generates categories to explain different forms of nationalism within a single national culture. One common argument, for example, portrays nationalism as mainly an ideology of liberals and the political Left until the mid-nineteenth century, when the political Right began to embrace nationalist ideas in the name of conservatism and tradition.[26] Nationalism in both France and Germany could thus be civic or political in one context and ethnic or linguistic in another. Similarly, nationalism could be the ideology of left-wing antico-lonialist movements and also the ideological justification for conservative regimes in postcolonial states. In short, nationalism moves widely across the political spectrum, sometimes promoting transnational ideas such as human rights and sometimes promoting the extreme particularism of ideas such as racial superiority.

Wherever nationalism has evolved on the left-right political spectrum, however, it has always promoted self-conscious cultural identities. As the cultural historian Gregory Jusdanis notes in a persuasive account of this process, "all nationalism takes on a cultural dimension" because cultural traditions, languages, and the arts "have served as stimulants in the construction of even the most quintessentially political nations." At the same time, both the cultural and political themes of nationalism evolve through comparisons with other nations, which helps to explain why nationalists have constantly warned their compatriots about the dangers of "lagging behind" or "falling behind" other nations. This theme of "belatedness," as Jusdanis also emphasizes, repeatedly shapes nationalist thought because transnational comparisons almost always imply the need to "catch up" with others—in education, in culture, in economic productivity, in national armaments, or in other symbolic aspects of national stature.[27] The belief in (and anxiety about) the variety of nations and nationalisms has thus been as common in the writings of self-conscious nationalists as in the scholarship of the historians who study them.

Analyzing the differences among nationalisms thus brings order to the contradictory themes within and among nationalist movements, but his-torical accounts of nationalism almost always find a similar political sig-nificance in the ideas and events of the American and French Revolutions. These late eighteenth-century revolutions claimed national sovereignty for the "people" rather than for kings or social elites, and similar rhetorical claims to represent the "people" would become one of the political themes in all later nationalisms. Yet this early affirmation of sovereign political rights, as most analysts describe it, soon evolved into a much stronger affirmation of the "people's" cultural rights and identity in Germany and other societies to the east. Nationalisms in eastern Europe and numerous other societies of Asia and Africa have thus been described in much Western scholarship as derivative variations of the claims for national sovereignty that emerged first in the West.[28]

Contemporary critics often challenge this view of "derivative" nationalist discourses, however, and note the autonomy of various nationalisms. Although the nationalist tendency to compare nations or express anxiety about "belatedness" can be used to define nationalist movements as "derivative" forms of earlier national states, it is also important to recognize the historical differences among nationalisms—including the diverse forms of political and cultural nationalisms that exist in various historical eras and national contexts. There are, for example, crucial differences that separate the rationale and objectives of the political violence in the French Revolution from the racist violence in Nazi Germany, though both forms of violence have some relation to nationalist ideologies. Historical differences are therefore often as important as the historical similarities of modern nationalisms, but the analysis of nationalism in this book gives more attention to the ideas and cultural themes that nationalisms share than to the specific political, economic, military, and cultural actions that also make them different.

I focus on the nationalism in Western societies (though many similar aspects of nationalist thought can be found throughout the modern world), and I refer most often to three particular national cultures: the "old" nation in France, a society whose national identity has usually been portrayed as an example of political nationalism; the "old" or "new" nation in Germany, a society whose national identity has usually been described as a cultural or ethnic nationalism; and the "new" nation in the United States, a society whose national identity has usually been described as a somewhat exceptional political nationalism that brought diverse ethnic and immigrant populations into a coherent nation-state. Setting aside many of the familiar distinctions between "old" and "new" nations, I stress similarities in the cultural components of political nationalisms and the political components of cultural nationalisms. More specifically, I look at how each of these national cultures defined collective identities in opposition to other cultures and developed their nationalist ideas through the active power of new national narratives. In contrast to an American historical tradition that separated the United States from the history of nationalism in Europe, I examine the similarities and continuities of nationalist thought on both sides of the Atlantic.

Isidore Pils, *Rouget de Lisle Singing "La Marseillaise,"* oil on canvas, 1849. This imagined scene of the composer's first rendition of France's national anthem (1792) provides an idealized representation of the nation's people, unified purpose, and bold young heroes. It also offers an example of how art helps to construct national memory. (Musée Historique, Strasbourg; Snark/Art Resource, New York)

I also stress the historical importance of the "long nineteenth century" (1789–1914) as the decisive period for the formulation and spread of nationalism's distinctive political and cultural themes. Joep Leerssen (whose insightful study of nationalist ideas was noted earlier) rightly emphasizes that "in the course of the nineteenth century we can see development of nationalism affecting Europe as a whole," but this argument should be extended to America as well.[29] The explosions of twentieth-century nationalist violence, racism, and warfare carry a long fuse from the ideas of the nineteenth century. The cultural history of nationalism must therefore look especially at the evolving nationalist ideas of that era, even though this history necessarily begins with the eighteenth century and leads also into the world wars and anticolonial revolutions of the twentieth century.

The Emergence of Nationalism in an Age of Revolutions

The similarities in different national movements became especially notable in the emergence of specific western European and American nationalisms during the era of early democratic revolutions (1775–1850)—a period of major changes in both the politics and cultures of Western societies. The "age of democratic revolutions" was also the first "age of nationalist revolutions," a link that suggests how much nationalism (even in its authoritarian forms) owes to the anti-aristocratic idea of democratic national sovereignty.[30] Early nationalisms were later transformed by modern technologies and communications, worldwide movements against colonialism, new kinds of violence and warfare, and other social movements, such as socialism and communism. The changing contexts of nationalism, however, never completely altered the complex political and cultural interactions that began to shape modern nationalisms and national identities after the 1770s.

The European and American political and cultural transitions of that revolutionary era drew on Western religious traditions, the eighteenth-century Enlightenment, and romantic philosophy to construct new nationalist ideologies. Needless to say, these nationalisms were not the only influential national movements in the modern world, but the identity-shaping cultural processes that emerged in late eighteenth-century writings and political conflicts (and in nineteenth-century memories of the recent revolutions) can be found in the diverse nationalisms of every subsequent generation and in every part of the world. The cultural history of modern nationalism thus began with new descriptions of cultural difference and new claims for the "sovereign people." It spread through famous new stories such as "Nathan Hale," "La Marseillaise," and the *Addresses to the German Nation*, and it gained political power in the violent upheavals of the American and French Revolutions.

CHAPTER TWO

Politics, Revolutions, & National Sovereignty

Modern nationalisms differ widely in their descriptions of national ideals and cultural traditions, but all nationalisms have developed political objectives, political institutions, and political claims for the sovereign rights of specific national populations. Nationalism thus began to emerge as a coherent political force or ideology when influential writers and other critics of royal power proposed a new conceptual framework to explain the proper relation between governments and the people whom they control. Arguing that national communities must be represented and protected by independent nation-states, a small group of eighteenth-century writers began to describe a national political identity that differed from older political entities such as empires (which often ruled diverse cultures and linguistic groups), city-states (which typically represented only small territories within larger cultures and linguistic groups), and traditional monarchies (which claimed legitimacy on grounds of family lineage or divine right rather than the political will of a nation). The political novelty of nationalism therefore emerged in the gradually spreading belief that state power should represent the collective will of a particular population or "citizenry" that lived within the borders of a large, well-defined territory.

Such ideas had occasionally appeared in Europe since the sixteenth century. Various kinds of "proto-nationalist" political thought appeared, for example, in Machiavelli's response to the foreign invasions of Italy after 1500, in the Dutch revolt against Spain during the 1580s, and in the English Protestant mobilization against the Spanish Armada in this same era; and even ancient or premodern empires had encouraged their diverse populations to identify with the specific institutions and laws of their imperial systems.[1] The new, more *democratic* argument for the sovereign rights of nations, however, did not really emerge until the American and French Revolutions. The revolutionary conflicts in France were especially important in shaping new accounts of the "nation" as a political community that expressed both the sovereignty and will of a large but specific national population. Although ideas about a distinctive American society or a distinctive French nation evolved over the course of the eighteenth century, the arguments for a new kind of "political nation" did not really shape national political institutions until the 1780s. A growing emphasis on the cultural themes in later nationalisms may have obscured the two essential political themes of eighteenth-century revolutionary nationalisms: the claim that a nation's sovereignty lies in its people rather than in a king or social elites and the claim that individuals who live in these sovereign nations have certain fundamental rights to liberty and legal equality. Elite social groups had sometimes argued in earlier centuries that they represented the nation in campaigns against foreign enemies or even against monarchs within their own countries, but the American and French Revolutions promoted new forms of national political identity by claiming to represent the sovereign will of entire national populations and the legal rights of all national citizens.[2]

Theoretical Arguments for
National Sovereignty and Human Rights

Ideas about national sovereignty and "natural" human rights emerged in the eighteenth-century political theories, economic relations, and cultural institutions that influenced the themes and practices of the Enlightenment. The critical thinkers who contributed to this famous, secularizing, eighteenth-century cultural movement—from John Locke to Montesquieu, Voltaire, and Jean-Jacques Rousseau—challenged earlier political theories that ascribed sovereignty to kings and royal power to the will of God. Enlightenment-era critics rejected the "divine rights" of kings, and the "sacred monarch," as Hans Kohn noted in his classic intellectual history of this early modern transition, "lost his symbolic value as the center and justification of society." This loss of divine-right, monarchical sovereignty occurred gradually, but the critique of royal sovereignty attracted support because it also carried a strong, new, positive claim for a political legitimacy that came entirely from the "people." Theorists drew on the ideas of Locke and others to argue that political institutions should embody a "contract" between governments and the governed, though the "people" or "the governed" carried more amorphous meanings than a king. "The sovereignty of the prince who had been one," Kohn explained, "was to be replaced by the sovereignty of the people, who had to become one in a higher sense of the word."[3]

This new sovereign entity would be entitled to rights and freedoms that had once been reserved for sovereign kings. The people of each nation, for example, must be independent of external control in order to act upon their collective national will, and this national independence could not be secure until it was embodied in a national state. New theories about the nation's sovereign political life appeared most forcefully in the writings of Rousseau (1712–78), who argued that collective and personal identities came together in the "general will" of the nation. *Each of us places his person and all his power in common under the supreme direction of the general will*," Rousseau wrote in *The Social Contract* (1762), "*and as one we receive each member as an indivisible part of the whole.*" This general will established the basis for national sovereignty, which for Rousseau was "inalienable" and "indivisible." The nation's indivisible sovereign existence thus acquired divine qualities that earlier generations had found in God and kings. As Rousseau explained it, "since sovereignty is merely the exercise of the general will, it can never be alienated, and . . . the sovereign, which is only a collective being, cannot be represented by anything but itself."[4] The early political meaning of what would eventually be called nationalism (the word "nationalism" did not emerge until the end of the century) therefore suggested that a new kind of state should represent the collective reality and political will of a sovereign community. Individual citizens within this community would find political meaning and freedom through their connections to the sovereign state in much the same way that religious people had long found spiritual meaning and purpose through their connections to God. Rousseau's abstract conception of the sovereign people's "general will" thus provided theoretical foundations for the later development of "nation-states," even as most eighteenth-century people continued to understand their collective identities through their local social lives or their occasional encounters with government officials.

Although the political arguments of Rousseau and other theorists may suggest that individuals would have no more personal freedom under sovereign nations than under sovereign kings, the new definitions of national sovereignty often became linked to new definitions of what are now called "human rights." Enlightenment ideas about the use of human reason required that autonomous, rational individuals, like sovereign peoples, should have rights to pursue the truth freely, no matter where the inquiry might lead in religion, society, or politics. These rights would be defined in famous documents during the late eighteenth-century revolutions, but the early modern definition of natural rights was already developing throughout the previous century. The breakdown of religious unity after the Protestant Reformation, the decline of belief in divine-right monarchy after the emergence of Enlightenment-era political theory, and the development of a popular new sentimental literature about human relationships all contributed to new definitions of individual knowledge and personal autonomy.

Challenges to the traditional religious and monarchical foundations of the European political order also overlapped with economic and social changes that were weakening another traditional base of European society: the hierarchical social order that had long rested on different legal rights and duties for nobles and commoners. A new social world evolved with the economic expansion and cultural themes of early capitalism. Put simply, the social theories that supported this emerging economic system merged with new political and cultural theories that called for the reward of individual merit or enterprise (the ideology that historians have often labeled "individualism"). The ideal state would therefore come to be viewed as a protector of individual rights as well as the defender of collective interests. By the late eighteenth century, there was a complex cultural interaction between what Louis Dumont has called the "holism" of traditional, hierarchical social life and the "individualism" of modernizing social relations.[5] These interactions produced polemical public debates and new social fusions, including new nationalisms that defined their political purposes and collective identities with the emerging language of individual rights.

The late eighteenth-century revolutions thus tended to combine theories of national rights and sovereign independence with declarations about individual rights and liberties—though the possible contradictions or tensions between the rights of nations and the rights of individuals soon became apparent in recurring conflicts over issues such as slavery, warfare, and the repression of dissent. Rousseau himself had envisioned the contradictions that could quickly develop in the overlapping claims for collective sovereignty and individual freedom (individuals who failed to accept the general will, he explained, could "be forced to be free"); but he also submerged such problems in confident affirmations of the sovereign nation's social equality. "The social compact," Rousseau wrote, "establishes among the citizens an equality of such a kind that they all commit themselves under the same conditions and should all enjoy the same rights. Thus by the

Jacques Réattu, *The Triumph of Liberty*, oil on canvas, 1793–94. Supporters of the new French republic celebrated the French Revolution as an unprecedented triumph for human liberty, which is represented in this painting by a symbolic republican woman who holds a tricolor flag and rides on the shoulders of heroic, classical soldiers. The sovereign power and liberty of nations, however, could threaten as well as support the liberty of specific persons; and the French Revolution helped to produce permanent connections *and* tensions between the rights of nations and the rights of individual citizens. (Musée Réattu, Arles; photograph by Michel Lacanaud)

very nature of the compact, every act of sovereignty (that is, every authentic act of the general will) obligates or favors all citizens equally, so that the sovereign knows only the nation as a body and does not draw distinctions between any of those members that make it up."[6]

Nationalism and individualism therefore evolved as related but potentially conflicting ideologies of human rights in the revolutionary political cultures of the era. As Kohn argued in his intellectual history of early nationalism, the increasing social autonomy of modern people seemed to require new political and cultural systems that would control individuals who were also becoming free: "In the eighteenth century the free personality emerged in all fields of human activity. . . . But this new order posited the grave problem of how to conciliate the liberty of the individual with the exigencies of social integration, how to subject man to a law which could no longer claim the authority of an absolute lawgiver outside and above men. In this situation nationalism was to become the tie binding the autonomous individual into the partnership of a community."[7] Rousseau's writings provided in this context a new account of sovereignty (the "general will" of the nation) and individual liberty (personal freedom realized in collective action) that would help fuse new conceptions of the nation with older religious or political allegiances and rituals in a new realm of revolutionary politics. The idea of the "nation" offered political integration for an emerging liberal society whose religious unity had disappeared, whose monarchs had lost the legitimating foundation of divine right, and whose individuals no longer deferred to a clearly delineated social hierarchy. Nationalism thus offered—from the beginning and in subsequent eras—a new structure for political order, social identity, and cultural coherence during the political and social transition to modernity.[8]

The key political themes of national sovereignty and individual rights suggest the novelty of nationalism and also its role in modernizing social processes. It was by no means a "throwback" to an earlier era. On the contrary, nationalist revolutions and movements began by defining their differences from the old, from what had come before. Nationalist movements generally sought to separate themselves from "old-regime" social and political institutions that were denounced for impeding the freedom of the nation and the individuals who comprised it. Such revolutions looked optimistically to a future that would differ from the old-regime policies of Britain's imperial monarchy, France's royal bureaucracy, or Germany's scattered princely states. The early political history of nationalism was thus mostly liberal and revolutionary rather than conservative and reactionary, in large part because the demands for popular national sovereignty and human rights challenged the traditional political order (even when such demands referred to earlier political ideas or cultural traditions). But to understand how these claims could move from political theory into new governments and national movements in America and Europe, we must look at specific examples of late eighteenth-century nationalist ideas and political practices, all of which depended on the new language and symbols of national identity.

Nationalism in the American Revolution

The characteristic political patterns of most modern nationalisms—claims for national sovereignty, claims for human rights, critiques of old-regime governments—gained early prominence and influence in the American Revolution. Although historians have often assumed that nationalism emerged first in late eighteenth-century Europe, most of the themes in modern political nationalisms actually appeared in the ideological justifications for America's revolutionary war against Britain. As Benedict Anderson notes in his influential account of the "creole" nationalisms that developed in both North and South America between 1775 and 1825, "It is an astonishing sign of the depth of Eurocentrism that so many European scholars persist, in the face of all the evidence, in regarding nationalism as a European invention."[9] Nationalism emerged gradually in the culture, religion, and economy of the Euro-American society that would become the United States of America (see chapter 6), but the major identity-shaping texts of the revolutionary era show that Americans began to describe their war with Britain as a *political* struggle for national sovereignty and independence in the earliest months of their violent resistance to British imperial forces.

The American Declaration of Independence (1776), for example, listed specific grievances to justify an armed insurrection, yet the most striking passages of that famous document insisted more generally on the sovereign rights of the American people. "We hold these truths to be self-evident," wrote Thomas Jefferson, "that all men are created equal, that they are endowed by their Creator with certain unalienable Rights, that among these are Life, Liberty and the Pursuit of Happiness." Jefferson thus began with assertions about individual equality and freedom that would reappear in other nationalist movements, but the claim for individual rights led immediately to a connected claim for the importance of national governments. "That to secure these rights, Governments are instituted among Men, deriving their just powers from the consent of the governed, That whenever any Form of Government becomes destructive of these ends, it is the Right of the People to alter or to abolish it, and to institute new Government, laying its foundation on such principles and organizing its powers in such form, as to them shall seem most to effect their Safety and Happiness." This argument for the rights of the sovereign "people" in America drew on earlier European ideas about the collective identity of specific populations and provided the theoretical rationale for establishing a new nation and new political institutions such as the Continental Congress. "We, therefore, the Representatives of the United States of America, in General Congress . . . do, in the Name, and by Authority of the good People of these Colonies, solemnly publish and declare, That

John Trumbull, *The Declaration of Independence*, oil on canvas, 1817–19. Trumbull's painting of the Continental Congress portrays America's declaration of national independence as the rational action of wise "founding fathers" (including the central figures of Thomas Jefferson, John Adams, and Benjamin Franklin). More generally, this iconic work contributed vivid imagery to the collective memory of a "sovereign people" claiming their political rights. (Architect of the Capitol, Washington, D.C.)

these United Colonies are, and of Right ought to be Free and Independent States."[10] America's Declaration of Independence thus offered a powerful rhetorical summary of how national governments should embody the sovereign rights of a "good people"—which also became the organizing theme for other early American national narratives in the popular works of Thomas Paine (1737–1809), David Ramsey (1749–1815), and Philip Freneau (1752–1832).

Paine's vehement arguments for national independence were published in *Common Sense* (1776), the famous political pamphlet that offered the most influential rationale for a definitive American separation from Britain. Although he had only recently arrived from England, Paine asserted that the "good people" of America were "grievously oppressed" by the British government, thereby helping to transform the local political conflicts of thirteen sparsely populated colonies into a coherent cause with universal significance. He thus promoted a new nationalist theme (the exceptional nation offers redemption for others) that would become common in European nationalist movements over the next century. "The cause of America is in a great measure the cause of all mankind," Paine noted in his call for national independence. "The laying a Country desolate with Fire and Sword, declaring War against the natural rights of all Mankind, and extirpating the Defenders thereof from the Face of the Earth, is the Concern of every Man to whom Nature hath given the Power of feeling." America's Revolution therefore took on moral clarity for Paine and his many sympathetic readers as a decisive struggle between the new and the old, freedom and oppression, national sovereignty and monarchical power. "O ye that love mankind," he wrote, "ye that dare oppose, not only the tyranny, but the tyrant, stand forth! Every spot of the old world is overrun with oppression." Standing against this decadent Old World history, the New World offered a refuge for freedom and for all those who wanted more freedom in their lives: "O receive the fugitive, and prepare in time an asylum for mankind."[11] Paine described an ambitious political mission for this small, isolated outpost of modern "mankind," but the ambition and optimism in his narrative helped create an "imagined community" that would define itself and its universal historical significance by opposing the corruption and oppression of long-established European states.

Paine's themes were repeated throughout the Revolution as American writers explained the meaning of the military violence and the political objectives of the war. A new nationalist narrative contrasted America's defense of freedom and popular sovereignty with the repressive policies of Old World monarchs and gave the Continental army a world-historical purpose. David Ramsay's "Oration on American Independence" (July 4, 1778), for example, helped to launch rituals of recurring celebration for the nation's unique achievements and identity. Calling America's war "the Cause of Human Nature," Ramsay assured an audience in South Carolina that "our independence will redeem one quarter of the globe from tyranny and oppression, and consecrate it the chosen Seat of Truth, Justice, Freedom, Learning and Religion. . . . Generations yet unborn will bless us for the blood-brought inheritance we are about to bequeath them."[12] The deaths in battle and the daily miseries of soldiers thus took on transcendent meaning and purpose in a developing story of American national identity, which explained why Americans had to wage war for their independence and how they differed from the British enemy they were fighting.

The revolutionary poems of Philip Freneau transformed similar national claims into popular literary commentaries on the moral dichotomies of the Revolution. Celebrating the naval victories of the American commander John Paul Jones (1781), for example, Freneau used the "brave Jones" to explain the political meaning of the war: "The rights of men demand thy care: / For *these* you dare the greedy waves." No monarch could withstand such a principled national opponent, Freneau argued, so the British "to our Thirteen Stars shall bend" and the "radiant" American flag would soon "ascend."[13] The final military victory at Yorktown could thus be interpreted as a moral confirmation of such poetic predictions, and the story of the American Revolution moved quickly from the identity-shaping narratives of warfare to the identity-shaping narratives of historical memory. The story of America's military/political victory also spread across the emerging nation at annual celebrations on the Fourth of July and in artwork, hand-sown quilts, and other material objects that reached Americans—who began to develop a political conception of the new republican nation even if they never read a history book or an urban newspaper.[14]

Americans therefore described the superiority of their new nation in a wide variety of texts, objects, and public events that linked the American right of national sovereignty to broad definitions of universal human rights. The successful campaign for the political rights of the American "people" (defined politically at the time as only "white males") was expected to provide the historical example for others who wanted to change their governments, so most American nationalists quickly embraced the French Revolution in 1789 as a European expression of the principles that had shaped their own war for national independence. Freneau was one of the many Americans who welcomed the revolutionary French ambassador to Philadelphia in 1793 with strong praise for the ideas of popular sovereignty and republicanism that now united France and America. "Thanks to our God," Freneau reminded his readers at a moment of bitter political conflicts within the new American government, "the *sovereignty* still resides with THE PEOPLE, and . . . neither proclamations, nor *royal demeanor and state* can prevent them from exercising it." France's revolution thus gave Freneau new reasons to praise the wisdom of America's political achievements, and his poems, like the writings of Paine and Ramsay, often celebrated the two nations and revolutions that had rejected Europe's most powerful kings.[15]

Freneau assumed that the well-lighted torch of American national freedom had shown the way for the later revolution in France—a popular political claim that appeared also in Paine's interpretations of the French Revolution. "One of the great advantages of the American revolution," Paine wrote from England in 1792, "has been, that it led to a discovery of the principles . . . of governments. All the revolutions till then had been worked within the atmosphere of a court, and never on the great floor of a nation." The American experience, by contrast, demonstrated the central political truth of nations and governments: "*That government is nothing more than a national association acting on the principles of society.*" With this truth now firmly established, it was, in Paine's view, "natural to expect that other revolutions will follow."[16] France's revolutionaries did in fact reiterate and extend the claims for national sovereignty and human rights that Americans had put forward during their revolutionary war against the British Empire, yet the national movement in France ultimately contributed far more directly and decisively to the emergence of other nationalisms in Europe.

Nationalism in the French Revolution

Despite a growing interest in the earlier emergence of "national identities" or conceptions of national sovereignty, most historians argue that the French Revolution made the most influential political contributions to modern nationalist theories and policies. For example, the French developed new definitions of national citizenship, established new duties for national military service, created new state institutions for education, and affirmed the sovereignty of the "nation" over the traditional sovereign power of the king and church. The political meaning of nationalism thus developed rapidly in France during the 1790s, when French revolutionaries referred constantly to the citizens and institutions of the "nation." The term "nationalism," however, did not enter political discourse until an antirevolutionary French priest used this new word derisively in 1798 as part of a polemical attack on all of the revolution's dangerous new ideas and actions.[17] The revolutionaries themselves talked about "patriotism," but their descriptions of a patriotic French national identity were not altogether new. Drawing on historical research that shows important continuities between old-regime France and the revolution, some historians have argued that French national identity had already emerged in the seventeenth and eighteenth centuries among nobles (who claimed to represent France's ancient historical traditions), in the centralizing state bureaucracy, in the French army, in

the French Catholic Church, in the expanding French press, and in official projects to codify the French language.[18]

This emphasis on continuities, which extends the nineteenth-century
arguments of Alexis de Tocqueville, suggests that revolutionary ideas
about the nation made sense after 1789 because they repeated familiar,
long-developing claims about the distinctive achievements of French culture and the centralizing aspirations of French kings. Yet France's revolutionary activists also introduced crucial new themes into their narratives of
the nation. They sought to create an entirely new political system and political identity in France, thereby moving politics from the royal court at Versailles into the new National Assembly in Paris and more generally into the
everyday life of French citizens. This political transformation had radical
consequences, as Lynn Hunt has explained, because the new national leaders "acted on the conviction that the regenerated Nation was a new community without precedent in history, and this community was based on an
ideal of transparent social and political relations." The nation became in
this revolutionary account a political entity that was always moving toward
a better future rather than defending an imaginary past. Such movement
required constant *political* activity in order to sustain the new political
culture of national identity and the new political ideal of citizen participation.[19] The "subjects" who had lived under old-regime kings, in short, had to
learn the meaning of "citizenship" in the new sovereign nation.

The guiding ideas in this new political culture referred, as in America,
to the collective rights of national sovereignty and the human rights of
individual citizens. These two strands of nationalist thought became part
of the French Revolution's call for "Liberty, Equality, Fraternity," and they
entered into other ideals such as republican "virtue," but they were stated
most clearly in the Declaration of the Rights of Man and Citizen. This
famous document, which the revolutionary National Assembly approved
in August 1789, asserted that "all sovereignty rests essentially in the nation.
No body and no individual may exercise authority which does not emanate expressly from the nation." The fundamental principle of national
sovereignty made laws an "expression of the general will," which would
emerge from the legal equality of all French citizens. Indeed, the theoretical starting point for every specific law and policy of the nation could be
found in article one of the declaration: "Men are born and remain free and
equal in rights."[20] The new sovereign nation would therefore differ from
the political structure of the traditional French state (where the king was
sovereign) and the legal system of the traditional French society (where

laws and obligations applied differently to persons in separate social categories). Although the National Assembly did not always adhere to its own
declared principles, the "Declaration of Rights" contributed decisively
to a new French nationalism by redefining the sovereignty of the French
nation and the equal legal rights of all French citizens.

These new definitions of the nation appeared also in the vast production of popular political pamphlets that shaped the rapidly expanding
sphere of national political debates. More than 2,000 French pamphlets
were published in the first four months of 1789, and the stream of political
polemics would continue to flood Paris over the next ten years.[21] Amid this
torrent of new political language, the famous pamphlet by the Abbé Sieyès
(1748–1836), "What Is the Third Estate?," stands out as the most influential description of a new French national identity. Much like Paine's *Common Sense* in America, Sieyès's pamphlet argued that it was entirely logical
for the French to separate themselves from an outdated subservience to
political elites who no longer represented the will or the interests of the
nation. Denouncing the French nobility's claim for special privileges on
the basis of their special service to the state, Sieyès argued that the commoners of the Third Estate actually performed the essential, productive
work of the nation. In contrast to the nobility, which had become "foreign
to the Nation" because "its mission does not emanate from the people,"
the Third Estate represented the sovereign identity of France. "The Third
Estate therefore contains everything that pertains to the Nation," Sieyès
wrote, "and nobody outside of the Third Estate can claim to be part of the
Nation. What is the Third Estate? EVERYTHING." But this "nation" of the
third estate understood the equality of individual human rights as well as
its own essential sovereignty, so within this nation, Sieyès argued, all citizens "are equally dependent on the law, all present it with their liberty and
their property to be protected; and this is what I call the *common rights* of
citizens, by which they are all alike."[22]

Theoretical equality before the law did not mean for Sieyès that all
citizens should have equal rights to participate in public life. In fact, like
almost all of the French men who would eventually lead the revolutionary movement, Sieyès would later support the political distinctions that
separated the rights of well-to-do, "active" voting citizens from the rights
of poor, "passive" nonvoting citizens and also separated the political
rights of men from the legal rights of women—who could not vote or hold
office.[23] (Similar distinctions were also present in American nationalism,
including even more radical divisions between masters and slaves.) Such

inequalities in political rights showed the persistence of older ideas about gender and social hierarchies in the revolutionary era, but the other political distinctions in Sieyès's argument expressed a more radical view of how the earlier French government and society differed from a modern nation. The difference for Sieyès was between a national sovereignty based on the people instead of a king and between individual rights based on national citizenship instead of the legal positions of various social estates.

Sieyès's dichotomies therefore expressed the evolving themes of a new French national identity, which emerged through endless accounts of the social and political changes that separated the new French nation from an "old regime" of privilege, hierarchy, and superstition. Seeking to demonstrate the new regime's radical opposition to its political and social predecessor (especially after the execution of King Louis XVI in early 1793), French revolutionaries proclaimed a new calendar in which "Year One" coincided with the creation of the French republic (1792), and the renamed months were divided "rationally" into ten-day weeks called *décades*. The decree that established the new calendar portrayed the revolution's definitive break with all previous history in metaphors that could be compared to early Christian accounts (or dating) of the world before and after Christ: "The French nation, oppressed, degraded during many centuries by the most insolent despotism, has finally awakened to a consciousness of its rights and of the power to which its destinies summon it." To make sure that French citizens remained "awake" to their national political rights, however, revolutionary leaders emphasized every possible differentiation from the hated past, including the reorganization of time itself. "It wishes its regeneration to be complete," the official decree on the calendar continued, "in order that its years of liberty and glory may betoken still more by their duration in the history of peoples than its years of slavery and humiliation in the history of kings."[24] The nation's time, like the nation's geographic space, was therefore redefined to convey the meaning of radical political change. It would nevertheless take more than the renamed days, months, and years of a new calendar to produce a new nation; and so the French revolutionaries set out to create new clothing, language, flags, festivals, songs, furniture, armies, clergy, and political institutions, all of which theoretically opposed the old regime and carried the meaning of the new nation into daily life.[25]

Condemnations of the old regime thus reached into every sphere of public and private life, but the new rituals and symbols failed to produce national unity or the final victory of liberty and equality. Opponents of

Unknown artist, *The Triumph of the French Republic under the Auspices of Liberty*, pen and ink with watercolor and gouache, ca. 1793. This image conveys the revolutionary belief that France was overturning the oppressive institutions of human history. The new republic (symbolized by the seated woman whose arm embraces liberty) and the heroic action of a new Hercules (standing with his club) have toppled the monarchy and church (which lie subdued in the foreground), inscribed the "rights of man" on an elevated tablet, and forced the crowned heads of Europe to flee in despair. (Ackland Fund, Ackland Art Museum, University of North Carolina at Chapel Hill)

the revolution could still be found in all parts of France and along every French frontier, so that successive revolutionary governments repressed internal dissent and waged almost constant warfare after 1792. The revolutionary wars promoted a vivid sense of French national identity as the dominant political narratives extended the attacks against the old regime at home into attacks against oppressive old regimes abroad. A declaration of war on Prussia and Austria in 1792, for example, offered an occasion for the National Assembly to explain the meaning of its conflicts in a general proclamation to the people of France and the kings of Europe: "The French nation is free, and . . . conscious of its liberty. It is free; it is armed; it cannot be enslaved." This freedom now had to be defended in military campaigns that pitted "the just defence of a free people against the unjust aggression of a king." Repeating the themes of America's earlier separation from Britain and anticipating the rationale for most modern national wars, the French described their war as the necessary response to the provocations of an enemy with whom it was impossible to compromise. "To arms!" began a Jacobin proclamation in the following year. "The terrible hour is at hand when the defenders of the Patrie must vanquish or bury themselves under the bloody ruins of the Republic. Frenchmen, never was your liberty in such great peril!"[26]

War was thus portrayed as a consequence of the national support for sovereignty and human rights, and the requisite sacrifices were justified through the stark opposition of freedom and slavery. In the words of a popular revolutionary song, "Chant du depart," French soldiers fought the forces of absolute despotism:

> Tremble, enemies of France,
> Kings drunk with blood and pride,
> The Sovereign people advance,
> Tyrants, descend into the Grave![27]

Such narratives about royal "enemies" and the sovereign French nation translated the abstractions of political oratory into a comprehensible story for even the most illiterate soldier and the most distant provincial citizen.[28]

The new political definition of warfare described a national campaign on behalf of shared political ideals and brought all citizens into the service of a fully mobilized nation. Faced with enemies and defeats on all fronts, the revolutionary government decreed its famous "levée en masse" in August 1793, thereby defining the duties of everyone in France and setting an example for the "total" wars of all modern nations: "The young men shall go to battle; the married men shall forge arms and transport provisions; the women shall make tents and clothes, and shall serve in the hospitals; the children shall turn old linen into lint; the old men shall repair to the public places, to stimulate the courage of the warriors and preach the unity of the Republic and hatred of kings."[29] This national call to arms proved successful in saving the revolution from its domestic and foreign enemies, but its significance extended far beyond specific battles of the 1790s. France demonstrated how a new national government could mobilize its population and material resources with coercion *and* ideology. Equally important, it waged its wars with a new kind of apocalyptic rhetoric—describing warfare as a struggle for national survival against radically evil, dangerous enemies—that would reappear in the justifications for "total war" among nationalists everywhere in future centuries.[30] Young men often joined the French army as conscripts, yet they were constantly told that they fought for universal political principles (sovereignty of the nation, freedom, equality) as well as the defense of their national territory. Like the Americans before them, French political activists believed their revolution carried universal rather than local significance, and they confidently assumed their own nation's victories would promote freedom and equality in every European state. Although some foreigners served the revolutionary cause, the wars were viewed in France as a distinctive *French* campaign for the fundamental rights of all "mankind."[31]

The political theories of the French Revolution thus spread rapidly across Europe, but the diffusion of such ideas required far more than successful military campaigns. New claims for national sovereignty, human rights, and legal reforms could only develop and spread in the language and symbols of a new political discourse, which the French mobilized earlier and even more effectively than they mobilized their armies. Political nationalism needed new images and narratives in order to define the nation's identity and to change both the French social order and the wider world of European politics. This social and political reconstruction could not possibly proceed without the reconstruction of symbols and languages that had long sustained the old-regime church and monarchy. In other words, as Rousseau had argued in *The Social Contract*, a new republican nation must have a new civil religion. Political abstractions such as "natural rights" could not match the traditional aura of a king or the rituals of a Catholic mass in generating emotional attachments and personal loyalties to the state. Revolutionary leaders therefore developed alternative rituals to bring the new nation's political themes into the various spheres of everyday life. They promoted a new national identity through festivals, monuments, artwork, plays, "liberty trees," liberty caps and clothing, tricolor cockades, and countless other symbols of a regenerated French nation. The saints of Catholicism gave way to national martyrs, and the traditional images of the Virgin Mary or the royal family gave way to the new goddess of liberty, "Marianne." Statues of Marianne or Hercules offered illiterate persons the visual imagery to understand that national liberty and equality had replaced the king and church at the symbolic center of French life. Lacking a George Washington to serve as the symbol of political unity, the French represented the nation's identity and political meaning in portraits, festivals, and statues of "Liberty" and the "Republic."[32]

Revolutionary festivals, for example, were designed to provide a continuing political education for people who now had to learn the new national catechism in much the same way that they had learned how to be religious. The moral purpose of national festivals, wrote one of their advocates, was to give individual citizens a lifelong emotional connection to France by showing them how the bonds of a nation resembled the most intimate personal attachments in a family. The nation should be "the mother of all citizens, who gives them all the same milk, who brings them up and treats them as brothers and who, by the care that she lavishes equally upon all, gives them that air of family resemblance that distinguishes a people brought up in this way from all the other peoples of the earth. . . . She takes hold of the man and never leaves him, so that the upbringing of the nation is an institution not only for childhood, but for the whole life."[33] Public rituals thus became a kind of "political school" that taught people how their individual lives were linked to the collective life of the nation; and a person without a nation would be like a person without a family.

This narrative of national identity was repeated constantly in visual icons, literature, poems, and songs. The songwriter François de Neufchâteau, for example, wrote a "Hymn to Liberty" that transformed traditional injunctions to serve God into new political commands to serve the nation:

Love one's country and one's brothers,
Serve the sovereign people,
These are the sacred characteristics,
And the faith of a Republican.[34]

The story of national allegiance in Neufchâteau's "Hymn" and in other songs such as Rouget de Lisle's "Marseillaise" offered visions of national unity and freedom that could never be completely fulfilled. This frustrated desire for a transcendent unity contributed to the violence and systematic Terror of the French Revolution because criticisms of specific government policies or laws could be interpreted as treasonous threats to the very survival of the new national state. More generally, narratives of political inclusion and equality within the nation also *excluded* groups (for example, women and foreigners) who were placed outside the nation's political institutions and public debates.

Yet the revolutionary narratives about "liberty, equality, fraternity" also created a new national identity for which large numbers of French people were willing to kill or die. Although the Terror and the subsequent

Le Coeur, after Swebach, *Oath of the Federation of 14 July 1790*, etching and aquatint, 1790. The French revolutionaries created numerous festivals to express the meaning of their new national identity. This view of the celebration on the first anniversary of the fall of the Bastille shows how the new nationalist rituals stressed the national unity of men and women from all social classes, professions, and generations. (Image courtesy of the Division of Rare and Manuscript Collections, Cornell University Libraries)

imperialism of French armies discredited many of the revolution's political theories, the national theme of "fraternity" continued to flourish in the Napoleonic French state after 1799. It also began to appear among the European critics of France's growing national power. Indeed, the expansive nationalism in France gradually helped to create its most dangerous rivals by stimulating anti-French nationalisms throughout Europe. No matter what they thought of "liberty" and "equality," Europeans could find ideals for their own states and cultures in the revolutionary concepts of national "fraternity" and national "sovereignty."

National Responses to the French Revolution

French revolutionaries proclaimed the human rights of national liberty and self-determination, but their military campaigns in the late 1790s increasingly denied these rights to other European societies. The French thus contributed a positive ideology (self-determination) to justify resistance to their own policies (conquest); and the resistance to French imperialism helped to produce a new self-consciousness about national identities throughout much of Europe. Within France itself, the revolutionary themes of national citizenship and political participation evolved into a Bonapartist nationalism that demanded service to the sovereign nation-state but dispensed with most of the other "Rights of Man and Citizen" that had been so important to the earlier liberal view of the nation.[35] Yet Napoleon and his emissaries claimed to bring the universal principles of Enlightenment reason and reform to the countries that fell under French control, thus creating a political context in which the evolving opposition to French imperialism could easily merge with a cultural critique of "French" Enlightenment theories. There were, of course, conservative, traditional strands in French nationalism (as Napoleon demonstrated in many of his own policies), but for most persons outside France, the critique of revolutionary and imperial France became also a critique of the liberal Enlightenment.[36]

This conservative critique developed in both the British and German responses to the French Revolution. Although most British and German intellectuals strongly supported the revolution's early liberal reforms, the subsequent Terror and military expansion rapidly eroded this early identification with France and helped to produce new ideologies that celebrated the unique value of British and German national traditions. British nationalists, for example, defined their national mission in defiant anti-French language (as one popular ballad put it, "God smash the French . . . We'll shoot them every one"), but the national mobilization of British soldiers may also have contributed to a more democratic British society. The anti-French struggle acquired some of the traits of a Jacobin *levée en masse*, and common soldiers who joined the national campaign would have new grounds for demanding and expecting more political participation in the postwar British state.[37] The French enemy was therefore both rejected and, in some respects, imitated during the long wars with revolutionary and Napoleonic France. For the most part, however, British ideological responses to the French Revolution and Napoleon pushed the evolving British nationalism toward conservative ideas about Britain's distinctive political and social institutions.

This newly defined British nationalism stressed the nation's political and cultural differences from the threatening new regime of the French Revolution, a theme that shaped both the theory and passion of Edmund Burke's (1729–97) famous *Reflections on the Revolution in France* (1790). Burke's book became a "founding text" of modern conservatism and provoked an angry critique in Thomas Paine's *Rights of Man* (1791–92), but it also provided the narrative for a new nationalism that defined Britain's collective identity by emphasizing its opposition to the French Revolution and the political theories of the French Enlightenment. In contrast to the French belief in natural rights, Burke wrote, the English were happy "to derive all we possess as *an inheritance from our forefathers*." Where the French blindly embraced reason, radicalism, and revolution, the English nation honored the wisdom of its ancestors and protected its historical legacy through the continuity of its traditional institutions. Comparing the English to a cud-chewing cow in the shadow of a "British oak," Burke assumed (or hoped) that England would never accept political ideas from France. "Thanks to our sullen resistance to innovation, thanks to the cold sluggishness of our national character, we still bear the stamp of our forefathers. . . . We are not the converts of Rousseau; we are not the disciples of Voltaire." More precisely, Burke continued, "we are generally men of untaught feelings, . . . [and] instead of casting away all our old prejudices, we cherish them to a very considerable degree, . . . and the longer they have lasted and the more generally they have prevailed, the more we cherish them."[38] In short, Burke's critique of the French Revolution developed an intellectual rationale for a new British nationalism that rejected Enlightenment universalism as well as the revolutionary confidence in radical reforms—and then praised the distinctiveness and mysteries of a specific national culture.

Unknown artist, *Britannia Blowing up the Corsican Bottle Conjurer,* etching with hand
coloring published by R. Ackerman, 1803. The British wars against revolutionary and
Napoleonic France contributed to the assertive nationalist identity that is depicted in this
caricature of Napoleon. "British spirits," which are "composed of True Liberty, Courage,
Loyalty & Religion," are destined to overpower the hapless, hatless "Corsican" general.
(From the copy in the Hoyt Collection, Rare Book Collection, University of North Carolina at Chapel Hill)

Burke's writings later attracted sympathetic readers in Germany, where a similar interest in the specificity of national cultures had already emerged in the work of Johann Gottfried von Herder (1744–1803) and other intellectuals who challenged Enlightenment claims for the transcultural truths of reason. In contrast to Burke, however, most German intellectuals at first welcomed the French Revolution because it represented what Friedrich von Gentz (1764–1832) called "the first practical triumph of philosophy, [and] the first example of a form of government founded upon principles and upon an integrated consistent system of thought." Gentz soon became a bitter critic of the revolution, but he was still praising the French in late 1790 for their assaults on the "many ancient evils" of tyranny and oppressive governments.[39]

Such views were by no means unusual among the many intellectuals who believed that the revolution offered philosophical and political lessons for Germany. A revolutionary republic was actually established at Mainz in the German Rhineland (October 1792), giving at least some German political activists reason to believe that a new era of international freedom and equality had begun.[40] Although the short-lived republicanism in Mainz did not inspire other Jacobin experiments in Germany, many Germans continued to admire certain aspects of what France achieved during the later revolutionary and Napoleonic wars because the French had shown how a unified, mobilized nation could enact reforms, protect its own territory, and also impose its political will on others. Prominent figures such as Wilhelm von Humboldt (reformer of Prussian education) and the military theorist Carl von Clausewitz drew on French ideas as they set about modernizing the Prussian state and reconstructing the Prussian army. Meanwhile, some of the most creative thinkers in Germany—including Goethe and Hegel—never embraced the more radical nationalist critiques of France or Napoleon. Early nineteenth-century German nationalism often promoted liberal ideas such as national sovereignty and individual rights, and liberal nationalists supported "enlightened" reform of the prevailing privileges and political hierarchies in the diverse German states.[41]

Despite the liberal political strands in German culture, however, a much stronger intellectual-political movement harshly condemned the French Revolution and developed a new account (mostly after 1800) of how German culture differed profoundly from the French. Friedrich von Gentz, whose transition from supporter to angry critic exemplified the changing German view of France, translated Burke's *Reflections* into German (1793) and began publishing his own dire warnings about the dangers of France's entire revolutionary project. Gentz decided that Germans could learn nothing from the French example except that such revolutions led to disastrous outcomes. "The French Revolution never had a definite object," Gentz wrote in 1800, so it "ran through the unbounded space of a fantastic arbitrary will, and of a bottomless anarchy." Denying the most basic human feelings and needs, the revolution could "only force its way by violence and crimes," all of which Germany must reject in order to protect its own institutions and society.[42]

A new generation of intellectuals thus moved (like Gentz) beyond the politics of the French Revolution to develop a new definition of the nation, stressing German differences from France and the Enlightenment. Although this emphasis on difference resembled the themes of Burke's work in England, German writers tended to emphasize their nation's distinctive culture, *Volk*, and philosophical insights more than their unique political institutions. Herder's influential earlier writings, for example, argued that "every nation is one people, having its own national form."[43] This view of the essential differences among nations offered an attractive theory for explaining why German culture could and should survive after Napoleon's crushing defeat of the Prussian and Austrian armies in 1806. This military-political catastrophe for the Prussian state became the context for Fichte's *Addresses to the German Nation*, which argued that Germans must come together "into a single close-knit power" and promote the "concord of spirit" within a regenerated national "fatherland."[44]

The new philosophical appeals to the German nation did not address specific questions of political or military reform, but they clarified the cultural meaning of Germany by stressing the German difference from France. Opposition to French politics and culture enabled German nationalists to describe what it meant to be "German," no matter how individual German states or persons might differ in less important ways among themselves. "Let the unanimity of your hearts be your church," wrote the poet Ernst Moritz Arndt (1769–1860) in 1814, "let hatred of the French be your religion, let Freedom and Fatherland be your saints, to whom you pray." Calls for German unity thus emerged from the constantly invoked dangers of a French enemy whose differences posed the starkest dangers to Germany's national existence. "France has become for us the true antithesis in the struggle in which all our moral forces are called forth," the journalist Joseph Görres (1776–1848) explained in a concise summary of the identity-shaping, apocalyptic oppositions of the era; "it is a center of devouring fire and the totality of all evil, . . . and the

The Napoleonic Empire in Europe, 1810. This map shows how the French expanded their imperial control into the Rhineland, the Low Countries, Italy, and even into the Balkans; and it suggests why Napoleon's military conquests provoked nationalist reactions from all directions.

struggle with it will . . . force the missing unity upon our people and thus avert us from civil war."[45]

The immediate object of such declarations was, of course, the military defeat of Napoleon, but the larger enemy in this campaign for the German nation could be found in the political ideas and policies of France's Enlightenment and revolution. Defined as an alien imposition on German culture, "French" ideas became an all-important object for critique in the construction of German nationalism. Similar nation-shaping interactions between France and Germany continued long after the Napoleonic era, though these interactions did not always point simply to absolute national differences. Nationalists in each society also drew on the other to develop new accounts or definitions of their own national cultures. There would always be Germans who invoked the French Enlightenment and liberal political ideas as alternatives to the cultural or philosophical themes of German nationalism, and French nationalists in later eras would draw on German ideas about the uniqueness of cultures and national populations to describe their own distinctive language, traditions, and *peuple*. Later descriptions of national similarities or (more commonly) national differences, however, continued to refer to the revolution that had so profoundly influenced the development of nationalisms in both England and Germany. The French interactions with these other nationalisms, in turn, helped to extend and redefine France's own evolving nationalist political culture, so that Europeans carried the nationalist legacy of the revolutionary era into all of their later wars, economic rivalries, and political disputes.

The Nationalist Political Legacy of the American and French Revolutions

The nearly universal modern belief that every nation must have its own state and that each state must represent a sovereign nation reiterates key political themes of the eighteenth-century revolutions in America and Europe. From that era until the present, national movements have claimed to express the sovereign political will of specific national populations, to defend the human rights of political or legal equality, and to protect the personal rights of individual citizens. The American and French Revolutions embodied for contemporaries and for later interpreters the political ideas and institutions of liberal nationalism. Although these ideas were constantly violated in both societies (for example, in America's brutal treatment of Indians and slaves, in France's imperialist wars and repression

Europe after the Congress of Vienna, 1815. The diplomatic settlements in 1815 pushed
France back within its prerevolutionary borders, expanded Prussian influence in western
Germany, gave new territories to both the Austrian and Russian empires, and further
reduced the lands and autonomy of Poland; but the postwar boundaries also created the
context for new nineteenth-century nationalist movements in central and southern Europe.

of dissent, and in the exclusion of women from the political institutions of both countries), the emerging theories of national sovereignty and human rights shaped both the American Declaration of Independence and the French Declaration of the Rights of Man and Citizen. More generally, such theories often reappeared in later national movements throughout Europe, South America, Asia, and Africa, where political leaders produced new narratives to describe the inherent rights of their nations and citizens as well as the political principles of their national cultures. National rights and individual rights have often collided, and every nation has violated the "universal" rights of its own citizens in various times, places, and crises. Yet the narratives that create modern, national political identities have always referred in some way to the ideas of national and human rights.

All nationalists have also described their nations with explicit or implicit references to other (past or present) nations whose ideas and actions differ from their own nation's political ideals, institutions, or achievements. Descriptions of difference have appeared as frequently as the claims for political rights in national narratives because the "imagined community" requires outsiders or enemies in order to define the imagined unity and coherence of the nation. Liberal nationalists, for example, defined their revolutionary national objectives in opposition to Old World monarchs and corrupt "old regimes," whereas the new conservative nationalists began to defend their distinctive national identities by opposing republican revolutions and Enlightenment intellectuals.

Later nationalisms often developed a much stronger emphasis on differences of race, ethnicity, religion, or language, but even the most militant cultural nationalisms have usually asserted theories of national political sovereignty that appeared earlier in America's Declaration of Independence or France's Declaration of the Rights of Man and Citizen. Modern nationalisms have also resembled the eighteenth-century revolutions in their use of national rituals, festivals, songs, art, and monuments to construct and narrate the meaning of the nation. These enduring contributions to nationalist theory and practice may therefore remain the most influential and far-reaching historical and political consequences of the American and French Revolutions. Nationalist ideals and institutions have differed enormously in various historical and cultural contexts, yet every modern nation has developed a political claim for national sovereignty, a legal description of national citizenship, a historical narrative of national differences, and a cultural collection of national symbols.

CHAPTER THREE

Land, Language, & Writing

All nations and nationalisms claim a homeland or bounded territory, and all use languages and literary narratives to describe their political and cultural identities. Political movements for national independence have therefore always referred to specific geographical places and specific national languages, thus connecting politics, land, and languages as overlapping components of a coherent national culture. Although historians have often made distinctions between cultural nationalisms (which emphasize language and ethnicity) and political nationalisms (which emphasize political rights), this account of differences obscures the crucial geographical claims and linguistic traits that all nationalisms share, including nationalist movements that are still struggling to establish an independent state. Nations assert their sovereign rights to defend particular territories and languages as well as certain political and human rights, but the *meaning* of national territories, national linguistic traditions, and national histories evolves in popular narratives that "nationalize" geographical spaces and the memory of past times. The political themes of modern nationalisms and sovereign states are thus forever entangled with the cultural nationalism of modern writing and education.

Lands and Boundaries

Nationhood can scarcely be imagined without reference to specific lands, just as selfhood cannot be understood without reference to specific human bodies. Nations evoke what the historian R. J. B. Bosworth calls the "religious sense of belonging to a land"—a modern theme that goes back to antiquity but gained new poetic and cultural dimensions in the nineteenth-century romantic fascination with nature and landscapes.[1] Modern nationalism spread across Europe and the Americas at the same time that writers and artists were celebrating sublime human encounters with natural beauty, creative geniuses, or historical ruins, all of which merged in romantic stories about national lands and national heroes. The German philosopher J. G. von Herder was especially influential in stressing that geography could be as important as languages and cultures in shaping the collective identities of national populations. Although Herder's discussion of nature and culture referred mostly to "sensual" peoples (that is, non-Europeans) who were deeply "attached to the soil" and "inseparable" from the natural climates in which they were born, others extended his assumptions about land and climate to almost every national population in the world. Geography and identity seemed to intersect, Herder explained in his famous *Reflections on the Philosophy of the History of Mankind* (1784), so that the "Arab of the desert" carries a connection with nature into his "simple clothing, his maxims of life, his manners, and his character." Deep attachments to the land could also explain the "lasting hatred of the natives of America toward Europeans," who had usurped the Indians' ancestral territories in the New World. Summarizing the response to this occupation with phrases that might also have described Europeans during their later wars with France, Herder wrote that Native Americans "cannot suppress the feeling: 'This land is ours; you have no business here.'" He conceded that Europeans had reason to complain about the violence of "savages," but he also argued that such violence was understandable whenever "despots" seized places that people had inherited from "their fathers."[2] All people (and not just "savages"), in other words, would use violence to defend their land against encroachments from outsiders.

This emphasis on lands and collective identities would reappear in all kinds of national movements throughout the nineteenth and twentieth centuries, beginning with the responses to France's imperial conquests in Germany and Italy. Johann Gottlieb Fichte's *Addresses to the German Nation* (1808), for example, referred to the German "Fatherland" and stressed that the earliest German people had always retained a close link to their own lands, whereas other ancient peoples lost their cultural essence as they wandered across Europe. "The first difference between the fate of the Germans and that of the other tribes," Fichte asserted in one of his historical lectures, was that "the former remained in the original homelands of the ancestral race, whereas the latter migrated to other territories." This allegiance to ancient lands may not have been so significant in itself, Fichte continued, but loyalty to their own territory helped Germans protect their distinctive language and institutions. Staying on the land was thus the first step toward retaining a unique cultural identity, and the boundaries of the homeland became also the border for an autonomous German culture.[3]

This emphasis on the link between territorial homelands and distinctive national cultures would become a common nationalist theme over the following century. In the early American republic, nationalists referred to the "manifest destiny" of a people who were ordained to occupy a vast continent "from sea to shining sea"; and European nationalists such as the Italian writer Giuseppe Mazzini (1805–72) advanced similar claims for "national lands" in the Old World. The older "divine right" of kings gave way to a new belief in the "divine right" of specific peoples to control well-bounded territories. Mazzini, among many others, thus argued in the 1830s and 1840s for the "natural" significance of national borders, which seemed also to coincide with the boundaries of linguistic communities. As he wrote in *The Duties of Man*:

> To you, who have been born in Italy[,] God has allotted . . . the best-defined country in Europe. . . . God has stretched round you sublime and indisputable boundaries; on one side the highest mountains of Europe, the Alps; on the other the sea, the immeasurable sea. . . . As far as this frontier your language is spoken and understood. . . . Brute force may for a little while contest these frontiers with you, but they have been recognized from of old by the tacit general consent of the peoples. . . .
>
> Your Country is one and indivisible. . . . [And] so you should have no repose as long as a portion of the territory upon which your language is spoken is separated from the Nation.[4]

Mazzini was writing well after Herder and Fichte, and his own nationalism was definitely more "cosmopolitan" than the nationalism in Fichte's *Addresses*. His imagined map of Italian lands, however, evoked ideas of national character, territory, and language that resembled the earlier cultural claims of the German philosophers. It was, of course, impossible to align national territories and languages along precise political boundaries, yet the cultural claims for both a national land and a national language became central themes of modern nationalist thought. The story of national lands that reached from mountains to seas was presented constantly in the books, newspapers, maps, and schools that helped people envision a coherent national space; and defense of the national lands was often linked to defense of a national language, as in Fichte and Mazzini.

Language and Identity

The connections between nationalisms and languages carry significantly different meanings for nationalists and critical-minded cultural historians. Nationalists have usually claimed that languages express essential national, cultural identities and that each distinctive linguistic culture should have its own nation-state. Although cultural historians also emphasize the importance of language, they tend to reject "essentialist" cultural and linguistic accounts of the nation and examine instead how nationalists have constructed the symbols and narratives that sustain national identities. People spoke languages before the emergence of modern nations, of course, but the nationalist use of language developed later to create social coherence within specific territories and to justify the modern exercise of political power. Where the nationalist sees a deep or premodern linguistic spirit emerging in modern nation-states, the cultural historian is likely to see modern nationalist institutions and states retrospectively constructing a cultural and linguistic coherence that past generations never recognized or understood. For the advocates of both arguments, however, language shapes the dynamic, evolving identities of nations and nationalisms.

Most nationalists therefore promote a single, unifying language and view this language, like the national land, as an essential aspect of the nation's political and cultural identity. Praise for the unique qualities of the English and French languages, for example, became an important early theme in the political nationalisms of England and France, so it would be wrong to assume that writers in central and eastern Europe were the only nationalists to justify their aspirations for political unity and independence on the basis of linguistic traditions. Many of the most notable *linguistic* explanations for national autonomy and identity nevertheless emerged first in central Europe, where authors such as Herder and Fichte argued that different cultural assumptions were embedded in different languages. Herder assumed that every nationality had "its own language" as well as its own lands; and although he did not deny that deep similarities could be found among people in various national cultures, his emphasis on the intricate overlap of language, culture, and ideas contributed a strong linguistic rationale to the political arguments for independent, sovereign states. When people speak different languages, nationalists would argue, they express different ideas and develop different institutions—all of which should be embodied in the governments of different nation-states. Fichte summarized the argument in this way: "[W]herever a particular language is found, there exists also a particular nation which has the right to run its own affairs and to govern itself."[5]

Nationalists therefore assumed that language both expressed and protected the life of a nation, and the loss of language would cause its death. Expanding these linguistic assumptions to the battlefield, nationalists could link the war against French armies to a broader national resistance against the French language. "When a nation's language falls into disrepute and decay," wrote one German patriot shortly after the Napoleonic wars, "the manner in which it observes and judges things is also lost." France's threat to the German language was thus even more dangerous than the destruction of Prussia's army because the suppression of the national language would destroy the essential, unifying bond of the German people.[6] Anti-Napoleonic nationalism in Germany portrayed linguistic identity as a foundation for the revival of independent political institutions, thereby developing a linguistic-political argument that later national movements would also use to promote linguistic autonomy from occupying powers. In this view, new nations evolved from old languages into social and political alliances that culminated in new political states. "Those who speak the same language," Fichte explained, "are already . . . joined together by mere nature with a multitude of invisible ties; . . . they belong together and are naturally one, an indivisible whole." These deep bonds also made it impossible for any "other nation of a different descent and language" to absorb or long control a unique linguistic community. The "men" of an occupied nation might "dwell within the confines of certain mountains and rivers," Fichte concluded, but their essential nationality survived in a shared language that created "a people . . . by a far higher law of nature."[7]

Fichte's account of how language sustained the "invisible ties" of a nation expressed a common nineteenth-century view of the nation's essential cultural identity. For most contemporary cultural historians, however, the arguments of Fichte and other like-minded authors suggest how modern nations were actually constructed or imagined by those who claimed to speak for the "people"—an amorphous entity that gained apparent coherence in the rhetoric of nationalist philosophers and political leaders. People lived in specific places and spoke specific languages, but they did not become a nation until nationalist writers, historians, and political leaders defined their collective identity as a "national" community.

Nations therefore acquired a new cultural prominence and identity through the new linguistic and historical studies of early nineteenth-century authors. These identity-shaping narratives entered the lives of literate people through new schools and other state institutions that taught a national language and spread cultural or political descriptions of the nation's history to communities that had rarely or never imagined themselves as part of a large national state. People in such scattered places did not "naturally" become French, German, Russian, or any other national identity, but they learned to describe themselves with these national adjectives as they attended schools, public festivals, church services, or military ceremonies and as they read national newspapers, novels, historical narratives, or travel books. The political and literary cultures of nations were thus shaped through countless "communicative acts" that gradually extended nationalist ideas and practices into almost every aspect of daily life.[8]

New forms of literature and history praised the distinctive national sacrifices of previous generations and explained how national heroes had served the universal progress of humanity as well as the specific interests of the nation. Adjusted to fit the circumstances of each nation, the themes of personal sacrifice and collective purpose became familiar in all the romantic nationalisms of the early nineteenth century. Philosophers, poets, novelists, and historians narrated the cultural meaning of their nations in popular writings that went far beyond the official declarations or policies of political leaders, yet the literary works also resembled the political speeches whenever they repeated the most straightforward political and military dichotomies of national difference. The language of the nation had to be defended against different languages and cultures that flourished like other national enemies both inside and outside the nation. The dangers and differences called for strong national action and unity, but the collective cultural identity also depended on the continued existence of such dangers. The nation's unifying identity and purpose emerged most clearly in its opposition to other people and cultures, so that the disappearance of national enemies could threaten the nation's cultural coherence and survival almost as profoundly as the enemies themselves.

The revolutionary activists in France, for example, defined their national language against both the hierarchical language of the old regime and the regional *patois* languages that seemed to threaten the political unity and cultural coherence of the nation. Local dialects represented a linguistic difference that could easily fuse with political differences to undermine the national revolution. As Abbé Grégoire (1750–1831) stressed in a report to the National Convention (1794) titled "On the necessity and the methods for destroying the Patois and making usage of the French language universal," the "universalizing" political aspirations of the revolution could only be accomplished in a shared French language. The new political nationalism in France thus linked political reforms to linguistic reforms and described French culture with repeated references to the enduring dangers of cultural and linguistic differences.[9]

Foreign critics of the revolution and France's subsequent imperial expansion also seized on the linguistic meaning of French politics, so that the attack on revolutionary ideas often overlapped with a wider cultural attack on the French language. German nationalists argued that French was a weak language whose derivation from the ancient Latin meant that it could never express the originality and creative strength of German. A strong, original nation, in this linguistic view, could only emerge from an original language. Much like the self-affirming dichotomies in France's revolutionary theory (national or republican versus local or monarchical), the description of national culture in Germany presumed a linguistic difference (original versus derivative) that gave German a higher position in the national cultural hierarchy. "It is only a daughter language," noted a typical German commentary on the gendered weakness of French, "a spurious language, deflected and subjected by tyrants." Language therefore produced and reflected the essential traits of a nation, including its creativity, its originality, and even its national virility. The best language, according to German theorists, emerged from the depths of a national population, whereas weaker languages evolved out of other cultures and the contrivances of superficial academic elites. "Naturalness on the German side," Fichte explained in his summary of the linguistic dichotomy, "arbitrariness and artificiality on the foreign side."[10]

Similar claims for cultural superiority could extend to the literature of a nation as well as its language, though the status of national literatures was typically established, like the status of languages, through comparisons with other cultures and a strong desire for cultural purity. The Polish poet Adam Mickiewicz (1798–1855), for example, asserted that Slavic literature grew directly out of "the soul" of the Slavic "people" and thus "differed completely" from the writers and books of other nations.[11] The problem for such linguistic and literary advocates of the nation, however, resembled the problem facing the political advocates of nationalism. Nationalist narratives described a unified, pure national language, yet the meaning of this linguistic identity depended on its relation to other languages that threatened both the purity and unity of the true national language. Given these problems of linguistic interaction and infiltration, national narratives about linguistic and cultural identity had to be constantly promoted and rewritten in nationalist publications, songs, art, and schools. The "people," in other words, had to learn how they were connected and why they were a nation.

Spreading the Language of the Nation

The nationalist belief in popular, unifying languages faced the disconcerting reality of linguistic diversity in almost every would-be national society. There were at least thirty regional *patois* languages in France, for example, and incomprehensible differences between the rural and urban languages in Germany. The call for national political and cultural unity was therefore stymied in practice by the fact that much of the "national" population could not understand what their national leaders said on their behalf. "The people," as the French reformer Grégoire explained in the midst of the French Revolution, "must understand the laws to approve and obey them."[12] Grégoire wanted to create a new republican nation, but he realized, like most of his revolutionary allies, that this new nation could not exist until the people of France shared a common language. He therefore developed ambitious proposals to diffuse a standardized republican French language into the villages of France, emphasizing the need for new schools and grammar books. The French nation was to be reformed through education, which meant that the French political revolution inevitably became also a prolonged campaign for national educational reforms.

This new "nationalization" of the masses might be compared to earlier conversions of European populations to Christianity. "Missionaries" went into the countryside to establish new schools, teach the alien national language, and combat older beliefs and sources of local identity. The language of elites had to be translated into the language of common people (and vice versa), though in theory the teachers were returning the national language to a population from which it had come. "We must popularize the language," wrote the French linguistic activist Barère; "we must destroy this aristocracy of language which seems to establish a polite nation in the middle of a barbarous nation. We have revolutionized the government . . . [and] we must now also revolutionize the language."[13]

Education thus became an enduring concern of France's successive revolutionary governments, but, as in other aspects of emerging modern nationalisms, the revolution's foreign critics also began promoting many of the French-style linguistic reforms in their own societies. Every nationalist movement wanted to revolutionize and nationalize education. Fichte's *Addresses to the German Nation* gave more attention to the need for a "new education" than to any other issue in German culture and society because education offered the specific institutional structure for national survival and regeneration. "Through the new education," Fichte argued, "we desire to form the Germans into a totality that in all its individual parts is driven and animated by the same single interest."[14] Utopian aspirations for national unity thus generated utopian proposals for teaching the German population how it might actually acquire the unified linguistic and philosophical qualities of the ideal German nation. But the Germans were by no means alone in looking to education for their national unity and salvation. "Without National Education," the exiled Italian nationalist Mazzini wrote in *The Duties of Man*, "a nation has no moral existence."[15]

The influence and success of nationalist plans for changing national education varied widely and depended, of course, on the relation between nationalist writers and the governments in their societies. An exiled Italian or Polish nationalist had less direct impact on education policies than, say, the intellectuals who worked for the ministry of public instruction in the French government. Even the most active intellectual intervention could not produce the national morality and unity that nationalists envisioned, but schools became increasingly important in the creation of new national identities. The French government's expenditure on education, for example, roughly quadrupled between 1789 and 1812. New textbooks taught national languages and national histories, new maps provided the visual imagery for students to place themselves within national boundaries, and new school examinations defined the national knowledge that people needed when they sought jobs in the national government or in the private businesses of the national economy. Education moved steadily from the churches into the hands of state bureaucracies, which opened the schools to far more people (at least at the elementary level) than in any previous era. Educated workers and soldiers were needed in new national economies and armies, where the citizens of nineteenth-century nations continued to learn about their national states and cultures long after they had left school. Young persons who entered national business enterprises or national military units quickly recognized that advancement in every sphere required knowledge of the national language, culture, and government. Elite national languages thus challenged and gradually displaced local vernacular languages, partly in the schools and partly in the other institutions of modernizing European states. Children learned and were rewarded for their national identities in school, but they continued to be rewarded for their national educations and identities throughout their adult lives.[16]

The collective activities of education, state bureaucracies, and national economic institutions all depended on written information and ideas, a universal pattern that connects the history of nationalism to the modern history of publishing, journalism, and mass communications. Some historians have in fact described the modern nation as a centralized communications network that carries national narratives of events and culture from major urban centers into all classes and geographical regions of a political state. Modern nationalism, in this view, entered public life through the publications industry and the newspapers that expanded rapidly before and after the eighteenth-century political revolutions. New books, pamphlets, journals, maps, engravings, and popular newspapers flowed from the printing presses of nations and nationalist movements, giving people the language to locate themselves within national territories and collective national stories. Literacy created a booming market for publishers, so that new nationalisms developed at the intersection of education, communications, and the new economy. As Benedict Anderson has argued in his account of this historical transition, "the convergence of capitalism and print technology on the fatal diversity of human language created the possibility of a new form of imagined community."[17] Daily newspapers brought the nation into the lives of individuals who had learned to read the national story at school, and national rituals (as reported in newspapers) provided continuities and meanings that had once come from the rituals and calendars of the church.

The rapid expansion of education, journalism, and other forms of national communication created the need for a growing number of writers to produce new narratives of the nation. Schools needed textbooks, language manuals, examinations, and teachers; newspapers needed journalists; publishing houses needed authors; and all nationalist movements and governments needed literary advocates. In short, a new class of intellectual experts and critics emerged along with the new nationalisms and demanded a special status within the state (or in exile) as defenders of the "people" and the culture of a national community. "The noblest privilege

Fiayn and Chaponnier, after a drawing by Lembert, *Crossing the Bridge at Arcole*, etching and engraving, ca. 1797. The French republic's wars became a popular subject for a new nationalist art that helped people learn their recent national history. This engraving depicts one of Napoleon's famous battles against Austrian forces during the Italian campaign in 1796 and portrays the heroic service that other French citizens should emulate; Napoleon leads his troops to victory beneath flags that represent the "French people" and "French Republic." (From the copy in the Hoyt Collection, Rare Book Collection, University of North Carolina at Chapel Hill)

and the most sacred office of the writer," wrote Fichte, "is . . . to assemble his nation and consult with it on its most important affairs." Writers could contribute even more than governments to the life of nations, particularly when they claimed (to quote Fichte again) that the nation was "held together as a common whole only by the spoken and written word."[18] This argument for the significance of writers was, of course, a flattering, self-referential view of how literature defined national life, but it was also at least partially accurate inasmuch as the nation took its imagined coherence from the narratives of its history and ideas and enemies. The need for writers was as great as the need for soldiers; and it would be impossible in this respect to separate "political" nationalisms from "cultural" nationalisms. Writers and their national texts defined every national identity, though the status and themes of writers who sought to create new nation-states often differed from the status and themes of writers who represented the nationalisms of established nation-states.

Fichte's description of writers gave them exceptional importance to the nation, but his views were not unusual. From the other side of the Atlantic, for example, Ralph Waldo Emerson (1803–82) was urging American writers to add their work to the new American nation's struggle for national independence. Calling for a new American culture in his famous essay "The American Scholar" (1837), Emerson described the scholar as a "man who must take up into himself all the ability of the time, all the contributions of the past, all the hopes of the future." This project required writing and thinking that could break free from the national cultures of Europe and produce new narratives for the New World. "We have listened too long to the courtly muses of Europe," he complained in this "American" essay that went on to describe what the writers of a new nation must do. "We will walk on our own feet; we will work with our own hands; we will speak our own minds. The study of letters shall be no longer a name for pity, for doubt, and for sensual indulgence." Instead, Emerson continued, the scholar (who was always male in this description) would provide practical national service by linking individuals to a higher world of national and spiritual transcendence: "A nation of men will for the first time exist, because each believes himself inspired by the Divine Soul which also inspires all men."[19]

Despite the differences between Fichte's faith in the national spirit and Emerson's faith in individualism, both authors wrote narratives of national identity that would long circulate in schools, books, and newspapers. They both lectured to university audiences, published their lectures for wider public spheres, and became prominent symbols of their national cultures. The diffusion of nationalist ideas in such writings suggests the influence of intellectuals in modern national movements—an influence that resembles the role of theologians and clergy in the diffusion of religions. Yet the self-conscious advocates of the nation could not simply proclaim the nation's existence in the language and independence of its people. They had to show how the continuities in their national literatures, religions, politics, and histories *separated* their nations from other cultures and *connected* their nations to the past as well as the spirit of their own era.

National Literatures and National Identities

The search for the distinctive traits of national cultures and languages raised questions about where the meaning of such cultures could be clearly identified. Although nationalists commonly referred to the "people" as the embodiment of unique cultural traditions, it was difficult to describe the specific qualities or ideas that gave diverse, anonymous populations their shared national identity. The history of writing and linguistic usage therefore provided some of the best evidence for the belief in coherent national cultures because literary works were interpreted as expressions of the enduring national spirit and ideals. An earlier, eighteenth-century Enlightenment desire to write about universal reason and general historical truths gave way in many places to a new romantic emphasis on the particular truths and national experiences that appeared in specific national literatures.

Romantic literature thus overlapped with romantic nationalism throughout much of Europe and America, linking the romantic literary belief in unique creative artists with the romantic nationalist belief in unique creative cultures. The romantic literary critique of the Enlightenment gained influence in all parts of the Western world, but many historians stress the exceptional appeal of romanticism for German intellectuals who resented their marginal position within both the fragmented German states and the wider intellectual networks of Europe. Critics of German nationalism have argued that unhappy writers celebrated their national literature and language in order to establish their own social status, resist the universalizing claims of the Enlightenment, and assert their independence from the political legacy of the French Revolution.[20] Although this argument for German intellectual *ressentiment* relies on debatable claims about the uniqueness of German nationalism, romanticism clearly helped to shape nationalism in Germany and other central European societies. More generally, however, romantic writers in all modern cultures argued that literature embodied the truth of the nation by representing the spirit of less articulate national populations. "Rustic popular culture," the historian Joep Leerssen notes in a concise summary of nineteenth-century nationalist ideas, was "canonized into the very essence and bedrock of the national identity."[21]

National writing about the "people" became a prominent component of nineteenth-century novels, dramas, literary criticism, philosophy, poetry, and history. Novelists such as Sir Walter Scott and James Fenimore Cooper, for example, wrote romantic stories about medieval Britain or early America (*Ivanhoe* and the *Leatherstocking Tales* were especially popular) and created national literary characters whom readers came to know like the national political characters in their newspapers. Benefiting from the growth of the publishing industry and the expanding market of readers, novelists described national heroes or traditions and often linked love of the nation to other forms of love in families and personal life. The imagined world of the novel helped people imagine the world of their nation because novels were filled (like newspapers) with accounts of different persons acting at the same time in a shared space and national story. Novels thus told past or present stories about nations, and the stories of nations evolved like literary plots in which the characters struggled against adversities and symbolized dramatic national sacrifices, conflicts, or triumphs.[22]

The rise of the novel helped to spawn new forms of literary criticism that evaluated and interpreted the national literature for a growing public audience. Prominent critics such as Charles Augustin Sainte-Beuve (1804–69) in France and William Hazlitt (1778–1830) in Britain described their national cultures in newspaper commentaries on canonical literary figures (for example, Molière and Shakespeare) and in critical reviews of new works by national writers in their own time. Literary criticism thus became part of the national story and national memory. Meanwhile, a new generation of scholars extended their research from literary history into the deeper, obscure history of language itself. Philology became a major branch of nineteenth-century academic research through the work of linguists such as Jacob Grimm (1785–1863), who provided systematic accounts of the history of words and grammar in national languages. Grimm's own philological research carried strong nationalist and political connotations because he assumed (like many of his academic colleagues in Germany) that the German language expressed a deep national unity, which should also be expressed and defended by an expansive German state. Linguistic researchers thus joined with novelists and literary critics in producing politicized stories of long-developing, essential national identities, though the philologists sometimes went beyond their literary compatriots in trying to identify the pure linguistic traits that separated their nation from foreign cultures.[23] Despite the often arcane themes of linguistic research, the study of national languages supported and reflected popular assumptions about the linguistic origins of distinctive cultural identities and geopolitical ambitions.

Yet the truths of a nation could not be understood until they appeared in the literary forms of philosophy and poetry. Nationalists therefore assumed that philosophers and poets shared a common responsibility to express the national spirit and give the nation a literary image of itself. This task gave writers an especially important role in national life, but it was a role that philosophers such as Fichte were happy to embrace. Fichte believed German philosophy enabled the German people to recognize their originality, freedom, morality, and historical destiny. To put it simply (as Fichte rarely did), philosophy was like a "mirror" that showed Germany the self-knowledge it needed "to make itself into what it ought to be." Fichte thus held the most optimistic expectations for his own national philosophy, though he also worried like other nationalists about the deadly foreign influences that were forever threatening the nation's distinctive culture and mind. German philosophy could only flourish when it resisted the derivative ideas of other languages or traditions and drew knowledge from its own national language. Philosophers could then give these national truths back to the people in the language of great poetry. Indeed, the thinker "is already a poet," Fichte wrote, because living ideas must be communicated in an imaginative, living language. "Such a language carries within it the capacity for an infinite poetry, eternally refreshed and renewed; for every stirring of living thought in it opens a new vein of poetic inspiration. And so for a living language poetry is the best means of transfusing into general life the spiritual development that has been accomplished."[24] A vital national culture therefore produced poetic philosophers and philosophical poets, all of whom described the spirit and ideals of "people" who could not describe their own identity so precisely or poetically for themselves.

German writers developed much of the early philosophical argument for this cultural interpretation of national identity, but similar themes spread through all the romantic nationalisms of the era. Adam Mickiewicz, for example, assumed like Fichte that true philosophers resembled great poets in drawing their wisdom from the distinctive spirit of a nation, but he complained (ironically) about Polish philosophers who embraced alien German ideas. As for the poets themselves, Mickiewicz argued that the most imaginative were always inspired by the "great life that animates the people" rather than by the lessons they learned in school. Mickiewicz was, of course, a poet, so it is not surprising to find him giving poets the cultural importance that Fichte gave to philosophers. No poet, Mickiewicz conceded, could completely describe the past or the future, yet imaginative poetic writers expressed the needs of their people and thus helped to create a better future for the nation. Poets must sometimes be "dominated by the masses," but they must also strive at other times to push the people toward a higher level of national understanding and action. In every case,

Unknown artist, *Fichte Addressing the German Nation*, date unknown. This image of Fichte speaking to an idealized audience of Germans suggests how later nationalist art represented the national philosopher's relationship with the "people." Fichte appears in this imaginary scene among a hardy cross-section of Germans who have gathered on the German land to hear the "voice" of their nation, even as an ominous, caped Frenchman looms darkly on the edge of the crowd. (Popperfoto/Getty images)

however, the poets derived their power "from the vital force of a *nationality*."[25] Great poets, in other words, needed nations just as surely as great nations needed poets.

Russia's political and military control of Poland forced Mickiewicz to live in Paris during the 1830s and 1840s, but this permanent exile brought him into contact with new ideas and sources that he used to define the distinctive meaning of Poland's "people" and national literature. One of his favorite writers was Ralph Waldo Emerson, whose nation was located, like Poland, on the margins of western Europe and whose vision of an autonomous American culture included a special role for poets. Following the romantic cultural assumptions of the era, Emerson assumed that the poet "sees and handles that which others dream of" in nature, daily life, and the complexities of language. Unlike Fichte and Mickiewicz, however, he could find no philosopher-poet in his own nation to summarize the essential national spirit—though he believed that new nations resembled old nations in needing such voices to describe their unique cultures. "We have yet had no genius in America," Emerson wrote in one of his essays, who could see "the value of our incomparable materials" and appreciate the poetic beauty of daily life in the New World. "Yet

America is a poem in our eyes; its ample geography dazzles the imagination, and it will not wait long for metres."[26] The nation and its poets would have to grow up together, but America's national material was now available for the kind of inspired national writer that Mickiewicz and his romantic allies were celebrating in Europe. If philosophy, literature, and poetry told the story of the people's truths, then every "people" could generate its own poets, stories, and truths; and the nation itself was a poem that "dazzles the imagination." This national poem still had to be written, however, in the imaginative prophecy of poets and the imaginative memory of historians.

National Histories and National Identities

Memory shapes national identities in many of the ways that it shapes individual identities: it gives order and meaning to selected events and people in the past and provides narratives of continuity to establish a coherent identity in the present. Neither nations nor individuals could sustain their identities if they had no memory of the past. Historians therefore contributed crucial literary service to modern nationalisms by describing the national meaning of the past and by showing how the living generations were always connected to the dead. Yet nations, like individuals, also protect their identities by forgetting or repressing the most painful conflicts of the past, so historians also contributed to national cultures when they helped people forget events that could challenge the dominant national story. As the French writer Ernest Renan (1823–92) pointed out in a famous nineteenth-century essay, "the essence of a nation is that all individuals have many things in common, and also that they have forgotten many things."[27] The bitterness of past conflicts, the violence against unpopular persons, the brutal conquests of national territories, and the personal flaws of "Founding Fathers" tended to disappear from history. Or, more precisely, such events and people lost most of their troubling complexity in popular national histories that celebrated the nation's unique destiny and virtuous early leaders. Forgetting was thus essential for the emergence of nationalisms because a *selective* memory promoted and protected popular stories of national unity.

This interplay of memory and forgetting produced the historical foundation for nationalist ideologies. Narratives about the national past gained coherence through a discrete silence on certain contentious issues, and the apparent coherence of the nation's shared history supported the belief in a common cultural identity that extended across many generations. "The nation," to continue with the themes of Renan's essay, "is the culmination of a long past of endeavours, sacrifice, and devotion," which means that "a heroic past . . . is the social capital upon which one bases a national idea."[28] Although Renan was not a typical romantic thinker, he clearly summarized the cultural themes that brought romanticism and nationalism together. Romanticism's emphasis on the specific rather than the universal traits of cultures, individuals, and historical eras became a recurring motif in both the amateur and professional histories that flooded the European literary market during the early nineteenth century.

Romantic assumptions helped to shape new theories of history (often called historicism) that emphasized the unique characteristics of each historical era and culture.[29] Historians thus staked out claims for their own essential national work as they brought the nation's past culture into the consciousness of subsequent generations. The new historicism stressed that each age of history had its own spirit (*Zeitgeist*), just as each group of people had its own distinctive spirit (*Volksgeist*), so historians provided a valuable, identity-affirming service by explaining how the spirit of a people expressed itself in particular eras and events that may have been misinterpreted or forgotten. Romantic history, like romantic poetry and philosophy, celebrated the creative expression and will of individual nations, whose character appeared in the personal actions of famous leaders as well as the collective actions of entire populations. In both cases, however, history became another "mirror" in which the "people" could see themselves acting heroically in past times. The nation could also "hear itself" in the voices of the dead, and nationalists could appeal for new sacrifices to honor the memory of long-deceased ancestors.

Such themes appeared implicitly or explicitly in the national histories of all modern nations, but the most influential new historical theories drew upon the new themes in German philosophy. Stressing the historical importance of languages and cultural differences, writers such as Herder and Fichte developed the philosophical underpinnings to support the study of distinctive national histories and to justify new actions in the name of old ideals. Fichte confidently assured his Berlin audiences that his philosophy of national regeneration expressed the will of those Germans who could not speak from their graves. "Your forefathers unite with these addresses," Fichte explained in a lyrical, concluding call for resistance to Napoleon's empire. "Imagine that in my voice are mingled the voices of your ancestors from the grey and distant past, who with their own bodies stemmed the tide of Roman world domination, who won with their own blood the independence of those mountains, plains and streams which under your charge have become the spoils of strangers. They call out to you: represent us, pass on our memory as honourably and blamelessly to future ages as it has come down to you."[30] Fichte evoked a specific "German" history, but the exemplary sacrifices of past generations reappeared as a theme in the histories of all modern nations, in part because such stories carried a strong political message. If ancestors had sacrificed their bodies and blood to save the nation (the images were often religious), the present generation must now make its own sacrifices for those who would come later.

The development of professional historical studies gradually pushed many nineteenth-century historians away from Fichte's philosophical passion and rhetoric, but his assumptions about national differences and national histories continued to influence even the most rigorous new scholarship—including the work of fellow German Leopold von Ranke (1795–1886). Although Ranke insisted that historians should base their arguments on the careful study of documents and should include comparative or even "universal" perspectives in their analysis of historical sources, he also portrayed nations as the central force in modern history. Equally important, Ranke viewed government institutions and leaders as the most vital forces in each specific national history, so his own important books typically dealt with the politics and diplomacy of national elites. He shared the historicist belief in the uniqueness of each historical era and culture ("History leads us to unspeakable sweetness and refreshment at every place"), but he assumed that the distinctive spirit of each era emerged most clearly in the history of the state. "It is obvious," he explained, "that each state has a completely definite character and a life of its own, which distinguishes it from all others."[31] This emphasis on the unique history of each nation-state became the starting point for modern historical scholarship, which soon channeled professional historians into specific "national" fields and stressed the historical importance of political events. Nationalism and historical scholarship thus came together almost everywhere in the academic institutions of modern nation-states.

Professional historians in nineteenth-century Germany and many other countries focused on the history of political elites because such people (kings, ministers, generals, judges, legislators) were viewed as embodiments of nations. Describing the "new development of the national spirit" in eighteenth-century Germany, for example, Ranke emphasized the distinctive accomplishments of the evolving Prussian state. Although he acknowledged that a "true politics can be sustained only by a great national existence," he attributed Germany's growing intellectual independence to a strong eighteenth-century king, Frederick II of Prussia. Like other cultures, Prussia needed political leadership: "For a nation must feel itself independent in order to develop freely; and no literature ever flourished save when a great moment of history prepared the way. But it was strange that Frederick himself knew nothing of this, and hardly expected it. He worked for the emancipation of the nation, and German literature worked with him, though he did not recognize his allies. But they knew him well. It made the Germans proud and bold to have had a hero arise from their midst."[32] Such arguments provided a professional historical account of how national leaders could represent national identities. Ranke's description of Frederick II thus noted the distinctiveness and independence of the German nation, suggested that cultures were connected to states, pointed to deep national allegiances that were not apparent to the past actors themselves, and traced a new sense of national pride and identity to the influence of an exceptional national leader. Ranke's academic approach to history, in short, reinforced the idea that nations were the decisive force in history, even as he rejected Fichte's philosophical rhetoric and wrote about state leaders or institutions rather than the spirit of a language and the soul of a people.

In contrast to Ranke's emphasis on national states and political elites, however, some national historians stayed closer to the poets and philosophers who found the nation's spirit in the "people." This non-Rankean view of national histories flourished among a wide range of national historians—especially when they described "nations" that lacked states—yet one of the most influential historians of the "people" lived in the long-established French state and worked at a famous state institution. Jules Michelet (1798–1874) told the story of the French nation in lectures at the Collège de France and in popular books that located the essential meaning of French history in the character of the French people. Although these people had revealed their strength and purpose in numerous events and historical eras, Michelet believed that the French Revolution represented the purest expression of France's deep, enduring national identity. He therefore celebrated the revolution as the climactic moment of French history and the nation's most generous contribution to modern world history. "The Revolution lives in ourselves,—in our souls," he explained at the beginning of a long book about its meaning and legacy, which he attributed to the grandeur of a "people" who were far more significant than the famous revolutionary leaders.

> Great, astonishing results! But how much greater was the heart which conceived them! The deeds themselves are as nothing in comparison. So astonishing, indeed, was that greatness of heart, that the future may draw upon it for ever, without fearing to exhaust its resources. No one can approach its contemplation, without retiring a better man. Every soul dejected, or crushed with grief, every human or national heart has but to look there in order to find comfort: it is a mirror wherein humanity, in beholding itself, becomes once more heroic, magnanimous, disinterested.[33]

The disinterested sacrifice of that heroic French generation could thus provide "comfort" for those who saw a "magnanimous" humanity in France's revolutionary "mirror," but it was the apparent unity of the French nation that elicited Michelet's strongest praise and nostalgia. Unlike the many historians who emphasized the revolution's violent internal conflicts, Michelet described a revolutionary era of harmony and shared purpose. "In the villages, especially, there are no longer either rich or poor, nobles or plebians; there is but one general table, and provisions are in common; social dissensions and quarrels have disappeared; enemies become reconciled."[34] Michelet's French Revolution became an imagined utopian community that somehow overcame the usual divisions of history or politics and momentarily constructed a society in which national similarities overwhelmed every significant internal difference. Writing the story of the nation with the rhetorical skills of a brilliant narrative historian, he remembered the French Revolution by forgetting the bitter conflicts that challenged his account of national unity and purpose.

The French "people" thus became a remarkably coherent entity in Michelet's influential books. He saw himself as the spokesman for those people (dead and alive) who embodied the exceptional virtues of the French nation, though they had never actually described themselves in the unifying language that Michelet provided. He believed that he was in fact able "to establish the personality of the people" and to describe national qualities "which they have but do not understand."[35] This specific understanding of the nation obviously required historians who could infuse their written texts with the soul of the people, as Michelet assumed he had done in a popular book entitled simply *The People* (1846). Summarizing

Unknown artist, *Teaching: Quinet, Villemain, Guizot, Cousin, Michelet, and Renan,* fresco in the Sorbonne, Paris, late nineteenth century. Historians played a key role in constructing modern national identities. This portrayal of an imaginary gathering of famous French historians (Michelet stands with a manuscript) provides a nationalist homage to writers who taught their compatriots the historical meaning and coherence of France. (Snark/Art Resource, New York)

his approach to history in the book's preface, Michelet explained that his writing went beyond a narrative or critical analysis to produce a "*resurrection*"; he brought the dead back to life. In an era when France's revolutionary achievements had been forgotten or denied, Michelet claimed to speak the national truths that were no longer heard. "I shall ever thank God for having given me this great France for my native land," he wrote in a typical statement of his national faith, "because I see her both as the representative of the liberties of all the world and as the country that links all the others together by sympathetic ties, the true introduction to universal love." As this passage suggests, Michelet invoked religious imagery to describe France's exceptional sacrifices and gifts to humanity. French history became for him the story of a messiah nation that had suffered and sacrificed its own life for the salvation of others, though the French people themselves often failed to remember how that sacrifice had set them free.

"So do not come and tell me how pale France is," Michelet wrote. "She has shed her blood for you." But this sacrifice was not just a gift to subsequent generations in France; it was also a sacrifice that offered life and freedom to the whole world, just as the death of Christ had offered hope for universal salvation. France "had to die and descend into the tomb in order that her living spirit might spread throughout the world. . . . The sword they plunged into her heart works miracles and heals. She converts her persecutors and teaches her enemies."[36]

The images of a sacrificed messiah nation may seem strange in the works of a prominent historian at the Collège de France, but such images indicate how historians could draw upon earlier religious languages to convey their vision of a revitalized national future. (Mickiewicz used similar metaphors in his lectures at the Collège de France, regularly referring to Poland as the "Christ" of nations.) Michelet's rhetorical style gradually disappeared from professional historical writing, but the claims for a distinctive national history, the references to exceptional national sacrifices, and the belief in unique national accomplishments would remain in all kinds of history books—including the textbooks that carried the national story of every modern state into schools and universities. These histories helped people place themselves within national cultures and also merged stories of the nation with familiar ancient narratives of religion and sacrifice. Michelet's history of France, like Fichte's history of Germany and Mickiewicz's history of Poland, repeated the oldest stories of life, death, and resurrection, though the salvation in these new historical stories came from the nation instead of God.

Writing, Identity, and Difference

Modern nationalisms emerged out of political theories and revolutions that cannot be separated from the cultural history of writing. Political arguments for national sovereignty and national independence gained adherents and historical influence as they became integrated into the much wider history of newspapers, novels, maps, poetry, philology, philosophy, and history. Writing about nations confirmed their existence in places where governments already claimed to defend national territories or national populations and also in places where nationalists hoped to create new national states. In most cases, national identities developed in conjunction with wars, border disputes, military occupations, revolutions, or economic rivalries, but in every case the survival and diffusion of nationalism required the literary work of journalists, philosophers, poets, literary critics, and historians.

The construction of nations in writing often fused with the construction of nations in military or political conflicts because the meaning of nations depended on narratives about cultural differences. According to nationalist writers, different languages, literatures, and histories created different nations and the rationale for different nation-states. Such differences could be obscure and complex, however, and they had to be constantly explained to people who might well overlook the political significance of Latin and Germanic languages or the national meaning of long-dead ancestors. Nationalism thus justified and shaped the intellectual labor of national writers and teachers, whose work in turn justified and shaped the nationalism that people learned from their newspapers, schools, and history books. To be sure, most persons in these emerging nineteenth-century national cultures did not understand the complex nuances of national philosophers and historians, in part because they did not yet have much education or even know the national literary language. The new national writing and cultural institutions nevertheless described unique national territories and histories in popular stories that carried the meaning of the nation far beyond the educated elites.

These cultural messages overlapped with the political themes of nationalist movements and governments, generating modern ideological claims that even the most isolated persons would eventually encounter. The nation's distinctive political, cultural, and literary traditions were constantly described anew in order to separate it from other nations and to justify new sacrifices from each generation—occasionally in blood and almost always in education, labor, military service, and taxes. Modern people still faced the ancient problems of cooperation, conflict, survival, and death, but the meaning of these problems and the organization of daily life became steadily more connected to the meaning and history of modern nations. Indeed, for some persons in almost every modern society (including prominent writers such as Fichte, Mickiewicz, Michelet, and Mazzini), the nation offered a personal and collective salvation that was anticipated or defended with all the fervor, poetry, and ritual of an ancient religion.

CHAPTER FOUR

Religion, Sacrifice, & National Life

Nationalism emerged in the overlapping spheres of politics, revolutions, state building, language, literature, historical writing, and education, but even the combined power of all these political and cultural forces cannot adequately account for the intense emotional identifications that link individuals to modern nations. More people have died for their nations in modern times than for any other creed or political ideal—a remarkable historical pattern that raises some of the most complex questions about the meaning of nationalist ideas and identities. How do nations acquire the transcendent meanings that can transform a national cause into a sacred cause? What commitments and emotions enable people to view their own likely death or the deaths of their children as necessary and acceptable sacrifices to the collective interests of a nation? Why have so many people been willing to kill others in the name of their national governments or in pursuit of abstract national ideals?

Many persons have, of course, been compelled to serve in modern national armies, so the "power of nation-states" could provide one answer to these questions. Yet the coercive force of state power and propaganda does not really explain how modern nations have successfully mobilized public opinion in support of national wars and other dangerous or disruptive enterprises. Warfare often provokes the strongest popular support for national governments (at least at the beginning of a war), but many nationalists also make comparable sacrifices before a nation-state has even been established. More generally, modern people often respond with strong emotions when they encounter national symbols (flags, national monuments, military memorials) in everyday life. Defacement of a national flag, for example, regularly produces intense anger among those who see their national symbol attacked. Official condemnations of flag defacements do not in themselves generate such strong feelings of moral revulsion. Indeed, the moral passion that is provoked by such defacements suggests that the modern identification with national symbols often expresses the deep reverence and anxiety that people have long expressed for their highest religious ideals and their gods. It is precisely this emotion-laden commitment to "God and Country" that expresses the complex interaction of nationalism and religion in most modern national cultures.[1]

One common account of the links between nationalism and religion emphasizes the importance of religion in defining the essential traits of a national identity. Irish nationalists, for example, might point to Catholicism as a crucial characteristic of the Irish nation, Israeli nationalists would insist on their nation's Judaism, some American nationalists have always claimed that Protestantism is the true creed of the United States, and many Iranians believe in the essential Islamic identity of their national state. Such connections between specific religions and national identities need to be examined in the historical analysis of particular nationalist ideologies, but the discussion of nationalism and religion here will stress the more general structural similarities of these two forms of thought. Instead of examining the Catholic components of Spanish national identity or the Protestant aspects of English identity, for example, this chapter will note some of the ways in which nationalisms repeated, transformed, and fused with traditional Jewish and Christian ideas during the "Age of Revolutions" (1775–1850). This era has often been described as a transitional period of "secularization," but much of the passionate commitment to nationalism and the willingness to die or kill for the nation emerged in the revolutionary and romantic fusion of national and religious narratives about life and death; and these religious aspects of modern nationalisms continue to influence "secular" nation-states throughout the contemporary world.

Although the connections between nationalism and religion have attracted attention in many scholarly disciplines, the American historian Carlton J. H. Hayes was one of the first to propose a comprehensive argument that continues to generate contemporary research. Writing shortly after the horrifying violence of the First World War and responding to a wave of American religious fundamentalism in the 1920s, Hayes argued in an influential essay ("Nationalism as a Religion") that modern nations and nationalisms provide an integrating social and philosophical coherence that resembles the cultural role of the Catholic Church in medieval Europe. From the day of their birth to the day of their death, modern people are registered, organized, mobilized, and consoled by nation-states and the ideological themes of nationalism. Hayes himself accounted for nationalism's power by referring to a "religious sense" in the human psyche. During all eras of human history, he argued, this "religious sense" in "man" has been expressed through "a mysterious faith in some power outside of himself, a faith always accompanied by feelings of reverence and usually attended by external acts and ceremonial." To be sure, many modern people have lost their faith in specific religious doctrines, yet Hayes argued that even the skeptics typically "seek some object outside of themselves to which they might pay reverence." This search for a power greater than the self, as Hayes described it, became a crucial source of nationalism's ideals and popularity. The nation thus offered connections to a transcendent reality and a system of beliefs to replace the faith in God that eighteenth-century skeptics had so famously questioned and rejected.[2]

Contemporary analysts have generally moved away from Hayes's emphasis on an essential human trait that can explain the historical power of nationalism. Stressing the interplay of religion, nationalism, and language rather than an inherent "religious sense," recent accounts suggest that nationalism tended to merge with or supplement religion rather than replace it.[3] Hayes nevertheless posed questions about the overlapping emotional power of religion and nationalism that even the most antiessentialist historian must still confront. Despite the changing perspectives of historical research, we can draw on his theory of cultural displacement—most notably, the transformation of earlier Christian themes or rituals into nationalism—to examine the important religious components of nineteenth-century nationalist theories. Placed in the context of religious traditions, nationalism can be compared to other beliefs that offer consolations and explanations for violence, sacrifice, and power. The intersection of religion and the nation thus carries the analysis of nationalism from politics and writing into the psychology and history of human anxieties about death.[4]

Nation as Salvation

Modern nationalisms first emerged in Western societies where monotheism and Christian ethical ideals had shaped the dominant religious traditions. In this ancient Judeo-Christian conception of the links between divinity and human beings, individuals derived their purpose and meaning from their personal relation to a God who had existed before they were born and who would exist forever after they died. This transcendent Being entered into every phase and sphere of life, giving support and protection but also demanding commitments, loyalty, respect, and service. God thus gave each person a profound connection to eternal realities and to other people. As the theologians and priests had explained since late antiquity, God understood the pains of human life, brought coherence and unity to human history, and offered the salvation of eternal life after human deaths.

The modern nation was not eternal, but it could rival religion in its comforting assurance of personal connections to a greater power that existed long before and after the life of every individual person. It could also resemble God insofar as it became the ultimate source of meaning, protection, or salvation and as it provided the ties that could bind otherwise isolated individuals into a shared (or imagined) community. Of course, the nation could also resemble God by demanding loyalty and service, but this was a familiar price that most people would pay for the benefits of protection, association, and identity. In any case, as Anthony D. Smith has noted in an influential analysis of collective identities, there is a "vital" aspect of nationalism and nations that draws on "the very core of traditional religions, their conception of the sacred and their rites of salvation."[5] Although modern historians have repeatedly noted the similarities in these religious-nationalist themes, the fusion of religion and nationalism was already recognized among the early nineteenth-century theorists who sought to establish the highest possible authority for their nationalist arguments.

This often-claimed link with religious truths gave nationalists an ontological proof for the existence of the nations they admired. Jules Michelet's account of the national "soul" in *The People*, for example, stressed a deep connection between individual persons and the creative power of their nation. "The Fatherland," Michelet argued, "is for that soul of the people which dwells there the single and all-powerful means of realizing its nature, because it supplies both a vital point of departure and freedom to develop." The nation therefore became the vehicle for God's divine vision of human creativity and cooperation, which Michelet, like most romantic nationalists, believed that modern nations could achieve on earth by cultivating their distinctive cultures *and* living in harmony with other nations: "The more man advances, the more he enters into the spirit of his country and the better he contributes to the harmony of the globe; he learns to recognize his country . . . as a note in the grand concert; through it he himself participates [in] and loves the world. The fatherland is the necessary initiation to the fatherland of all mankind."[6] Metaphors of the "father" were thus transferred from God to the Nation as Michelet described the personal spiritual development that led the individual to a higher world beyond the self; and it was the "Fatherland" that offered modern access to the ancient religious ideal of human cooperation.

The nation provided more than transcendence and human bonds, however, because romantic nationalists often assumed that it gave people a kind of cultural or political "bridge" to divine power. In fact, duty to the nation was often described as a religious duty, and serving the nation was viewed as a new opportunity for serving God. Nobody promoted this fusion of God and country more fervently than the famous Italian writer Giuseppe Mazzini. In contrast to Michelet, Mazzini lived (like many romantic nationalists) outside the national culture that he sought to represent and unify. His strongest national weapon was therefore a pen rather than a sword, but he had no doubt that he was wielding his weapon on behalf of a sacred cause. The Italian nation was for Mazzini an almost eternal being whose origins were older than ancient Rome and whose future lay beyond the vision of the most imaginative modern writers. Yet this extraordinary nation also required committed action from its people, as he explained constantly in writings that exhorted his compatriots to follow God's plan for their national destiny.

> The cry which rang out in all the great revolutions—the cry of
> the Crusades, *God wills it! God wills it!*—alone can rouse the inert
> to action, give courage to the fearful, enthusiasm of self-sacrifice
> to the calculating, faith to those who reject with distrust all merely
> human ideas. Prove to men that the work of emancipation and of
> progressive development to which you call them is part of God's
> design....
>
> God wills it—God wills it! It is the cry of the People, O Brothers!
> it is the cry of *your* People, the cry of the Italian Nation.[7]

Mazzini thus invoked divine will as the most compelling justification for his imagined society of Italian unity and republicanism, thereby translating the oldest religious duty—serving God—into the national political campaigns and conflicts of nineteenth-century Europe.

Although Mazzini accepted the romantic assumption that different nationalities could cooperate in a "harmonious concert" of nations, he also assumed that God had given Italy an exceptionally important responsibility in world history. Similar assumptions about unique national destinies or missions became typical religious themes among many other nationalists who described their own national populations as the "Chosen People" of history. This particular strand of nationalist thought drew especially on the ancient Hebrew belief in God's unique concern for (and covenant with) the people of Israel, but it first became a central theme in the modern nationalisms of Protestant societies.

The emergence of early national feeling in Britain owed a great deal to the Protestant opposition to Catholicism and Catholic Spain during the sixteenth century; and the Protestant influence on early American national identity may have become even more pronounced.[8] Puritan religious accounts of a new "City on the Hill," for example, helped to generate a narrative of the "Chosen People" that would contribute decisively to the American Revolution and the subsequent development of America's national ideology. Early American "patriots" thus promoted what the historian Nicholas Guyatt has called the "providential thinking" in American culture—a widely held belief that "God had given America a special role in history and that independence had been providentially determined."[9] European Protestants had meanwhile established national churches that depended upon and enhanced the power of national governments. Church-state alliances provided strong institutional support for the fusion of religion and nationalism in northern European nations such as England and Germany. The popular religious traditions of pietism merged with a new national movement to produce typical descriptions of German society as a privileged center of God's plan for the world. "I can never despair of my fatherland," wrote the German philosopher Friedrich Schleiermacher (1768–1834) in a letter that resembled the way English and American writers also portrayed *their* nations. "I believe too firmly in it, I know too definitely that it is an instrument and a people chosen by God."[10]

The religious images of a Chosen People offered another opportunity to define the differences that gave each national culture its own identity. Although these religious definitions of difference first became especially important in Protestant nationalisms, they also contributed to new nationalisms in predominantly Catholic countries such as Italy and Poland. Adam Mickiewicz's Polish nationalism, for example, rested on a whole series of messianic claims about the unique spiritual achievements and sufferings of the Polish people, all of which separated their Slavic identity from the identities of other people and promised future achievements for a united Polish nation. In contrast to modern secular nations, Mickiewicz explained from exile in Paris, Slavs had "the humility, the gentleness, [and] the patience that characterized the martyrs of the early medieval church." Such traits gave the Slavic religion an unparalleled "purity" that might well show modern people the way to a new, higher morality. "The Slavs alone have the advantage of having conserved the early [Christian] tradition in all the purity [and] natural sentiment of the divinity," Mickiewicz argued in a narrative about the overlapping histories of religion, literature, and nationality. This legacy of "pure" religion sustained an identity that later Slavs were obliged to honor through their defense of a distinctive national culture, but Mickiewicz believed they possessed both the will and the knowledge to uphold their religious traditions. In contrast to other nations, the Slavs had never abandoned their religious beliefs for the false gods of science, literature, and philosophy. "They therefore truly form a separate race."[11]

Religious history thus gave Mickiewicz and other nationalists a narrative to explain the unique sufferings of specific nations—all Chosen People had to undergo special tribulations—but the millennial perspectives in the Christian tradition could also be used to portray past or present crises as the prelude to a happier future. The Chosen People always had good spiritual and national reasons to expect that present-day suffering would lead toward a coming millennium of peace, prosperity, justice, and freedom.

The nationalists' belief in the special mission of their own nations gave universal significance to what might otherwise appear to be the local problems of a small population or specific culture. Situated in a religious narrative of collective suffering and redemption, the endless struggle for national independence and unity became an essential contribution to the progressive development of world history. Each generation faced the tasks of identifying the national mission and promoting this mission in a wider world of politics, culture, and work. The national mission might well seem daunting to the would-be nationalist, but it was precisely the grandeur of the mission that accounted for the sacrifices and suffering on its behalf. Here again, the ancient religious language of witnessing for one's faith in the world offered models for nationalists who translated the religious injunction into a new call for service to the nation. Mazzini's commentary on Italian duties to the nation, for example, included repeated assurances that Italy's mission carried hope and implications for the entire modern world. "Our country is our field of labour," he wrote; "the products of our activity must go forth from it for the benefit of the whole earth. . . . In labouring according to true principles for our country we are labouring for Humanity. . . . Your Country is the token of the mission which God has given you to fulfill in humanity."[12]

But what was this unique Italian mission, and what did it require? Mazzini informed his readers that Italy was to provide "the moral unity of Europe." This task obviously imposed "immense duties" on all Italians, yet Mazzini claimed it was a mission for which Italians were uniquely prepared. A long history of unifying achievements in ancient Rome and early medieval Christianity had shown that the Italians knew how to bring moral unity to all the people of Europe—though this unique Italian mission also called for the strictest moral virtue. "Your duties to your Country are proportioned to the loftiness of this mission. You have to keep it pure from egoism, [and] uncontaminated by falsehood."[13] The new servants of the nation were, for Mazzini, the successors of the ancient missionaries of the church, and their new national mission required the kind of devotion and piety that had given moral purpose to the early Christians.

Such rhetoric offered little more than asceticism and a futile idealism for modern, skeptical readers, but the reward for Mazzini or Mickiewicz (and their many sympathetic followers) would come in the exalted status of the nation. If devotion to God could bring salvation for the loyal believer, then surely devotion to God's country could assure a similar salvation for the new nationalist. In fact, nationalists such as Michelet and Mickiewicz regularly compared the suffering of a nation and its believers to the sufferings of Christ and His believers. The consolations in both cases came in the expectation of ultimate redemption for all who shared in the pain. The story of the nation thus became the story of Christ, as Mickiewicz explicitly claimed in his famous account of messianic Poland (1832):

On the third day the soul shall return to the body, and
the Nation shall arise and free all the peoples of Europe
from slavery.

And already two days have gone by. One day ended with the
first capture of Warsaw, and the second day ended with the
second capture of Warsaw, and the third day shall begin, but
shall not end.

And as after the resurrection of Christ blood sacrifices ceased in all
the world, so after the resurrection of the Polish nation wars
shall cease in all Christendom.[14]

Mickiewicz extended the narrative of the Chosen People, national mission, and national salvation farther into the realm of religious speculation than many of his contemporaries, but the themes of his messianic nationalism could also be found in more muted forms throughout the writings of most early nineteenth-century nationalists: national sacrifices, in short, would lead to a better place or time and also provide models of virtue for future generations.

Claims for the universal significance of national events or movements reappeared in diverse nationalisms from America to Russia as national writers translated religious conceptions of transcendence, unity, duty, and mission into stories of national purpose and destiny. Successful nationalisms therefore merged with and sometimes replaced many of the oldest religious aspirations in Western cultures, including the desire to emulate Christ and the desire to find life after death. At the same time, however, the replication or translation of ancient religious traditions went beyond nationalist theologies into the equally important symbols and rituals of new nations and nationalisms.

The Symbols and Rituals of Religions and Nations

The images and metaphors that nationalists used to describe their nations in the early nineteenth century drew upon the familiar icons and languages of Christian churches. As Mazzini noted in one of his typical summaries of the new faith: "Your country should be your Temple. God at the summit, a People of equals at the base."[15] This image ignored the possible conflicts between nations and the will of God; indeed, it suggested a remarkable continuity in these two transcendent entities, both of which could be honored in the service to a truly national state. Although some theologians still debated ancient questions about conflicting human duties to "Caesar and Christ," most nationalists assumed that the fusion of national and religious ideals confirmed the overlapping authority and wisdom in both forms of truth. "Heaven and earth must unite themselves in Germany," a patriotic German pastor explained to his parishioners during the Napoleonic wars. "The church must become a state in order to gain power and the state must become a church in order to be the kingdom of God."[16] Given such assumptions among the clergy, it was easy enough for nationalists in Germany and other modern cultures to extend the emotional meaning of religious beliefs into a deep reverence for the new symbols of a nation.

As Carlton Hayes and other analysts have noted, there were nationalist analogues for almost every traditional religious symbol, book, ritual, saint, holiday, and moral lesson.[17] The national flag of each national movement, for example, became a powerful, sacred symbol, evoking the kind of respect that had long been directed toward the symbolic Christian Cross or the religious relics in famous churches. Elaborate rituals were developed to honor national flags, and the desecration of flags became a new form of sacrilege or blasphemy. Most national movements represented themselves with a flag before they had established an independent state, which meant that flags expressed symbolic political challenges to reigning regimes as well as the power of well-established nation-states. The famous red, white, and blue tricolor flag in France, for example, symbolized a liberal opposition to the conservative Bourbon government that had restored both the monarchy and the traditional royal flag after the fall of Napoleon (1814–30). German nationalists were also using an illegal black, red, and gold tricolor flag during these same years to express their opposition to the Austrian Prince Metternich and to symbolize their political and cultural aspirations for a new unified German state. Other nationalisms turned to the natural world for symbols such as the eagle, which could represent the autonomy or aspirations of distinctive national cultures.

In addition to their flags and other symbolic icons, nationalists regularly praised national documents or literary works with the reverence that religious leaders brought to their study of the Bible and other ancient religious texts. Every nationalism and nation identified essential sources of national unity and truth in a canon of written texts that included declarations of national independence and rights, national constitutions, great works of national literature, the words of national anthems, and even the famous speeches of national orators. Students read the sanctified national texts at school, and nationalist leaders invoked their authority to explain or justify all kinds of public action. The American Declaration of Independence and national Constitution, for example, quickly became sacred texts in the United States, where the typical nineteenth-century Independence Day rituals celebrated the wisdom and virtue of both the documents and their authors.[18] Political documents were also important in European nationalisms, but literature was often a more valuable resource for defining national unity. Despite the divisive political conflicts within each nation or national movement, the English could celebrate Shakespeare as their national literary treasure; the French could praise Molière, Racine, or Voltaire; the Italians could honor Dante; and the Germans could remember Luther. The famous political and literary texts of various national cultures thus came to resemble canonical religious works

Unknown artist, *French-Polish Committee Flags*, illustration for the committee, 1831. National flags represented collective identities and new political movements such as the campaign for Polish independence from Russia in the early 1830s (strongly supported by a French-Polish committee in France). The flags of France and Poland are joined here to show a transnational collaboration, and they evoke national liberty with typical nationalist allusions to nature—as symbolized by the images of a French cock and Polish eagle. (Marquis de Lafayette Manuscript Collection, David Bishop Skillman Library, Lafayette College)

insofar as they defined a national creed and provided a shared cultural resource for citations, reinterpretations, and praise. Nobody could denounce the sacred texts of his or her own nation and retain political or cultural influence in the nationalist movement. The sacred national texts often attracted even more respect than the older religious texts because people who disagreed about religion could still agree on the wisdom of a national constitution or the genius of Shakespeare. Religious education thus evolved into national education, and the recitation of religious catechisms gave way to the recitation of national poets, the oratory of national heroes, or the dying words of national martyrs.

The sanctified texts of the nation often fused with images of sacred national figures who symbolically embodied the highest national ideals. Like the stories of saints and virtuous actions in the religious tradition, the stories of George Washington, Joan of Arc, or Martin Luther showed how the virtuous figures in a national culture served the national cause with unbending commitment and integrity. "Founding Fathers" and other exemplary national leaders therefore represented or interpreted the meaning of the nation in the same way that Moses, Jesus, and Mohammed had interpreted the meaning of God. The status of such national leaders in the civil religions of nationalism could in fact be compared to the status of the great founding figures in the ancient religious traditions.

National heroes might have expressed the national spirit in the realm of politics, warfare, religion, or literature, but their achievements in every case offered inspiration for nationalists who might despair about the status or survival of the nation in their own time. J. G. Fichte's account of Luther, for example, suggested that this national hero had confronted and overcome sixteenth-century dangers that were every bit as threatening as the dangers facing Germans in the Napoleonic era. Luther "went fearlessly and in good earnest to do battle with all the demons of hell," Fichte wrote, and yet this struggle was "natural and certainly no cause for wonder. This, then, is proof of German seriousness and German soul." But how did Luther embody the qualities of a whole nation? According to Fichte, the Germans "renounced everything and bore every torment and fought in bloody wars of doubtful outcome" in order to maintain their independence and their reformed religion; neither Luther nor the German people would surrender their religious principles to foreign leaders or outside forces. Luther was therefore the highest expression of a distinctive national soul ("Here you see proof of the particularity of the German people") and a model for new struggles against Napoleon and those who accepted the French occupation of Berlin.[19]

The history of national heroes in the writings of Fichte and other nationalist authors always stood in stark contrast to the history of skeptics or traitors who had lost their national faith. In fact, nationalists typically identified evil figures whose corruption or betrayal of the nation would be familiar to anyone who knew the biblical story of Judas Iscariot. National traitors were the modern heretics—persons who went astray, deceived others, and deserved the most severe punishments. These national heretics could be famous people (for example, General Benedict Arnold in America) or part of a secret conspiracy (émigrés and spies in revolutionary

France), but their role in national narratives resembled the role of Satan in religious narratives. Nationalists were therefore eager to expose and revile all presumed national traitors and heretics, especially since such traitors could be expected to operate with satanic deception. Unmasking the most conspicuous national heretics was not enough to assure the national survival, however, because there were other, more widespread dangers in the general indifference to national ideals and national objectives. Like the prophets in ancient Israel or the pastors in modern Protestant pulpits, nationalists often warned that their own generation lacked the faith and commitments of earlier generations.

The national story could thus become a religious story of dangerous moral decline in which people betrayed the national cause to pursue their own selfish gains or to adopt the ideas and customs of other nations. To be sure, nationalists anticipated a better future for their nations much like religious leaders anticipated a better world to come, but the road to that better world was filled with temptations to abandon the higher cause. In short, people could forget about the nation as readily as they could forget about God. Anxious "jeremiads" in nationalist literatures therefore used the rhetorical structures and moral admonitions of a vivid church sermon. When Mazzini warned against those who would no longer defend the national cause, for example, he urged his allies to "thrust them from your ranks; for whoso is not ready to testify to his faith with his blood is no believer." The temptations of lethargy and despair could easily undermine the faith in a better future, but Mazzini insisted that the nineteenth-century "cross of misfortune and persecution" was simply the prelude to a coming age of harmony and cooperation. "Let your lips not utter the cry of hate, nor the conspirator's hollow phrase," he counseled in an essay ("Faith and the Future") for those who might have lost faith in the cause, "but the tranquil, solemn word of the days that are to come."[20] Mazzini's good nationalists therefore needed vigilance and perseverance to withstand the dangers of decline and betrayal, but the steadfast believers would ultimately arrive in a better, more harmonious future.

The sacred texts and prophets of nationalisms were remembered and honored in public places that became the national equivalents of the sanctified spaces in which religious believers had always expressed their devotion to God. Advocates of national creeds sanctified the birthplaces or tombs of national heroes, the sites of famous battles, and the cemeteries of unknown soldiers. Every nation-state created monuments and memorials to celebrate the achievements and sacrifices of national armies or great generals (for example, the Arc de Triomphe in France, Trafalgar Square in Britain, Arlington National Cemetery in the United States, and the Walhalla in Germany).[21] The greatest monuments were usually erected in capital cities, but even small towns would eventually construct memorials to deceased soldiers and heroes. Such monuments attracted visitors and symbolized national identities in the same way that famous cathedrals had symbolized the ideals and identities of medieval towns. Visits to places such as Napoleon's tomb in Paris (constructed in 1840) or George Washington's home at Mount Vernon appeared on the itineraries of modern tourists, whose pilgrimages to national monuments became as common as medieval pilgrimages to sacred shrines. National monuments conveyed the lessons of national histories and sacrifices in images that could be compared to the representations of Christian history and sacrifices in great churches. Indeed, the rituals at national monuments on national holidays often resembled the rituals of religious holidays in urging remembrance of deaths that had given life to the nation. Such rituals promoted the ideals of national unity and offered annual opportunities for nationalists to remind their compatriots about the duties and rewards of national identity.

The calls for national sacrifice did not simply replace older religious rituals, however, because the churches remained important nongovernmental gathering places for national messages and remembrances. Linking religious duty to national duty, the clergy often helped the nationalist cause by adding theological justifications for national sacrifices, especially during times of war. Religious leaders in late eighteenth-century America, for example, regularly interpreted the American Revolutionary War as a divinely inspired event in which good patriots could serve God by joining the struggle against Britain. In 1777 a Protestant pastor named Abraham Keteltas offered this kind of providential interpretation when he assured his congregation in Massachusetts that the American cause was also "the cause of God." Noting the evils and oppressions of the British government, Keteltas claimed that Americans were defending and promoting the divine plan for justice and freedom on earth. "It is the cause of heaven against hell," he explained. "It is the cause for which heroes have fought, patriots bled, prophets, apostles, martyrs, confessors, and righteous men have died. Nay, it is a cause for which the Son of God came down from his celestial throne and expired on the cross."[22]

This image of Christ's sacrifice for humanity provided the most compelling precedent or model for those many nationalists who merged the cause of God with the cause of the nation. Comparisons between Christ and

Victor Adam, *Procession of Napoleon's Funeral Cortege*, lithograph, ca. 1840. The procession that carried Napoleon's body to an elaborate new Parisian tomb in 1840 suggests the neo-religious aspects of French nationalist rituals; and a visit to places such as Napoleon's tomb became a new kind of nationalist pilgrimage. An inscription on this image describes the public event as a "triumphal procession worthy of the great People who attended . . . and of the hero who was honored." (From the copy in the Hoyt Collection, Rare Book Collection, University of North Carolina at Chapel Hill)

modern human sacrifices for the nation gave a messianic dimension even to national ideologies that have never been called "messianic nationalisms"— though their advocates repeatedly invoked ancient religious conceptions of death and resurrection. Among all the overlapping symbols and rituals of religion and nationalism, the Christlike images of sacrifice and death for others provided the most powerful summary of what nations could ulti-mately require from their people. Those who gave their lives to save the nation were thus the most hallowed figures in every nationalist ideology— and the story of the nation was always a story about life and death.

Death, Sacrifice, and Warfare

Nationalist accounts of the connection between individual lives and the nation often argued that nations provided a consoling form of immortal-ity. Although individuals inevitably had to die, they could, by dying for their nation, continue to live in a collective national memory that preserved their language, their ideas, and their institutions. Ancient human desires for a life after death could thus evolve from the realm of theology into the realm of nationalism, where people could find strong moral inducements for risking their own lives or the lives of their children in long national wars. Breaking with older patterns of monarchical warfare that mostly promoted royal dynastic interests or the military careers of nobles, modern wars came to be seen as national crusades against infidels whose alien customs and beliefs threatened the existence of one's own nation. Death in battle against such enemies might not send the soul to heaven, but it would definitely earn eternal gratitude from a nation whose survival depended on the sacrifices of its soldiers. Nationalism therefore joined with religion to provide explanations and meanings for the traumatic violence and deaths in modern national wars.[23]

The military force that could bring death to the nation's youth and the nation's enemies acquired religious significance because the soldiers' sacrifices gave life to the nation as a whole. Images of immortality and resurrection abounded in early nineteenth-century nationalist commentaries that celebrated the life-giving force of national communities. Ernst Moritz Arndt reported from Germany during the anti-Napoleonic wars (1813), for example, that a military parade gave him a sense of eternal life that he could find nowhere else. "I feel the indestructible life," he wrote in a description of the national army, "the eternal spirit, and the eternal God. . . . [In this moment] I am no longer a single suffering man, I am one with the Volk and God."[24] Arndt's desire to connect himself to an immortal national existence suggests the deep emotional anxiety (fear of death) that nationalism helped to assuage in Germany and other modern, secularizing societies: people die, but their nations can live forever.

Fichte developed a more philosophical summary of this emotional desire for immortality in his *Addresses to the German Nation*. Individuals placed the survival of the nation above the mere physical survival of themselves, Fichte explained, because they knew that future generations would remember and honor their sacrifices for the national cause. "The belief of the noble man in the eternal continuance of his activity even on this earth is . . . based on the hope for the eternal continuance of the people from which he has sprung." Individual lives and deaths, as Fichte described them, thus acquired enduring purpose through this link to the nation. The individual who sought "to plant something imperishable" and to comprehend "his own life as an eternal life" was thus connected "most intimately with his own nation." Indeed, this personal stake in national immortality could make death itself an entirely acceptable sacrifice for the continuing life of the nation. The person who achieved national consciousness would therefore be "sacrificing himself on behalf of his people. Life, simply as life, as the continuation of changing existence, has never possessed value for him; he desired life only as the source of what is permanent; but this permanence is promised to him only by the independent perpetuation of his nation; to save it he must be willing to die, so that it may live and he live in it the only life he has ever wanted."[25] Fichte's description of immortality, in other words, shows how traditional Christian conceptions of salvation entered into new beliefs about the saving grace of nations. Human beings needed nations in order to find the "permanence" that physical existence could never provide, but this eternal source of meaning (like God) required service and sacrifice. Although serving the nation might well cause personal pain, it was the kind of virtuous action that ennobled human beings and assured their life after death.

Nationalist narratives about sacrifice thus merged with the nationalist narratives about history; and it was the national memory that gave immortality to deceased patriots. Given this moral duty to remember the virtues of the dead, historians contributed to the nationalist ideology by urging later generations to emulate the commitments and sacrifices of their ancestors. Fichte reminded his audiences of courageous Germans who had "willingly spilt their blood" for posterity, thereby saving the nation and giving nineteenth-century Germans an example of what they must do for *their* descendents.[26] The gift of blood and bodies was, of course, a familiar religious theme in all nationalisms, but the blood was simply the prelude to a new national life or resurrection. "Fight as Italians," Mazzini told his compatriots, "so that the blood which you shed may win honour and love, not for you only, but for your Country. And may the constant thought of your soul be for Italy."[27]

The images of blood, sacrifice, and death suggest how the links between nationalism and religion could transform warfare into the highest expression of national identity. Wars revealed the dangers of evil enemies and the coherent purpose of one's own nation more clearly than any other historical event. No matter how much a nation's people might differ or disagree among themselves, their essential unity appeared forcefully in their opposition to foreign dangers. The unity and survival of every nation therefore depended on people who were willing to fight the nation's enemies, even if—or especially if—they must sacrifice their own lives in the struggle.

Pinçon, after a painting by Horace Vernet, *Grenadier on Elba Island*, lithograph, ca. 1840. Nationalist imagery and writings have often praised soldiers as the ideal embodiment of the nation's virtues and strengths, in part because soldiers sacrifice their blood and bodies to protect the national population from foreign dangers. This portrait conveys the determination of a French grenadier who stands ready to defend the national leader and tricolor flag that loom over him and his well-armed compatriots. (From the copy in the Hoyt Collection, Rare Book Collection, University of North Carolina at Chapel Hill)

Soldiers became the highest embodiment of the national ideal when they died to protect the lives and freedom of others.

Nationalism's link to warfare gave a strong military flavor to many forms of nationalist culture, including historical writing, art, flags, parades, monuments, uniforms, and national anthems. The words of national anthems, for example, frequently referred to the military struggles that defined or clarified the meaning of nations. Songs such as "The Star-Spangled Banner" in America (1814) and "La Marseillaise" in France (1792) clearly indicated that nations ultimately survived armed conflicts with flags waving in the "rockets' red glare" and "bombs bursting in air." Rouget de Lisle described the French national mission in "La Marseillaise" by emphasizing the dangers of an enemy that came "to cut the throats of your sons." In typical nationalist optimism, however, he insisted that the violence would lead to a final French victory. "Fight with your defenders," he implored,

> under our flags, so that victory
> Will rush to your manly strains;
> That your dying enemies
> Should see your triumph and glory![28]

National wars thus offered a high road to national salvation. To be sure, the nation's military struggles could be as dangerous and difficult as the Christian's struggle against evil, yet both the patriot and the believer could see the battle as a necessary sacrifice for the better world to come.

Meanwhile, service to the nation was a "manly" task for soldiers who set out to defend their "mother country" or "Fatherland" with all the passion of a child defending a beloved parent. Indeed, the nation would often be compared to a family, thus linking conceptions of gender and sexuality with religious conceptions of duty, immortality, and sacrifice. Men could make the highest sacrifices to the nation in warfare, but women proved their own extraordinary commitment by sacrificing their children to the national cause. For every "Christlike" soldier's death, there was a "Madonnalike" mother or wife. In short, the overlapping themes of nationalism, religion, and war fused also with social, cultural, and political definitions of men and women.

The Fusion of Nationalism and Religion

Some analysts of nationalism have argued that the faith in nations replaced ancient religious beliefs and became a new secular religion. This kind of "replacement theory" may accurately describe the ideology of a few fervent nationalists, but most modern nationalisms have managed to fuse religious and political ideals. Nationalists have often retained numerous religious assumptions, including a belief in God and clearly delineated ethical conceptions of good and evil. More generally, most nationalisms attracted adherents by expanding rather than replacing religious accounts of transcendence, unity, and sacrifice. Belief in a higher, metaphysical world had always given Europeans a way to understand their place in the material world, so the "nation" could take its place within this cultural tradition as a new mediating link between individuals and the higher realm of virtue and immortality. Nationalisms drew on religious traditions to praise what Anthony Smith has called the "sacred communion of the people" or the "sacrificial virtue of heroes and prophets," but national movements did not usually flourish by attacking religious beliefs.[29] The resistance to "de-Christianization" during the French Revolution suggests why later nationalisms tended to merge with rather than replace traditional religions.

This nationalist-religious fusion may well explain why the first systematic narratives of nationalism appeared in Western societies, where the ancient biblical narratives (Hebrew and Christian alike) had long influenced philosophy, literature, political theory, historical writing, and social rituals. Almost all of the ancient religious themes could be adapted to fit into stories about nations: descriptions of a "chosen people," beliefs in a distinctive moral mission, explanations of current sufferings as the path to a more harmonious future, and reverence for the life-giving sacrifice of blood and bodies. Such ideas circulated in modern national cultures through sanctified flags, texts, liturgies, holidays, monuments, and memorials to national heroes, all of which also resembled the symbols and rituals of Judeo-Christian religious traditions. The identity-shaping power of national-religious ideas and symbols appeared most conspicuously in the "total wars" of modern nations, when nationalist movements and nation-states used the language of religious crusades to justify their violent conflicts with national enemies. In the French revolutionary wars against old-regime Europe and the German wars against Napoleonic France, for example, nationalist leaders urged the "nation" to purify itself and make painful sacrifices. In return for this commitment, good patriots received assurances about the survival of the nation after their deaths; immortality would be found in a culture that could not die. Indeed, popular images of soldiers (who gave their lives for others) and their nations (which suffered for the greater good of humanity) drew meaning from ancient Christian images of Christ, so that the story of the Messiah often reappeared implicitly or explicitly in the stories of nations.

This fusion of nationalist and biblical ideas could, of course, produce tensions and contradictions as well as an ideological merger—and there were always religious thinkers who questioned or rejected the "false gods" of nationalism. Roman Catholic conceptions of the universal church, for example, offered attractive alternatives to nationalist conceptions of competing, conflicting nations. Similarly, Christian injunctions to love one's enemies could be invoked in opposition to national wars. Yet the religious plea to respect and love enemies was typically ignored in the nationalist embrace of other ancient religious ideas that could be readily translated into modern narratives of national destiny. Nationalists found valuable religious parallels to their own creeds in historical dichotomies that contrasted good against evil, eternal against temporary, and sacrifice against self-interest.

Political abstractions and the desire for national economic development simply could not generate the nationalist moral passion that made death an acceptable sacrifice for national causes. And even the most comprehensive knowledge of national histories and literatures was unlikely to sustain a soldier in battle. For most people, therefore, the national cause could only evoke the requisite emotional attachments when it became linked to the oldest human anxieties about survival, death, and immortality. Religious accounts of God and life after death had long provided the most important, consoling explanations for the inevitable limitations and pains of human existence, and nationalism could destroy neither the anxieties nor the traditional responses to them.

Nationalist ideologies and rituals nevertheless offered new consolations for death and new justifications for moral crusades; nationalist moral dichotomies fused with religious moral dichotomies to define the transcendent meaning of national identities; and new definitions of national identity and difference drew on familiar religious definitions of cultural identity and difference to deepen the emotional meaning of nationalism. At the same time, however, both nationalism and religion became deeply entangled with identity-shaping conceptions of gender, family, ethnicity, and race, each of which added other emotions and psychological complexities to the quest for national unity and coherence.

CHAPTER FIVE

Gender, Family, & Race

Nationalism has always generated the strongest emotional power when nationalist ideas have overlapped with other components of individual and group identities. Although all national ideologies and identities evolve through the symbols and conflicts of human cultures, the individuals within a national culture often merge their national identities with other traits or realities that seem to be "natural" rather than historical. National identities can thus become associated with climate or geography, for example, and they have regularly been linked with the apparently natural realities of sexuality, gender, family, and race. Ideas about gender and race resemble ideas about nations in that a person's gender and racial traits are taken to be rooted in nature, like the primordial history of a national population. In this view, people are simply born as girls or boys—and as "black," "red," "yellow," or "white"—just as they are born German or Chinese, French or American.

Recent historical studies generally challenge such conceptions of gender and race by stressing that the so-called natural traits of individuals and groups are in fact shaped more by culture than by biological inheritance.[1] People learn the meaning of their gender and race through the families, schools, religions, laws, and political systems that also teach them the meaning of their nationality. There are, of course, physical characteristics that differentiate the sexes, and people inherit different skin pigmentations, but these physical differences acquire their historical significance through the ideologies and hierarchies of social and cultural institutions. As these institutions became "nationalized" during the nineteenth century, the meaning of both gender and race became increasingly entwined with the ideologies of modern nationalism.

Nationalism flourished by connecting the intimate, personal spheres of individual lives with the public spheres of politics and collective identity. Such connections developed most powerfully in modern conceptions of the family, reproduction, and personal respectability, all of which suggested that a "good" citizen was also a responsible member of a family (and vice versa). Ideas and anxieties about the family also fused with other ideas and anxieties about the biological meaning of race or racial purity, so that nationalist claims about distinctive histories, languages, religions, and political institutions gradually merged in the nineteenth century with other claims about distinctive national families or racial traits. Descriptions of sexuality, gender, and race thus overlapped with descriptions of national identity, especially when nationalists sought to define the (imagined) purity of a nation's culture or the prospects for a nation's future development. The meaning of gender and race also evolved, like the meaning of nations, through definitions of difference or "otherness." The differences of gender and racial groups were therefore used to define *internal* social categories within nations in much the same way that differences were used to define *external* cultural boundaries between nations. The existence of a nation required ideas about the relations between women and men as surely as it required national schools or memories of past events, and each generation had to learn the meaning of sexuality, gender, family, and race while it was also learning the meaning of national history.

Gender Identities, Families, and Nationalist Ideologies

Narratives about the "imagined communities" of modern nations rely constantly on metaphorical and political allusions to families and family relationships. Evoking the emotions of complex family attachments, nationalist writers have always referred affectionately to the "Fatherland," "mother tongue" and "Mother Country," "brothers in arms," "Founding Fathers," and the "national family." Celebrations of "fraternity," for example, continued to be an important theme in a postrevolutionary French political culture that remained profoundly divided over other revolutionary ideas about liberty and equality; and the new legal management of families in the Napoleonic Code became a more permanent component of French national life than all of the military campaigns during the Napoleonic wars. The nation-state entered widely into all phases of family life (from births and marriages to deaths and inheritances), thus displacing the church from various domestic spheres that—like education—had long been the province of religion.

More generally, nationalist writers and political activists often used stereotypical gender traits to emphasize the "manly" virtues of good nations in contrast to the deceptions and corruptions of bad nations. The British portrayed their wars against revolutionary and Napoleonic France, for example, as a masculine opposition to an essentially effeminate French society. This image of Britain's "masculinity," as the historian Linda Colley notes, appeared in the self-defined British tendency to be "bluff, forthright, rational, [and] down-to-earth," whereas the "feminine" French were said to be "subtle, intellectually devious, preoccupied with high fashion, fine cuisine and etiquette, and . . . obsessed with sex."[2] Interpreted from this perspective, the military conflict between Britain and France could be linked to other strong feelings among British nationalists who saw the national struggle as a kind of war between the sexes in which positive (male) and negative (female) sexual characteristics shaped the combatants on both sides of the battlefield.

Most modern nations and nationalist movements developed male or female national symbols that were supposed to represent national strengths and virtues to the citizens at home as well as foreigners. The meaning of England appeared in images of Britannia and John Bull, the Germans represented themselves with Germania, and the Americans eventually produced Uncle Sam. French revolutionaries embraced the famous allegorical figure of "Marianne," who symbolized national virtue for republican groups throughout France during the nineteenth century. This "personification of the Republic as a female allegory," notes the leading historian of Marianne's importance in French culture, became an "object of affection that sometimes reached quasi-religious proportions."[3] If the various national populations found it difficult to understand the abstract meanings of their national histories or political institutions, they could turn to the reassuring, gendered images of national identities that gradually replaced religious saints and monarchs in the symbolic representation of national cultures.

This fusion of gender and national identities provided analytical categories for all kinds of nineteenth-century writers, including social theorists, historians, and the authors of travel books. When the French theorist Arthur de Gobineau (1816–82) published his ideas on race and nationality, for example, he also defined nations according to their characteristic gender traits—arguing that where "the male nations look principally for material well-being, the female nations were more taken up with the needs of the imagination."[4] Other theorists sometimes argued that an ideal nation might well combine male and female attributes, as the American Ralph Waldo Emerson (writing at the same time as Gobineau)

Le Petit Journal

TOUS LES VENDREDIS
Le Supplément illustré
5 Centimes

SUPPLÉMENT ILLUSTRÉ
Huit pages : CINQ centimes

TOUS LES JOURS
Le Petit Journal
5 Centimes

Deuxième Année   SAMEDI 21 FÉVRIER 1891   Numéro 13

LE NOUVEAU BUSTE OFFICIEL DE LA RÉPUBLIQUE
(Projet de MM. Jacques France et Charles Gauthier)

The New Marianne, illustration in *Le Petit Journal* (21 February 1891), designed by Jacques France and Charles Gauthier. This symbol of French republicanism appeared in a late nineteenth-century newspaper, but representations of "Marianne" first became popular during the French Revolution in the 1790s. The strong, youthful female embodied the imagined virtues of a republic and nationalized an artistic tradition that had long used the Virgin Mary to symbolize family devotion and religious morality. (Getty Images) suggested in his account of the well-balanced English national identity. "They are rather manly than warlike," Emerson wrote. "When the war is over, the mask falls from the affectionate and domestic tastes, which make them women in kindness. . . . The two sexes are co-present in the English mind." Indeed, according to Emerson, the fundamental traits of English culture could be found in the gendered traditions that had merged to form English society: "Mixture is a secret of the English island; and, in their dialect, the male principle is the Saxon; the female, the Latin; and they are combined in every discourse."[5] Emerson generally admired English culture, and his gendered explanations of nationhood pointed to specific historical achievements from which America's own dominant culture had evolved, but his wider social and cultural themes exemplified a typical nineteenth-century inclination to connect national identities to the identities of women and men.

The contrasting and connected identities of women, men, and nations thus became a prominent theme in nationalist writings about families. Indeed, as the historian Ida Blom has emphasized, "it was common for Western European nations to conceive of themselves as families," thereby linking the "timeless" emotional meanings of the family to the modern meaning of national cultures.[6] Most nationalists therefore compared the imagined "family" of a whole nation to the domestic "families" of specific grandparents, parents, children, and households that people knew in their personal lives. These two concepts of family were inseparable for most nationalists because they assumed that a strong national society needed deep personal commitments to families, and strong families developed their coherence or continuity through shared commitments to the nation; but the possible conflicts between love of nation and love of family were inevitably downplayed in the popular images of ideal families nurturing future national citizens.

Families were thus recognized (like schools) as crucial mediating institutions where nationalist ideas could help shape the lives and commitments of each individual. The Italian nationalist Giuseppe Mazzini, for example, sought to link the ideal national and domestic families through images of a "home" that brought all Italians into a collective family network. "Our country is our home," Mazzini explained with a common domestic metaphor, "the home which God has given us, placing therein a numerous family which we love and are loved by, and with which we have a more intimate and quicker communion of feeling and thought than with others." This domestic national union was nevertheless threatened like other families by separations and distances that must be overcome in order for the national family to achieve the unity that all good families required. "As the members of a family cannot rejoice at the common table if one of their number is far away," Mazzini continued, "so you should have no joy or repose as long as a portion of the territory upon which your language is spoken is separated from the Nation."[7] Such images of a lost or separated national "family member" reappeared often in nationalist writings about still-unformed nation-states or the territories that well-established national states had lost to other governments. In short, the emotional complexities of a grieving, divided, or united family could be invoked to support every call for national sacrifice and commitment. At the same time, however, Mazzini and other nationalists moved easily from these general metaphors of family identity into specific recommendations for individual behavior and personal domestic life that might now be called national "family values."

The rise of nationalism in the decades after the French Revolution coincided with the development of new ideas about the political significance of respectable families and sexual mores. Breaking with the reputed immorality of traditional aristocratic societies, the new leaders of sovereign nations promoted devotion to family and nation as the surest path to good morality and social order. This new alliance of moral reformers and nationalists has been described by the historian George Mosse, who argues that nationalism "sanctioned middle-class manners and morals and played a crucial part in spreading respectability to all classes of the population." Nationalist writers thus contributed to a wider bourgeois aspiration for well-regulated sexual behavior by praising marriage as the only appropriate venue for sexual relations and by advocating sexual restraint as the model for virtuous, "manly" national behavior. "Manliness meant freedom from sexual passion," Mosse explains, "the sublimation of sensuality into leadership of society and the nation."[8] This concept of sublimated sensuality became most pronounced in the Protestant cultures of northern Europe, but Mosse argues that ideas about manliness also appeared more generally in most modern accounts of strong nations—whose masculine strength was contrasted to women and weak or "abnormal" men.

There could, of course, be no nation without women, yet the women came to represent the "passive" and "immutable" element of national societies. According to this binary description of gendered national duties, men acted, used their reason for public causes, and made history; women embodied the deep, unchanging, natural force of the nation and made babies. Although women were responsible for the eternal moral values that respectable families and nations passed on to their children, they entered public life as symbols of timeless national virtue rather than as actors in the political and social processes of a dynamic national history. "The female embodiments of the nation [Marianne, Germania] stood for eternal forces," Mosse notes in his persuasive summary of how womanhood was linked to nationhood. "They looked backward in their ancient armor and medieval dress. Woman as a preindustrial symbol suggested innocence and chastity, a kind of moral rigor directed against modernity."[9] Placed on the pedestal of national purity, idealized national women were unable to participate in most of the political, social, and military institutions that represented and directed public life in the new national states; indeed, they were not even allowed to vote until the twentieth century.

Despite these restrictions on their public action, women loomed large in the nationalist imagination as the guardians of a crucial domestic sphere wherein boys and girls alike learned the meaning of their national culture. Weak families (as nationalists perceived them) would steadily weaken the whole nation, whereas good, strong families would create good, strong nations. The Polish nationalist Adam Mickiewicz described this family-nation connection as a system of mutual dependence and warned that domestic life suffered disruption and disorientation whenever national commitments or identities disappeared within families. National life must therefore overlap with family life, in Mickiewicz's view, and each family should share in the public goals of the nation by cultivating the memory of past national and family achievements. Women and men might have different roles in this nationalized family identity, Mickiewicz wrote in an account of the ideal family, and yet they fostered the same national and familial objectives: "In the Middle Ages, the wife prayed in her chapel for the same cause that her husband fought for on the battlefield; she was certain that her prayers brought aid to her husband. They needed each other: working for the same goal, they felt united in the same spiritual work. The memories of dead parents continued to live among the children; they invoked the memory of their mother as a saint and learned by heart the history of their father."[10]

Unfortunately, Mickiewicz went on to explain, such commitments to a shared family and national history no longer existed in most parts of Europe—except in Poland, where "families still nourish within themselves the great national life" and where even the wife "sometimes mounts a horse to defend the country."[11] Poland's national superiority thus emerged

Philipp Veit, *Germania*, oil on canvas, 1835. Veit portrayed the meaning of Germany in this idealized, symbolic portrait of a medieval woman. Seated on a throne with both rural and urban landscapes behind her, "Germania" holds a sword, a book, and an emblazoned shield as she looks toward an imperial crown. Although the image suggests the character of a medieval Madonna, she symbolically represents the sanctity of the nation rather than the mother of Christ. (Städel Museum [Frankfurt am Main]/ARTOTHEK)

for Mickiewicz in the strength of a distinctive family life that fused private memories with public causes and personal religion with national aspirations. Other nationalists claimed similar or different family virtues for their own nations, but in almost every case, the family stood at the mediating juncture of private and public life. "To sanctify the Family more and more and to link it ever closer to the Country," Mazzini reminded the Italians, "this is your mission."[12]

The widespread emphasis on the national significance of families gave women an honorable and essential role in national life. Most nationalists assumed that women must be carefully prepared to serve as guardians of family and national morality because their virtue provided the decisive first step toward a national education for the nation's children. Yet the education of women, as most nationalists interpreted it, could only build on those essential, immutable qualities that lay deep within the nation's women and mothers. When Jules Michelet wrote about the need for national education in France, for example, he suggested that the all-important early lessons could be learned in the homes of workers and artisans who already understood the domestic order that sustained a great nation. Michelet's account of working-class French families in his book *The People* thus described the relationships between women and men that nationalists liked to portray as the vital, creative source of successful national cultures. Returning home from a day of hard work, the French working man could find his wife and children in the blissful surroundings of a simple home. "This woman is virtue itself," Michelet explained in the language of nationalist gender stereotypes; she embodies "the particular charm of unaffected reason and tact that enable her to govern strength without being aware of it. This man is the strong, the patient, and courageous [worker], who bears for society the heaviest load of human life." Indeed, Michelet explained that the weary French worker went off to bed while his wife put the children to sleep and completed all the domestic chores, because he had to prepare himself for another day of labor in the world outside his home. "Early in the morning, long before he opens his eyes, she is up. Soon everything is ready—the warm food he eats at home and that which he takes with him. He goes off with his heart satisfied after kissing his wife and sleeping children, with no worries about what he is leaving."[13]

Michelet's idealized, male portrait of the happy French family thus emphasized the dichotomy of male and female labor, ascribed public action to men and domestic virtue to women, and placed the family at the center of a vibrant national life. Like many nationalists of the era, he complained about decadent aristocrats and bourgeois hedonists who did not follow the example of decent peasants and workers, but he had no doubt that virtuous families embodied the deepest values of the virtuous French nation; and no task was more important to these families than raising the children who would become the citizens and inheritors of the nation.

Reproducing the Nation

Nationalist writers frequently worried about how families were producing and shaping the nation's children. The essential biological labor depended, of course, on women, whose service to the nation was analogous to the mostly male labor of historians and writers. National cultures could only survive and flourish through a well-cultivated collective memory of the nation's past heroes and achievements, but there could be no national future without the constant reproduction of citizens. Men therefore took care of the nation's memory and current public problems, while women took care of the nation's biological survival. As Mazzini explained it, the woman's national duty was to "create the future . . . of which the living symbol is the child, [the] link between us and the generations to come. Through her the Family, with its divine mystery of reproduction, points to eternity."[14] National history provided the much-desired immortality for people who had already died; children sustained the hope of national (and personal) immortality for those who were still alive.

The anxieties about death that contributed much of the emotional force to the memories of soldiers or the fusions of religion and nationalism thus appeared also in the anxieties about reproduction, families, and children. Births and deaths—the ultimate boundaries in the lives of individuals—shaped the future and past meaning of nations as well as families, so even the most philosophical nationalists speculated on the mysteries and pleasures of childhood and child rearing. "What nobly thinking man," J. G. Fichte asked rhetorically, "does not wish and aspire to repeat afresh his own life . . . in his children and his children's children, and to live on even on this earth, ennobled and perfected in their lives, long after he is dead? . . . What nobly thinking man does not desire . . . to sow a seed that will bring the endless, continuous perfection of his race . . . [and leave] reminders that he too once moved on this mortal round?" Fichte raised his questions with the specific perspectives of a father, but he was certain that children offered the essential path to immortality for all individuals and nations alike. National struggles were therefore always in some sense about the survival of the children. When the German Protestants fought to establish their new religion, for example, they were thinking about what Fichte called "the blessedness of their children, of their grandchildren as yet unborn, and of all posterity."[15] For Fichte and most nationalists in all modern societies, this view of children and the "yet unborn" became an ultimate justification for every national sacrifice, including wars and campaigns for national independence.

Children were hence the most precious national resource, and the ultimate genocidal crime against any national society would be to kill its children. The death of children meant the death of a nation, whereas virtually every other national catastrophe could eventually be overcome through the survival of the children in whom a nation would continue to exist. Children were often described as the pure embodiment of national virtues (resembling in this respect a good soldier), and images of happy or endangered children were a common motif in nationalist writings and art. As Michelet noted in one of his many evocations of French virtues, "The child is the people themselves in their native truth before they are deformed; it is the people without vulgarity, rudeness, or envy." Indeed, no matter what problems or setbacks might afflict the French, the nation's children brought them back to their most profound national realities and national obligations. "In the name of our children," Michelet reminded his French readers, "we must not allow our country to perish."[16] The rhetorical references to children thus resembled the constant references to forefathers in nationalist literature and speeches, because children, like ancestors, seemed to carry the nation's virtue and original innocence. These virtuous, innocent young people, however, still had to learn about the meaning of the nation in their schools and families.

The family was therefore a site of cultural reproduction as well as biological reproduction, and it gave women a cultural labor to complement their biological work. Like Mickiewicz, who claimed superiority for Polish families on the grounds that they best sustained the memory of national accomplishments, nationalists everywhere called for a domestic cultural training that would assure a deep national consciousness in every child. In this respect, as in so many others, the Italian writer Mazzini summarized the almost universal nationalist preoccupation with a kind of national "home schooling." Stressing the profound public responsibility of all parents, Mazzini explained that "the task of the family is to educate *citizens*. Family and Country are the two extreme points of the same line. And where this is not so the Family degenerates into egoism." The successful, virtuous family celebrated its connection to a wider national community and gave conscientious attention to the children's understanding of their national identity. Take the children on your knee, Mazzini advised his compatriots, and "speak to them of their Country, of what it was, of what it ought to be." Children could learn these national truths better from their parents than from anybody else, but only if they heard constantly about their own place in a long history of ancestors. "Tell them over again the great deeds of the common people in our ancient republics," Mazzini implored, "teach them the names of the good men who loved Italy and her people, and endeavoured through suffering, calumny, and persecution to improve their destinies." The ideal national family thus helped each child understand his or her own intimate connection to the past in order to generate committed national actions in the future. Mazzini's authentic national family would always be united by personal love, yet the best parents would also make the family "a temple in which you may sacrifice together to the country."[17]

The nationalist concerns about children, reproduction, and families often led to an interest in sexual behaviors, which carried many nationalists beyond the problems of education into evolving debates about sexual mores and gender roles. Most nationalists regarded "nonproductive" sexual activity as a threat to national life—an idea for which they found confirmation in new medical literatures on the dangers of homosexuality, masturbation, and sexual promiscuity.[18] Nationalisms celebrated well-regulated heterosexuality, and homosexuals were regularly deemed "abnormal" within ideologies that praised "good" citizens for marrying, producing children, and fostering national identities in their domestic relations. Even late marriages caused concern among some nationalists, who worried that such marriages produced fewer children. Reflecting on the population in France (a country where declining birth rates generated early and enduring nationalist concern), Michelet urged the bourgeoisie to marry at a younger age and to seek partners among the more vital lower classes. "That is the path to strength, beauty, and a bright future," Michelet told his readers. "Our young men marry late, already worn out, and generally take a sickly young lady. Their children die or live in poor health. After two or three generations our bourgeoisie will be as puny as our nobility before the Revolution." The national struggle of life against death, in short, posed new challenges for every generation, though the biological threats always appeared to be most dangerous in the cities. Michelet and many

After I. A. Atkinson, *Russian Loyalty and Heroism*, etching and aquatint, hand colored by Clark and Dubourgh, 1816. Children learned the history of their nations through their families as well as their schools. This English image conveys the meaning of national sacrifice by portraying a Russian father who severed his own hand as he resisted orders to collaborate with the French advance on Moscow in 1812. A child observes the father's heroic action, thereby learning about honorable national duties that may be required for the future protection of his family and nation. (From the copy in the Hoyt Collection, Rare Book Collection, University of North Carolina at Chapel Hill)

other nationalists, in fact, extended their anxieties about sexuality into a wider anxiety about national degeneration as the (imagined) hardy, rural populations moved from the countryside into new urban centers. "Not only is the body failing," Michelet noted in his warnings to the French bourgeoisie, "but so is the mind."[19]

Although Michelet did not push his commentaries on reproduction and families toward a detailed discussion of "race" and "blood," other writers began to speculate on the complex intersection of sex, families, and racial identities as they worried about degeneration or national purity. The status of women was also crucial in the more race-conscious forms of nationalism, because a nation whose women "fell" to the men of other nations was a nation at risk of losing its national identity. National soldiers were thus portrayed as "protectors" of the nation's women, and national enemies in war became a menace to the nation's biological foundation as well as its politics or culture; indeed, violation of the nation's women represented, like the murder of children, an ultimate assault on the sanctity and survival of the nation. In the United States, for example, one of the most popular genres of national writing took the form of "captivity narratives" about European women who were taken prisoner by Indians. Portraying the "savage" as a sexual threat to European-American women, these stories helped establish an early American national identity by connecting sexual behavior to the boundaries of race and culture.[20]

Similar anxieties about sexual violation or racial mixing also appeared in European nationalist descriptions of warfare, overseas colonies, and threats of foreign invasion. Such fears surfaced dramatically in France when German soldiers poured across the Rhine in 1870 and 1914, threatening French women and the French nation with both a sexual assault and a protracted military occupation. Writers and artists in France portrayed the German seizure of French territory in the Franco-Prussian War as a literal and figurative rape of French mothers and "Mother" France, and French nationalists would emphasize the brutal, sexual aggression of German soldiers throughout the First World War.[21] The biological reproduction of nations thus seemed to be most endangered during wars, but nationalists also worried in peacetime about sexual behaviors, national-minded child rearing, national "fertility," and the domestic responsibilities of women. Meanwhile, the biological themes in the nationalist writing about families became even more prominent in the growing nationalist concern with race.

Racial Theories and Nationalist Identities

Theories about the racial differences that separated nations developed somewhat later than the nationalist theories about distinctive national histories, political institutions, religions, and languages. Beginning in the 1840s and 1850s, however, nationalists increasingly turned to new biological sciences and pseudosciences to support their claims for unique national characteristics. Biological conceptions of national identities spread rapidly after the appearance of Charles Darwin's *The Origin of Species* (1859), and the subsequent development of "Social Darwinism" in European and American cultures provided ideological support for a new wave of nationalist imperialism. The new biological theories were invoked to bolster racist ideas that transformed or expanded the political and cultural themes of earlier nationalisms. Where political nationalists might stress the political will and history of a sovereign people, racists stressed physical or biological traits that existed outside of history, political institutions, or literary traditions; and they assumed that the racial traits of a national population both shaped and reflected specific national histories.

Theoretical distinctions between nationalism and racism often enter into the historical dichotomies that separate Western (political) nationalisms from Eastern (racial, ethnic) nationalisms, yet some of the most influential racist theories actually appeared first among English and French writers. Although Fichte's *Addresses to the German Nation* referred to the "Teutonic race," he generally described national differences by emphasizing the contrasts between a vibrant German language and the stagnant or "derivative" languages of other European nations.[22] There was, of course, much racism in various strands of German nationalism by the late nineteenth century, but the German nationalist historian Friedrich Meinecke (who suggested that the existence of a nation required a "blood relationship") was still arguing in the early twentieth century that "there are no racially pure nations."[23]

The most complete expression of racist nationalism would emerge later in the twentieth-century policies of German Nazism, which transformed race into the central feature of all national identities. Although there were many older nationalist themes in Nazi propaganda, "races" tended to replace "nations" whenever Nazis set out to explain historical conflicts or justify their political-cultural policies. This kind of racist thinking had catastrophic, genocidal consequences when it became the reigning political ideology in Europe's most powerful twentieth-century nation-state. It is therefore difficult to understand earlier racial theories in the context of nineteenth-century nationalisms when we know the horrific, violent history of racism in Nazi Germany and in other modern imperialisms (discussed in chapter 7). Although it would be inaccurate to describe all nineteenth-century ideas about race as "proto-Nazi" ideologies, racial theories clearly gained wide influence in most nationalisms of that era, including the nationalisms that have often been linked to politics and history rather than to ethnicity or race.

Racial theories offered nationalist writers an apparently scientific perspective for characterizing the national cultures they wanted to define. Drawing on Enlightenment traditions that categorized the natural world according to various "objective" criteria, analysts identified the racial traits of different nationalities and ascribed social or intellectual characteristics to physical differences. Among the early leaders in this new racial theorizing, the English writer Robert Knox (1791–1862) emerged as a popular pre-Darwinian lecturer and advocate for racial interpretations of world history. "The results of the physical and mental qualities of a race are naturally manifested in its civilization," Knox assured the readers of his book, *The Races of Men* (1850), "for every race has its own form of civilization." This alleged historical truth could be seen clearly in England, where the population was divided between the "Saxons" and the "Normans." The latter were a French "Celtic" race that had conquered England in the eleventh century (the "greatest calamity that ever befel [sic] England—perhaps, the human race," Knox complained), but the racial qualities of Saxon England had never been destroyed. The Saxons were "thoughtful, plodding, [and] industrious beyond all other races," Knox reported, and they were a remarkably "tall, powerful, athletic race of men; the strongest, as a race, on the earth"; indeed, they were the "only absolutely fair race on the face of the globe."[24] Equally important for Knox, these strong Saxon "men" loved freedom and abhorred feudalism, thereby distinguishing themselves from the Celtic (French) deference to chiefs and social elites.

This Celtic racial trait of obedience, as Knox described it, ran so deep in the French soul that even their most dramatic revolutionary demands for freedom always ended with deference to a new chief (for example, Napoleon). "The world thought Celtic France a great and free people," Knox wrote in a commentary on the French Revolution, but "the world forgot the element of race . . . [in] the probable destinies of the French Celt."[25] Expressing their inherent racial instincts, the French preferred their military heroes over parliamentary governments and their Celtic deference over Saxon freedom. The whole course of French history was thus for Knox a perfect example of his pseudoscientific racial theories: political institutions and leaders might change over time, yet history could never transform habits that flowed from the essential nature of a race.

One could perhaps dismiss Knox's absurd racial explanations for historical events if they were a marginal or insignificant aspect of modern nationalism, but his images of Saxon strength and freedom soon became popular themes in much nineteenth-century writing about England and America. Many white Americans took "racial" pride in their historical links to "Saxon" England, thus giving English authors like Knox a market on both sides of the Atlantic. When Ralph Waldo Emerson wrote a book on "English Traits" (1856), for example, he read Knox's racial theories and found himself referring to race as he pursued his subject. Despite his skepticism about Knox's racial absolutisms, Emerson noted that "it is in the deep traits of race that the fortunes of nations are written," and he portrayed the English as "more intellectual than other races." This intellectual superiority explained why the English nation tended to "assimilate other races to themselves" and why other peoples who came in contact with the English generally deferred to English dominance and learned the English language. Yet Emerson also suspected that England's dominance might be ending, that the nation had entered "her old age," and that the most dynamic, modern activity of the "British race" might well be found on the plains and mountains of America rather than on the ancient island itself. Like aging parents, Emerson concluded, the English could find their future glory and strength in their American "children," whose "elasticity" would become the "hope of mankind" if or when the "old race" lost its expansive energy in Britain.[26]

Such comments do not make Emerson a racist or a racial determinist like Knox, but they do indicate how the language of race influenced both the English and American conceptions of national identity. Indeed, even before Knox and Emerson were writing about the Saxon and English races, the American historian George Bancroft (1800–1891) had used racial explanations in the 1840s to account for certain aspects of early American history. Developing sharp contrasts between the Native Americans and the English settlers who displaced them, Bancroft argued that the Indians, "naked and feeble compared with the Europeans," could not possibly match the Europeans in civilized skills or military prowess. To be sure, he saw in the Indians a common humanity, but their racial differences seemed to have more historical influence than the deeper human qualities they shared with "Caucasians." Bancroft's narrative of America's emerging national culture thus established clear distinctions between the "races" on the North American continent and showed why racial characteristics helped the "Caucasians" to prevail. Descended from "that Germanic race most famed for the love of personal independence," the "Anglo-Saxons" had carried their traditional racial strengths into the remote forests of America. "The Anglo-Saxon mind," Bancroft explained, "in its serenest nationality, . . . fondly cherishing the active instinct for personal freedom . . . and legislative power . . . had made its dwelling-place in the empire of Powhatán."[27]

As for the Indians, Bancroft believed that they could not respond creatively to the intrusions from Europe because "the red man has aptitude at imitation rather than invention." Although the Indian could think about objects, he lacked the "faculty of abstraction to lift himself out of the dominion of his immediate experience . . . and he is inferior in reason and the moral qualities." Some sympathetic observers might assume that such flaws appeared only in certain individuals, but Bancroft reported that "this inferiority" was in fact "the characteristic of the race."[28] Bancroft was a strong Jacksonian Democrat who celebrated the virtues of political equality, and yet his racial assumptions led him to portray the conquest (or death) of Native Americans as an inevitable consequence of inescapable racial differences and inequalities. Like many other nationalisms of the era, Bancroft's expansive vision of America's destiny presumed a racial hierarchy and placed his own favorite racial category ("Anglo-Saxon") in a privileged historical position. He was by no means a proto-Nazi, but his support for America's national expansion clearly expressed influential, popular forms of racism. Similar racist theories were also used in this same era to exclude both free and enslaved Africans from the social and political rights of American national citizenship, and most European Americans viewed the nation's essential identity as the political, cultural, and economic expression of the white (or "Anglo-Saxon") race.[29]

The growing racial consciousness in nineteenth-century Western culture spread across both Europe and North America, but the most comprehensive summary of the ostensible links between races and nations may have appeared in the works of the French writer Arthur de Gobineau. A longtime critic of the French Revolution and of subsequent movements for democratic political reforms, Gobineau developed a racial explanation for France's past achievements and recent problems in a book called *Essay on the Inequality of the Human Races* (1853–55). Although he was a contemporary of Knox and other pre-Darwinian racial theorists, he was more concerned with the decline of races and nations than with the limitless possibilities for future racial achievements. Gobineau therefore helped to launch a new form of racist writing that emphasized the national dangers of mixing races (themes that did begin to resemble the ideas of twentieth-century Nazism), the decisive influence of race in all spheres of history, and the consequences of what he called racial degeneration. "The word *degenerate*," Gobineau wrote, "when applied to a people, means . . . that the people has no longer the same intrinsic value as it had before, because it has no longer the same blood in its veins, continual adulterations having gradually affected the quality of that blood. In other words, though the nation bears the name given by its founders, the name no longer connotes the same race."[30]

The meaning of a nation for Gobineau was thus inseparable from the purity of its "blood"—an alleged historical fact that posed grave problems for old nations in which generations of racial "mixing" had transformed an ancient or original population. "So long as the blood and institutions of a nation keep to a sufficient degree the impress of the original race," Gobineau argued, "that nation exists." This imagined racial purity provided the only secure defense against assaults on the nation's ancient institutions, yet Gobineau assumed that the most powerful nations were also the most vulnerable to the racial mixing that would cause their decline. Strong nations tended to conquer less powerful peoples, whereupon the fateful processes of racial mixing immediately began to weaken the conquering nation. "From the very day when the conquest is accomplished and the fusion begins," Gobineau explained in a typical sociobiological generalization, "there appears a noticeable change of quality in the blood of the masters."[31] Since "mixed" nations inevitably lost their vitality and strength, Gobineau assumed that Europe's once-pure nations would gradually decline and that racial mixing in the United States would undermine its national growth and power.

Gobineau's historical conception of national accomplishments and decline rested on typical racist theories about inherent racial traits and racial hierarchies. Predictably enough, he placed the northern "white" European race at the top of a racial pyramid that descended steadily down toward the populations of America, Africa, and Asia. Developing some of the most extreme racist claims of the era, Gobineau told his readers that "all civilizations derive from the white race, that none can exist without its help, and that a society is great and brilliant only so far as it preserves the blood of the noble group that created it." Such theories fit comfortably with European assumptions about their own imperialist projects, the growing belief in biological causality, and the pretensions of European social elites, but they also suggested the dangers that Gobineau saw lurking in France and other European nations. The expanding power of the "white" race was also expanding the racial mixtures that destroyed national traditions and creativity. "This [racial mixing] will lead eventually to mediocrity in all fields," Gobineau warned, "mediocrity of physical strength, mediocrity of beauty, mediocrity of intellectual capacities."[32]

Gobineau's pessimism about his nation's future diverged from the usual optimism of nineteenth-century nationalists, most of whom saw their nations' distinctive "racial" traits as the foundation for future expansion and influence. In fact, few nationalists went as far as Gobineau or Knox in stressing the racial essence of national identities, though they commonly attributed at least some of their nation's achievements to superior racial traits such as "physical strength," "intelligence," or "love of freedom." Extreme theories of racial determinism, however, did not give enough attention to the individual choices and historical agency that most liberal nationalists invoked to rally their compatriots to political action and national causes. Gobineau's pessimism thus anticipated another kind of conservative, fin-de-siècle nationalism in France and elsewhere that focused obsessively on the dangers of national decline instead of the prospects for exceptional national progress.

The Belief in National Exceptionalism

Nineteenth-century nationalists used the prestige of the biological sciences to reinforce other ideas about national identities that had already developed in historical studies, philology, literary criticism, and religious rituals. Long-term continuities in the "nature" of women and men, the relations within families, and the racial traits of national populations were described as embodiments of inherent national virtues and as distinctive characteristics that separated each nation from all others. Although the meaning of gender, family, and race steadily evolved through the same cultural systems that constructed the meaning of history, literature, and religion, nationalists typically claimed that women, children, and "manly" citizens expressed the immutable, transcendental, or natural essence of national identities.

These apparently "natural" attributes nevertheless had to be cultivated in homes and schools that taught young people how their various gender roles, racial characteristics, and social obligations merged with the history of their nation. Nationalists wanted to link collective, public identities with the emerging personal identities of children by immersing students in the nation's history and traditions; and parents were expected to extend the work of schools into their homes by teaching the emotion-laden lesson that each child was fortunate to have been born into a unique national family. This theme of national "exceptionalism" ran through every nationalist ideology, in part because the belief in national identity and difference usually rested on claims for national superiority in language, politics, culture, religion, or race. When people believed that their nation embodied the highest level of achievement in some or many spheres of human civilization, they also assumed that their nation's history carried universal significance and that the well-being or survival of their national population carried consequences for the whole world. The themes of biology and history came together on this point because the constant reproduction of future generations was, of course, the essential precondition for the national pursuit of world-historical destinies and duties.

The belief in national exceptionalism drew on old religious ideas about chosen peoples and collective missions, but it took on new intensity when it merged with biological metaphors of birth and death, growth and degeneration. No matter how much a nation's specific conflicts and enemies might evolve across time, nationalists could always use the "exceptionalism" of their nation's history or mission to justify renewed national commitment and action. Fichte's call for action against Napoleon, for example, portrayed the struggle as a test for all of humanity. Among "all modern peoples," Fichte assured his German audience, "it is you in whom the seed of human perfection most decidedly lies and to whom the lead in its development is assigned. If you perish . . . then all the hopes of the entire human race for salvation from the depths of its miseries perish with you. . . . If you sink, all humanity sinks with you, without hope of future restoration."[33] Where historical "realists" might have described Germany's conflict with France as simply another episode in a long struggle for resources, territory, and international power, the nationalist philosopher interpreted Germany's cause as a campaign for the whole moral future of humanity. It was a huge responsibility—the development of this "seed of human perfection"—yet it was also in Fichte's view a decisive opportunity for the Germans to show their unique commitment to the most elevated human aspirations for freedom and salvation.

Across the Rhine, however, nineteenth-century French nationalists conceded nothing to the Germans when it came to claiming exceptional national destinies. Michelet's commentaries on French history and the French people constantly proclaimed France's universal significance (mirroring in this respect Fichte's claims for Germany) and located the whole course of world history in the victories and defeats of the French nation. Describing this extraordinary nation as "the salvation of mankind," Michelet wrote proudly that "the national legend of France is an immense unbroken stream of light, a veritable Milky Way which the world has always fixed its eyes upon." The universal human interest in French achievements was, of course, a great honor, but it also produced exceptional obligations because the world could be "lost perhaps for a thousand years if France succumbs" to those who opposed or ignored its unique national history.[34] Michelet's concluding calls for national action in *The People* thus repeated in French the same apocalyptic, quasi-religious assumptions about human salvation that Fichte had developed earlier in Germany. In both cases, a specific nation became a kind of mediating messiah for people everywhere. "The fatherland, my fatherland," Michelet wrote, "can alone save the world."[35]

A long century of such writings about "exceptional" national missions helps to explain why the national hatreds were much stronger in the French-German war of 1914–18 than they had been in the French-German wars of the Napoleonic era, but it would be wrong to assume that grandiose claims for world-historical nations appeared only in the heated imaginations of European intellectuals. The modern discourse of national exceptionalism and chosen peoples also emerged very early in the history of America ("the city on a hill"), and American confidence in a unique national destiny only grew stronger during the century after the American Revolution. By the end of the nineteenth century, the United States was claiming its place as one of the major imperial nations of the world, though some Americans worried about whether they should take control of people in distant lands such as the Philippines. Responding to these doubts in early 1900, Senator Albert Beveridge (1826–1927) of Indiana delivered a speech on America's exceptional destiny in which he justified the colonization of the Philippines and asserted the "universalizing" national claims for America that Fichte and Michelet had long since made for their countries in Europe.

Beveridge believed that America's imperial expansion was a "racial" question because God had made the "English-speaking and Teutonic peoples" the talented "master organizers of the world." More specifically, "He has made us adept in government that we may administer government among savage and senile peoples. . . . And of all our race He has marked the American people as His chosen nation to finally lead in the regeneration of the world. This is the divine mission of America, and it holds for us all the profit, all the glory, all the happiness possible to man. We are the trustees of the world's progress."[36] Americans had always believed in the uniqueness of their national calling, so an American nationalist hardly needed the European intellectual contributions of Fichte, Michelet,

Mazzini, Mickiewicz, Knox, or Gobineau to claim an exceptional mission for the United States. Yet Beveridge repeated many of the most common themes in the increasingly "biological" nationalisms of late nineteenth-century cultures as he evoked images of race, senility, regeneration, and the "divine mission" of a "chosen nation" to advocate the American occupation of the Philippines. Earlier political and religious conceptions of American exceptionalism had by no means disappeared during the nineteenth century, but the nationalism of Beveridge and many other Americans resembled the nationalisms of modern Europe in more ways than the historical dichotomies of "Western" and "Eastern" nationalisms suggest. American nationalists, like their European counterparts, drew on biology, worried about families and gender roles, promoted racial stereotypes, and affirmed the unique natural and historical qualities of their national society. Placed in the wider context of European nationalist ideas, the emergence and cultural evolution of America's nationalism tends to exemplify rather than differ from the nationalist movements and political cultures in almost every modern "Western" or "Eastern" society.

CHAPTER SIX

The Cultural Construction of Nationalism in Early America

Earlier chapters of this book argue that nationalism has always grown out of specific cultural histories and that the nationalisms in Europe and America had more similarities than the traditional dichotomies of "Western" and "Eastern" nationalisms suggest. Each previous chapter has also focused on important themes in the nationalist political movements, cultural ideologies, and collective identities that helped to reshape modern governments and societies during the century after 1775. All of the main thematic components of modern nationalism had gained wide historical influence by 1900, and these nationalist themes would remain important almost everywhere in the twentieth century: the political claims for national sovereignty, the resistance to empires, the interest in national languages and histories, the fusion with religious traditions, the "nationalizing" of family and gender identities, the emphasis on land and race, the belief in national "missions," and the praise for national heroes.

Although these themes (and others) reappeared throughout the modern world and could be further explored through very wide-ranging historical examples, the final chapters in this survey of nationalist cultures will turn from general political and cultural themes to a more specific discussion of nationalism in early American history and to a brief overview of how nationalism evolved in the twentieth century. The broad themes of nationalism, in short, will be examined in "historical snapshots" of particular nations, modern wars, and historical changes that exemplified or transformed the nationalist ideas and practices that had mostly emerged in Europe and America before 1850. This chapter therefore focuses on the construction of American nationalism, partly because Americans have tended to deny or ignore their own political/cultural overlap with European nationalisms and partly because the modern, international power of the United States has given its nationalism the most significant global presence in contemporary history. No other nation now matches the cultural influence or military campaigns that flow from American nationalism and America's nationalist view of international affairs.

Americans managed to construct a national identity and nationalist ideology quite rapidly in the decades between their break from Britain (1776) and their painful, bloody Civil War (1861–65), so their early national history shows how a diverse, scattered population could be "narrated" into a nation in political institutions, schools, religious rituals, public celebrations, family memories, literature, and history books. These aspects of modern nationalist ideology can all be seen in the writings of authors and public figures who contributed significantly to the popular narratives that helped Americans invent their national traditions and imagine their nation. The discussion here will focus especially on the poet Philip Freneau (1752–1832), the historian George Bancroft (1800–1891), and President Abraham Lincoln (1809–65), but their recurring themes became important because they expressed an emerging national identity rather than simply the personal views of a few individuals. American nationalism, like all others, developed through new national stories that helped people identify with specific political and cultural traditions.

The new American nation's lack of ancient history, unique language, or exclusive ethnic identity pushed the American search for national distinctiveness toward politics, religion, geography, economic prosperity, and domestic virtue. At the same time, however, there was a strong racial component in early American nationalism because the "true" American had to be distinguished from both Native Americans (whose land was taken) and African Americans (whose civil rights were completely denied in slavery). Early American nationalists thus constructed their ideology by emphasizing political and cultural themes that could also be found in virtually every nationalist movement of the era: they assumed that the United States had a unique destiny or mission in world history and that this destiny was manifested in cultural differences that separated America from all of the world's other nations, peoples, and systems of government. American "exceptionalism" presumed that the United States had broken decisively with Old World values and institutions, but it also emphasized fundamental racial differences that divided European Americans from enslaved African Americans as well as from Native Americans—who were, of course, the only ancient or truly "territorial" Americans.

Historians have long pointed to the religious character of early American claims for a unique national mission. Drawing on the Bible and a deep sense of Puritan moral rectitude, Americans saw themselves as the Chosen People from whom God expected the highest human virtues and to whom God had promised a unique political and religious influence on the future history of the world.[1] Religious leaders frequently referred to this God-given mission in sermons that interpreted American victories or defeats during the Revolutionary War as part of God's plan for the emerging nation (see chapter 4), but the belief in America's divine destiny remained as strong among nineteenth-century nationalists as it had been among eighteenth-century ministers. When John O'Sullivan, the editor of *The United States Magazine and Democratic Review,* summarized America's identity in the late 1830s, he was certain that the divine will could be discerned everywhere. "We are the nation of human progress," O'Sullivan assured his readers. "Providence is with us. . . . We point to the everlasting truths on the first page of our national declaration. . . . In its magnificent domain of space and time, the nation of many nations is destined to manifest to mankind the excellence of divine principles."[2] This belief in an exceptional historical mission was shared by all fervent American nationalists, who assumed—as O'Sullivan himself explained in later arguments for the annexation of Texas—that America's territorial expansion fulfilled a "manifest destiny to overspread the continent allotted by Providence for the free development of our yearly multiplying millions."[3]

Such claims for the nation's "manifest destiny" echoed through political speeches, newspaper editorials, poems, and novels, thereby encouraging Americans in every region and economic condition to believe that they lived in God's favorite nation. Readers of Herman Melville's novel *White-Jacket* (1850), for example, came across the following summary of America's unique national destiny in a passage on the evils of flogging sailors: "We Americans are the peculiar, chosen people—the Israel of our time; we bear the ark of the liberties of the world. . . . God has predestinated, mankind expects, great things from our race. . . . We are the pioneers of the world; the advance-guard, sent on through the wilderness of untried things, to break a new path in the New World that is ours. In our youth is our strength; in our inexperience our wisdom."[4] Although Melville later developed a much more skeptical view of American national culture, his novel in 1850 expressed some of the most prominent themes in America's antebellum nationalist ideology, including confident assertions that the New World differed profoundly from the Old World and that God wanted this New World to belong to the advancing European Americans.

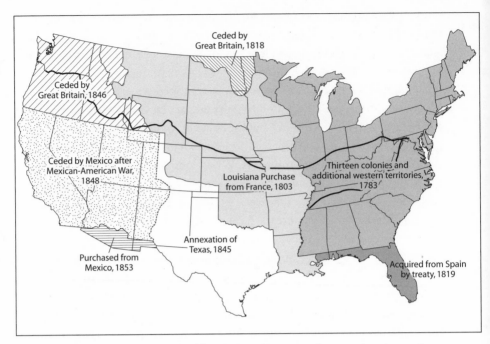

Territorial Expansion of the United States from the 1780s to the 1850s. American nationalists in the early nineteenth century claimed that the United States had a "manifest destiny" to expand across the entire North American continent. This map shows how the new American government rapidly accomplished this ambitious nationalist goal through diplomatic negotiations, land purchases from other nations, and decisive military victories in a war against Mexico.

American conceptions of a divinely ordained national mission contributed to a widely held belief that the new nation's cultural and political differences from the Old World also made it morally superior. In contrast to the corrupt hierarchies of European kings and aristocrats, nationalist orators explained, Americans were building a more virtuous society on the foundation of social equality, public honesty, and political democracy. This simple dichotomy of "Old" corruptions and "New" virtues shaped American self-images throughout the Revolutionary War against Britain and the subsequent era of France's revolutionary and Napoleonic wars, which culminated for the Americans in another war with Britain. The War of 1812 aroused strong opposition as well as a new wave of nationalist optimism, but the nationalist account of the conflict constantly reiterated the contrast between a peace-loving, democratic America and a belligerent, aristocratic Britain.

The British government thus came to symbolize anti-American, Old World hostilities that seemed to persist and even grow after the Americans had established their own successful institutions and economy. Complaining about the British arrogance toward America, one congressman from Kentucky summarized the English threat that seemed forever to separate the United States from dangerous enemies across the sea. "This deep rooted [American] enmity to Great Britain arises from her insidious policy, the offspring of her perfidious conduct towards the United States," Richard Johnson argued in a congressional speech. "Her disposition is unfriendly; her enmity is implacable; she sickens at our prosperity and happiness."[5] It was, of course, difficult to defeat this jealous, haughty enemy, but the very intensity of the struggle gave Americans a strong sense of their difference from Europeans and a deep pride in their national victories. "The proudest people in the world," one editorialist reported in an 1815 commentary on America's war with the British, "have been met and defeated, single-handed too, by a nation they had affected to despise."[6] This desire to affirm American triumphs over Britain's far-reaching, global power suggests how the emerging national identity depended on a firm belief in America's decisive break from the history and conflicts of the Old World. Most Americans therefore believed that isolation from European societies, ideas, and wars provided the surest protection for American virtues and the safest path toward a secure national future. "Our national birth," the journalist John O'Sullivan wrote in 1839, "was the beginning of a new history." It was, above all, America's anti-aristocratic political system that "separates us from the past and connects us with the future only," O'Sullivan went on to explain, so that "we may confidently assume that our country is destined to be *the great nation* of futurity."[7]

Yet the American nationalists had to do more than simply separate the United States from Europe, because they were equally engaged on their western frontier with Indians who claimed "American" lands as their own territory. The cultural defense of American distinctiveness thus drew clear boundaries both inside and outside the North American continent, but the national superiority was defined in each case by emphasizing the characteristics of national difference. Whereas the American nationalist narrative about Europe stressed the dangers of an aging, corrupt civilization, the descriptions of Native Americans developed a different dichotomy of civilization (now identified as American) and savagery that inevitably placed Native Americans on the "uncivilized" side of a cultural frontier.

Ironically enough, when Americans fought against Indians, they quickly linked themselves to the European cultures that they otherwise condemned in their political or cultural declarations of independence. As the writer Timothy Flint asserted during a period of intense hostility toward (and forced removal of) Native Americans in the early 1830s, the blame for frontier conflicts lay entirely with "uncivilized" Indians, who "were not sufficient civilians to distinguish between the right of empire and the right of soil." No compromise could be arranged with people who failed to understand the "right of empire," Flint argued, because their institutions and beliefs were completely alien to the good sense of progress and civilization: "Our industry, fixed residences, modes, laws, institutions, schools, [and] religions rendered a union with them as incompatible as with animals of another nature." This deep incompatibility meant that the United States must displace the entire Indian population; indeed, the vast European-American assault on the Indians should be understood as part of God's unfolding plan for the American continent. "In the unchangeable order of things," wrote Flint, "two such races can not exist together, each preserving a co-ordinate identity. Either this great continent, in the order of Providence, should have remained in the occupancy of half a million of savages, . . . or it must have become, as it has, the domain of civilized millions."[8] Flint did not yet refer explicitly to "Manifest Destiny" (the term that O'Sullivan began using in 1845), but the nationalist ideology that justified American expansion had long since established the reigning assumption that Indians could never hold legitimate claims to lands that Providence had reserved for the United States.

Popular nationalist accounts of America's destiny and cultural achievements thus shaped a powerful, reassuring national identity for a new nation that was defining itself against other people in both the Old and New Worlds. The new nation's unity faced constant threats from the enormous geographical space, the rivalries of different regions, the constant influx of new immigrants, the relative weakness of the national government, the debates about slavery, and the growth of a rival southern nationalism in the mid-nineteenth century; and yet these enduring dangers also gave American nationalists good reasons to continue their nation-building work. New narratives about America's national identity, unity, and history retold the story of a national past and a much-anticipated national future that justified deep personal commitments and frequent public action. Nationalist writers celebrated America's unique political and cultural achievements, its religious devotion to God or to deceased national heroes, and its distinctive domestic virtues or racial strengths. This vast national narrative appeared in art, music, literature, newspapers, political campaigns, schoolbooks, holiday celebrations, and religious services. It also flourished in more social contexts than even the most comprehensive historical account could fully describe, but the writings of Freneau, Bancroft, and Lincoln expressed all of the key nationalist themes in poetry and prose.

Philip Freneau's American Future

Philip Freneau grew up in New Jersey, attended college at Princeton, and lived through the American Revolution as a merchant seaman, a member of the New Jersey militia, a temporary prisoner on a British prison ship, and a poet. Following the war, he continued to write poems about America, but he also became a journalist and later edited the *National Gazette*, a Jeffersonian newspaper that was published in Philadelphia during the early 1790s. Many of his poems and newspaper articles were collected and later published in books, including *The Poems of Philip Freneau* (1786), *The Miscellaneous Works of Philip Freneau* (1788), and *Letters on Various Interesting and Important Subjects* (1799). Although much of his work reflected journalistic haste or the passing political issues of the day, Freneau's writing provided important, early definitions of American national identity and attracted respectful support from national leaders such as Thomas Jefferson and James Madison.[9] He was, in short, a typical nationalist narrator; and his "stories" came back constantly to America's distinctive political achievements, the modern concept of national sovereignty, the cultural distance from Europe, the quasi-religious reverence for deceased soldiers, and the virtuous domestic lives of humble Americans.

Freneau's political commentaries celebrated the brilliance of America's revolutionary political leaders and the nation's unparalleled commitment to human freedom and popular sovereignty. Like every American nationalist of his own time and later, Freneau portrayed George Washington as a uniquely talented, virtuous commander whose personal traits placed him in the highest rank of world-historical heroes and whose extraordinary resistance to British tyranny gave him a saintly status among his compatriots in the emerging American nation. "What few presum'd, you boldly atchiev'd," Freneau wrote in 1781, "A tyrant humbled, and a world reliev'd."[10] Despite some later doubts about the policies of Washington's

Unknown artist, *Washington Giving the Laws to America*, etching and engraving, ca. 1800. George Washington's quasi-religious status in early American nationalism can be seen in this image of a lawgiver who replicates the biblical role of Moses. Holding the new Constitution in his strong arms, Washington receives the acclaim of a united people and sits firmly amid his fellow citizens as a wise "father" of the nation. (Print Collection, Miriam and Ira D. Wallach Division of Art, Prints and Photographs, New York Public Library, Astor, Lenox and Tilden Foundations)

presidential administration, Freneau's praise for Washington remained a leitmotif through all of his nationalist poetry and contributed to the pride in the "Founding Fathers" that united almost all Americans—no matter how much they disagreed about specific government actions. At the time of Washington's death, for example, Freneau published the kind of popular eulogy that assured the national "Father" his permanent stature in America's national ideology:

O *Washington*! thy honoured dust,
To Parent Nature we entrust;
Convinc'd that thy exalted mind
Still lives, but soars beyond mankind;
Still acts in Virtue's sacred cause,
Nor asks from man his vain applause.[11]

Washington was by no means the only national leader to earn Freneau's admiration (other poems praised the genius of Franklin and Jefferson), yet the "honoured" commander and first president stood above all others in defending the righteous cause of American independence. Washington thus became for Freneau "the brightest name on *Freedom's* page, / And the first Honour of our Age."[12]

Even the greatest general, however, could not win a battle without his troops, and Freneau was certain that America's common people had contributed as much as the famous public leaders to the nation's military and political achievements. Freneau insisted in his newspaper articles that Americans understood the meaning of national freedom more profoundly than any other people in the world. "In a free government," he explained, "every man is a king, every woman is a queen," which meant that America would never accept Old World hierarchies, privileges, or exclusions. Rejecting European prejudices, Americans proclaimed that "ALL MEN ARE BORN EQUALLY FREE" and thus refused to give special homage to ancient elites. This strong American preference for the sovereignty of equal people pointed toward the republican political systems of the future, all of which would reject the traditional prerogatives of monarchs and their courtiers. As Freneau argued in a political poem of the early 1790s, republican America provided the best defense of human rights and also the best hope for eventual world peace.

Be ours the task, the ambitious to restrain,
And this great lesson teach, That kings are vain,
That warring realms to certain ruin haste,
That kings subsist on war, and wars are waste;
So shall our nation, form'd on Reason's plan,
Remain the guardian of the Rights of man,
A vast republic, fam'd thro' every clime,
Without a king, to see the end of time![13]

Freneau's poems often lacked political subtlety and aesthetic nuance, but they conveyed the story of America's republican political mission clearly enough to reach anyone who picked up a newspaper or wondered how America differed from the old monarchical states of Europe.

According to Freneau, American independence and virtue could flourish because the new nation was far removed from the European continent and cultures. Indeed, he joined with many Americans in celebrating the great width of the Atlantic Ocean, which seemed to shield the New World from all the agonies of the Old: "Remov'd from Europe's feuds, a hateful scene / (Thank heaven, such wastes of ocean roll between)."[14] The cultural distance from Europe was no less significant than the geographical separation, however, and Freneau strongly believed that these cultural differences provided the most enduring protection of individual freedoms. Each stranger arrived in America to find a free land, "Where no proud despot holds him down, / No slaves insult him with a crown,"[15] but the sovereign freedom of America could only survive through steadfast opposition to England's aristocratic privileges and imperial ambitions. American vigilance was thus essential for national survival because the nation's aristocratic, European enemies never disappeared ("All Tyranny's engines again are at work, / To make you as poor and as base as the Turk");[16] and yet Freneau seemed never to doubt that America's egalitarian principles would ultimately prevail.

America's future victories over European despotism would emerge from the superiority of its political institutions, but these institutions also fostered an economic growth that became both the product of a free government and the foundation for future national power. Like most early American nationalists, Freneau conceded that the new nation could not yet challenge the cultural superiority of Europe's artists and poets. It could, however, use the advantages of its national political freedoms to challenge Europeans in agriculture, commerce, and trade. Freneau's vision of America's continuing rivalry with Europe therefore included an imagined future in which the American economy reached unprecedented levels of prosperity and international influence. "It is not easy to conceive what will be the greatness and importance of North America in a century or two to come," he wrote in the 1780s, "if the present fabric of Nature is upheld, and the people retain those bold and manly sentiments of freedom, which actuate them at this day. Agriculture, the basis of a nation's greatness, will here, most probably, be advanced to its summit of perfection; and its attendant, commerce, will so agreeably and usefully employ mankind, that wars will be forgotten."[17] Freedom would produce prosperity, and the subsequent development of America would show the whole world how republican government and economics could remove warfare from human history. In the end, this American achievement would be recognized and embraced even in Europe, though it might take time: "'Til Europe, humbled, greets our western wave / And owns an equal—whom she wish'd a slave."[18]

America's economic growth could thus be linked to the military and political achievements that Freneau liked to describe whenever he tried to imagine the nation's limitless future development. It was nevertheless important in Freneau's view to build this national future with reverent remembrance of the people who had sacrificed their lives in the revolutionary struggle for national independence. Some of his best poems therefore invoked memories of the dead as he reflected, for example, on English prison ships in which "the ardent brave / Too often met an early grave," or as he wrote about old battlefields and cemeteries. Deaths in battle were not the same as other deaths, because soldiers were assured an honorable immortality in the life of a grateful nation. "Ah, what is death, when fame like *this* endears," Freneau wrote in a poem about a soldier who had died in South Carolina, "*The brave man's favourite, and his country's tears*."[19] Freneau may have harbored Jeffersonian doubts about Christian conceptions of life after death, but he believed, like other modern nationalists, in the immortality of all who died for the nation's cause.

The life of the nation thus flourished in the continuing existence of a whole people, whose soul shaped the domestic arrangements of families and local communities as well as the much-celebrated heroism on battlefields. Indeed, the common people became national heroes in Freneau's account of the social traits that distinguished America from Europe. Unlike corrupt European nobles, Freneau noted in one of his articles, "our AMERICAN FARMERS are virtuous, not in name but in REALITY. Vice has not been able to entice them from the standard of VIRTUE, INDEPENDENCE, and FREEDOM." These freedom-loving farmers guarded America's rights, embodied America's dignity, and supported the national Constitution. America's independence was thus assured if the nation's leaders continued to rely on such hardy persons for political guidance. Although the people's natural virtues would have to be steadfastly encouraged and supported in an era when European aristocrats plotted constantly to destroy democratic institutions, the national good sense could survive because the common people insisted that "AMERICA SHALL STILL BE FREE."[20]

The future held little promise, however, for the other people of America—the Indians who faced the endless, overwhelming expansion of a prosperous European-American population. Freneau predicted in one of his commentaries that the Indians might eventually disappear from the continent, though he tried to show some sympathy for their plight by placing his reflections in the voice of an imaginary Indian king named Opay Mico. "*We* are a miserable people," King Mico explained, "our numbers decreasing from year to year, and our country gradually contracting itself into a very small circle." Despite Mico's clear vision of what was happening, his people's decline was apparently beyond anyone's control, and the imaginary monologue ended with the unhappy Mico's lament that his people would one day "be reckoned among the lost things of the world."[21] Freneau's description of this loss (published in 1790) suggested that America's progress toward a prosperous, republican future carried catastrophic costs for some of the world's most abused people, but his recognition of the Native American tragedy did not destroy his nationalist optimism. An imaginative, fanciful account of how people would likely be living in New York in 1940, for example, portrayed a flourishing future city where (as Freneau described it) George Washington would be the most esteemed historical figure, slavery would have been abolished, superstition would have disappeared, and religious tolerance would guarantee a peaceful harmony for all. There would also be merchants and traders from all nations of the world, except for the Native Americans who would have unfortunately vanished from history.[22]

Such descriptions of an expansive national future would become a common feature of almost all nineteenth-century nationalisms, so Freneau's imaginary twentieth-century America represents an early example of the popular new narratives about the progressive meaning of national time. Optimistic visions of the future could not really sustain a strong national identity, however, if they lacked a parallel narrative about the nation's past. Good nationalists always stressed that history provided the surest evidence of a nation's identity or mission, which suggests why Freneau's optimism about America's future would be greatly expanded in Bancroft's confident, optimistic narrative about America's past.

George Bancroft's American Past

George Bancroft grew up in Massachusetts, graduated from Harvard, studied in Germany, became a state leader in the Democratic Party during the antebellum era, served as American ambassador to England (1846–49) and Germany (1867–73), and also found time along the way to produce a steady stream of articles and books on politics, history, and culture.[23] His greatest contribution to the evolving narrative of American national identity appeared in his monumental ten-volume *History of the United States, from the Discovery of the American Continent*, which was published over four decades between 1834 and 1874. Despite the title's reference to the "United States," the books actually dealt with the nation's emergence during the colonial and revolutionary era, ending with the British recognition of American independence in the early 1780s. The key point of Bancroft's massive work was thus to show the development of a political, cultural, and religious identity that had united the European Americans of the future United States in a heroic campaign for national independence. Bancroft expressed great confidence in America's progressive development, emphasized the growing separation from Old World institutions and ideas, and celebrated the emerging nation's independence with characteristic nationalist pride in its exceptional leaders and ideals. He therefore reiterated the common themes of early American nationalism, but his account of an essential "American character" also resembled typical nineteenth-century European histories of deep-seated ethnic or premodern national traits.

According to Bancroft, the essence of America lay in its energetic, freedom-loving people, whose sovereign will established a firm foundation for the nation's government and laws. Bancroft shared the typical nationalist respect for all of the individual "Founding Fathers," and his praise for Washington placed America's most famous national "Father" above virtually every leader in world history. "Never in the tide of time," Bancroft wrote, "has any man lived who had in so great a degree the almost divine faculty to command the confidence of his fellow-men and rule the willing."[24] Yet even Washington and his many talented associates could not have succeeded without the widely shared love of freedom that flourished among the common people of America. The unique meaning of America's Revolution therefore developed in the popular movement for self-government, wherein "the equality of all men was declared; personal freedom secured in its complete individuality; and common consent recognized as the only just origin of fundamental laws."[25]

This respect for individual freedom and popular sovereignty separated America from Europe because Europeans deferred to political and social hierarchies in which "power moved from a superior to inferiors and subjects."[26] If Europeans worried about what would happen when people acted freely to shape their own government, Bancroft offered confident assurance that democratic political principles in America had produced a rapidly growing population, an expanding economy, a strong system of education, and a lively free press—all of which made America "an asylum to the virtuous, the unfortunate, and the oppressed of every nation." Other societies were beginning to accept the new principles of self-government, Bancroft noted in the introduction to the first volume of his *History* (1834), but no other nation had gone nearly so far in accepting the central theme of American public life: "The sovereignty of the people is here a conceded axiom, and the laws, established upon that basis, are cherished with faithful patriotism."[27] Like most nationalists, Bancroft stressed the unity of this shared "patriotism" rather than the internal conflicts that emerged whenever Americans extended their political discussions from general pieties into debates about slavery, tariffs, or government expenditures. Bancroft's description of shared ideals thus offered valuable historical support for the belief in a coherent American national identity, which could not have survived if the reigning historical paradigm had stressed the differences in America's population or regions. (Southern nationalists would, of course, soon build their arguments for an independent new nation on contrasting narratives about the irreconcilable differences within the United States.)

America's unity and uniqueness became most apparent to Bancroft through comparisons with the politics and cultures of Europe. Although he frequently noted that Americans drew on earlier British conceptions of liberty to develop their own distinctive national faith, he insisted that such principles had never been fully developed or instituted until the Americans launched their new nation; indeed, the British turned against their own traditions when they sent their armies against the American patriots who "refused conformity to foreign laws and external rule." Americans had thus used "their vigorous vitality" to claim the freedom that people in other nations could only dream about. "When all Europe slumbered over questions of liberty," America's hardy pioneers on the frontier of civilization took charge of their providential destiny. "They were not only able to govern themselves," Bancroft argued, "they alone were able to do so; subordination visibly repressed their energies."[28]

And what had been the consequences of this exceptional campaign for national freedom? Bancroft found the answers to that question in the astonishing achievements of early American society, which included remarkable economic growth, the financial solvency of government institutions, and the constant expansion into western territories. Where lands had long remained dormant in the hands of "feeble barbarians," the new

American settlers quickly developed a flourishing agriculture and trade that carried the United States to "the first rank of nations" and attracted "an immense concourse of emigrants" from all the nations of Europe. Contrary to the expectations of monarchs in Old World societies, the new nation had retained its unity, defended its freedom, and become a model for the rest of the world. Americans in fact "possessed beyond any other portion of the world the great ideas of their age," Bancroft explained, and they had generously shared their ideas with anyone who would listen. The new truths of politics and society therefore flowed back to Europe, providing instruction and inspiration for people who had never understood how they could be free. "And the astonished nations," Bancroft reported, "as they read that all men are created equal, started out of their lethargy."[29]

America's world-historical contributions to the advance of human freedom reflected for Bancroft the unique experience and actions of its people, but his historical conception of American identity also fused with older religious strands in American thought to suggest that the new nation's triumphs must also have expressed the will of God. Momentous events did not occur simply by chance, in Bancroft's view, so he wanted Americans to see the purposeful direction of their own history in his books—which sought "to follow the steps by which a favoring Providence, calling our institutions into being, has conducted the country to its present happiness and glory." Belief in the divine guidance of history was, of course, a prominent theme in the New England Puritanism that had fostered popular confidence in the justice of America's revolutionary cause. As Bancroft described it, however, this American religious tradition was also a key source for the national belief in personal freedom because Protestantism encouraged the "right of private judgment." Drawing confidence from this faith, Americans avoided the philosophical skepticism that afflicted Europeans and also found a sensible religious justification for their passionate belief in civic freedom. Calvinist churches helped prevent the political excesses that accompanied the outbreak of revolutions in Europe, Bancroft argued, but the divine spirit in America spread far beyond the churches to give spiritual meaning to the whole society. "The spirit of God breathes through the combined intelligence of the people," Bancroft wrote in one of his enthusiastic summaries of America's distinctive national achievements. The British had inevitably tried to repress America's revolutionary movement in the 1770s, and yet all the power of Britain's army and navy failed to stop a "change which Divine Wisdom ordained, and which no human policy or force could hold back."[30]

Although God supported the national mission, America needed revolutionary soldiers and militiamen to carry the divine will into historical reality. Bancroft therefore invoked familiar religious images as he described America's wartime casualties in national stories that could be compared to older narratives about holy martyrs and the deaths of good Christians. The first militiamen to die at Lexington in 1775, for example, "gave their lives in testimony to the rights of mankind" and thereby demonstrated their steadfast allegiance to the most enduring moral principles of human history. Their deaths had been a tragedy for their grieving families, but the nation would always remember these "lowly men who proved themselves worthy of their forerunners, and whose children rise up and call them blessed."[31] Death led to immortality for these militiamen, Bancroft explained, because a thankful nation would never forget how their sacrifices had ultimately brought freedom to America. The dead "Minutemen" of Lexington continued to inspire their children and every subsequent defender of American independence, just as they had drawn courage from the ideals and actions of *their* ancestors. The continuity of the nation, in other words, appeared in the deaths as well as the lives of its most honored heroes.

Soldiers who rallied to their nation's defense, however, were protecting more than the ideals of political freedom or national sovereignty because the intrusion of British soldiers was also a physical assault on the families, livelihoods, and homes of the American people. When messengers warned the scattered population of Massachusetts about the advancing British troops in 1775, the "children trembled as they were scared out of their sleep" and the "wives with heaving breasts bravely seconded their husbands" as the men marched off to face the enemy. Using the typical nationalist rhetoric of family honor, Bancroft portrayed the domestic fears in Massachusetts to stress the decisive public and personal issues that came together in America's struggle against hostile British troops. "Come forth, champions of liberty," he wrote in one of his lyrical passages; "now free your country; protect your sons and daughters, your wives and homesteads; rescue the houses of the God of your fathers, the franchises handed down from your ancestors. Now all is at stake; the battle is for all."[32] The first brief battles at Lexington and Concord would be followed by long, difficult years of warfare, but from the beginning, there was no historical honor for those weak men who wanted to hide or compromise or abandon their families to the fury of hostile soldiers. As Bancroft told the story, everyone had to choose sides, and history showed clearly which side was right.

Emanuel Leutze, *Washington Crossing the Delaware*, oil on canvas, 1851. Leutze's paint-ing provided a visual representation of the nationalist themes that George Bancroft and other writers described in popular history books. The heroic Washington leads American soldiers across a swirling, treacherous river, but his extraordinary national victory will also depend on the many unknown people who support him and sacrifice themselves to the shared national cause. (Gift of John Stewart Kennedy, Metropolitan Museum of Art, New York/ Art Resource, New York)

Most Americans saw the justice of the revolutionary resistance, Ban-croft reported, so they rallied in 1775 to the patriot cause with exemplary unity and commitment. To be sure, some people in every region of the country remained loyal to the British king, yet Americans from South Carolina to New Hampshire had joined together in a shared revolution-ary commitment to the national ideals of freedom and self-government. This remarkable (retrospective) eighteenth-century national unity car-ried obvious implications for a nineteenth-century America that was fall-ing into bitter sectional conflicts while Bancroft was writing his history of revolutionary events. These latter-day conflicts seemed to push Bancroft toward a growing emphasis on an imagined, former unity that had dis-appeared amid the angry national debates about slavery. When Bancroft discussed the political conflicts in prerevolutionary Boston, for example, he stressed the unified support that came to Bostonians from people in the Carolinas and Virginia. All good patriots in the North *and* the South had rallied to the same cause and supported the same American principles. "But the love of liberty in America did not flash like electricity on the surface," Bancroft explained in 1858; "it penetrated the mass with magnetic energy. . . . [And] the continent, as 'one great commonwealth,' made the cause of Boston its own."[33] Here, then, was the historical model for later generations, if only they would recognize the national ideals they shared instead of harping on how they differed and disagreed. The history of America was for Bancroft a history of growing national unity, which developed out of a common belief in the nation's egalitarian political creed. Yet the political bonds that connected white people in the North and South did not cross the boundaries of racial difference, and the realities of "race" collided with the imagined unity of political ideals.

Bancroft assumed that deep differences of history, culture, and race separated African Americans from the "Anglo-Saxons" who constituted what he saw as the vital core of American national life; and he was certain that racial and cultural differences separated Native Americans from European Americans (see chapter 5). Whereas the European Americans arrived in the New World with strong cultural legacies, religious traditions, and a dynamic language, the Africans were brought to America with none of the essential tools of civilization. In fact, Bancroft argued in one of his early volumes, "they came with the limited faculties of uncivilized man," which meant they had "no common language, no abiding usages, no worship, no nationality." Such people could thus learn about civilization only through the skills and language of their "masters," Bancroft claimed (ignoring the strong African legacies that enslaved people had carried to America); and despite all the "horrors of slavery and the slave trade, the masters had, in part at least, performed the office of advancing and civilizing the Negro."[34]

The weakness of both the African and Native American civilizations, as Bancroft described them, placed the destiny of America in the hands of the "Anglo-Saxon" race, whose institutions and language soon dominated the continent and gave America its distinctive national identity. Once the French had been driven from North America in the 1760s, the whole continent lay open to "the Teutonic race, with its strong tendency to individuality and freedom" and with its distinctive English language. "Go forth, then, language of Milton and Hampden, language of my country," Bancroft wrote in his concluding summary of the Seven Years War, "take possession of the North American Continent! . . . Utter boldly and spread widely . . . the thoughts of the coming apostles of the people's liberty."[35]

English became the language of early American culture, freedom, and expansion; and, as Bancroft reminded his readers, English provided an enduring language for the unbreakable American Union.

Bancroft was a strong Unionist during the American Civil War, and, despite his criticisms of some abolitionists, he definitely wanted slavery to disappear—in part because he thought it was an immoral institution and in part because he saw slavery as a major obstacle to the national unity he cherished. At the end of the Civil War, Bancroft aligned himself with President Andrew Johnson in opposition to the proposals for Radical Reconstruction, and he gave Johnson advice as he prepared his first presidential speech to Congress. Even more significant for a staunch advocate of national union, Bancroft delivered the official memorial oration on Abraham Lincoln's life in the U.S. Congress on February 12, 1866, using the occasion to show how Lincoln had expressed the highest ideals of the American people.[36] Yet Bancroft's conception of America remained closely connected to the Jacksonian nationalism of the 1830s, which may partly explain why the most influential statement of America's national ideology in the 1860s came from Lincoln himself rather than from his congressional eulogist. No historian or political leader would duplicate Bancroft's ten-volume account of the American past, but Lincoln managed to turn the themes of Bancroft's historical narrative into 267 words that summarized the self-defined meaning of American nationalism more memorably and eloquently than all the volumes that Bancroft (or other historians) ever produced.

The Gettysburg Address and American National Identity

Authors such as Philip Freneau and George Bancroft made significant contributions to the evolving, early descriptions of America that enabled people to "imagine" their national identity and territory. Although the specific American themes often differed from the nationalist narratives in Europe, American writers also developed the usual claims for the political, historical, and cultural uniqueness of their own national society. They filled their texts with typical nationalist allusions to religion, literature, military heroes, and virtuous families—and even the allegedly eastern European themes of race and language appeared frequently in the "Anglo-Saxon" discussions of Indians, African Americans, and immigrants. Yet the writings of American poets and historians did not become part of the "sacred canon" of national texts that included the Declaration of Independence, the Constitution, the Bill of Rights, and (after the 1860s) Abraham Lincoln's Gettysburg Address. The famous, concise speech that Lincoln delivered in November 1863 at the site America's greatest Civil War battle quickly became one of the defining texts of American national identity and, as such, a canonical example of the political and emotional themes that have given nationalism its power in the public and personal lives of modern people.

Lincoln's speech at the commemoration of the dead at Gettysburg lasted about two minutes and consisted of the following three paragraphs:

> Four score and seven years ago our fathers brought forth on this continent, a new nation, conceived in Liberty, and dedicated to the proposition that all men are created equal.
>
> Now we are engaged in a great civil war, testing whether that nation, or any nation so conceived and so dedicated, can long endure. We are met on a great battlefield of that war. We have come to dedicate a portion of that field, as a final resting place for those who gave their lives that that nation might live. It is altogether fitting and proper that we should do this.
>
> But, in a larger sense, we can not dedicate—we can not consecrate—we can not hallow—this ground. The brave men, living and dead, who struggled here, have consecrated it, far above our poor power to add or detract. The world will little note, nor long remember what we say here, but it can never forget what they did here. It is for us the living, rather, to be dedicated here to the unfinished work which they who fought here have thus far so nobly advanced. It is rather for us to be here dedicated to the great task remaining before us—that from these honored dead we take increased devotion to that cause for which they gave the last full measure of devotion—that we here highly resolve that these dead shall not have died in vain—that this nation, under God, shall have a new birth of freedom—and that government of the people, by the people, for the people, shall not perish from the earth.[37]

Contemporaries immediately recognized Lincoln's brief speech as a dramatic summary of the American national creed (George Bancroft asked for and received from Lincoln a copy for a volume on "American authors" he published in 1864), and later generations would recite these words at countless celebrations of America's distinctive national history.

When one places the address in the more general context of modern nationalism, however, it becomes a remarkably succinct account of the

Timothy H. O'Sullivan, photographer, *Incidents of the War: A Harvest of Death. Gettysburg, July 1863*. America's national identity and collective memories were affirmed most specifically in the praise for soldiers who gave their lives to defend the nation and its enduring political ideals. Abraham Lincoln's Gettysburg Address became the most famous American summary of this respect for deceased soldiers and of the need for future national sacrifices; and O'Sullivan's battlefield photograph starkly conveys the painful human losses that Lincoln recognized and that also flowed from every national war. (Print Collection, Miriam and Ira D. Wallach Division of Art, Prints and Photographs, New York Public Library, Astor, Lenox and Tilden Foundations)

life-and-death themes that have inspired emotional allegiances in every successful nationalist movement or nation-state. Delivered on a battlefield (always a privileged, "hallowed" ground for nationalists), it began with references to both the national "fathers" and the central claims of the national political culture—that the nation was "conceived in Liberty" and "that all men are created equal." The historical significance of these claims then emerged in the following paragraph, which stressed that (1) the national legacy was now facing its greatest challenge; and (2) the living generation must honor "those who here gave their lives that that nation might live." Lincoln's phrase thus evoked the ancient, Christlike image of sacrifice that has long given powerful religious force to the nationalist reverence for dead soldiers.

The ultimate lesson of this sacrifice, though, went beyond the memory of the dead to the essential message of the final paragraph, in which Lincoln urged his compatriots to recommit themselves to new action and new sacrifices in the future. The long struggle was not yet over; indeed, it required an "increased devotion" to make sure that the dead "shall not have died in vain." This new, resolute devotion to the cause of the national "fathers" and the deceased soldiers would inevitably be difficult, but such commitments would give new meaning to both the sacrifice of the dead and the future work of the living. In the end, "this nation, under God," could achieve a great triumph for its national mission through a "new birth of freedom." It could bring new life out of painful deaths and a new historical message to the whole world. The victory of the national, Unionist cause, in short, would prove "that government of the people, by the people, for the people, shall not perish from the earth."

Lincoln's speech therefore became a canonical nationalist text because it provided a brief, affirming summary of the nation's political creed; a brief, moving homage to the nation's dead; and a brief, inspiring vision of the nation's future mission. It would appeal to later generations as a compelling statement of unifying national ideas and as an exemplary recognition of virtuous soldiers; but it also offered stark reminders of the national dangers that must always be opposed. Although Lincoln never mentioned specific enemies (for example, Confederate generals or evil slaveholders), he issued clear warnings about insufficient commitment to the national cause and insufficient honor to the sacrifices of the dead. These broad themes gave Lincoln's address its distinguished place in the endless nationalist campaign to link the nation's living generation to the dead, celebrate the nation's distinctive historical destiny, and promote the nation's future virtue and influence. More generally, the Gettysburg Address suggests why the nationalisms and nationalist identities that have generated and sustained so much of the modern world's violence have also generated and sustained many of the modern world's most valuable aspirations for freedom and human rights.

CHAPTER SEVEN

Nationalism & Nation-States in the Modern World, 1870–1945

Modern nationalism's political and cultural power produced the most far-reaching historical consequences in the seven decades between 1870 and 1945. The national political cultures, imperial expansions, and global wars in this era became the culmination of nationalist ideas and practices that had evolved steadily since the late eighteenth century—from the militant political assertion of national sovereignty to the spread of national education and systems of communication; the development of national celebrations and symbolic rituals; the encouragement of national beliefs in family, race, and ethnicity; and the violence of "total wars." Among nationalism's many historical influences in this era, it should be stressed that approximately 100 million people died in nationalist-inspired wars during the first half of the twentieth century (the exact number can never be known) and that these wars significantly reduced Europe's earlier global power.[1] The Europeans who had contributed so much to the emergence of nationalist ideas and political systems suffered enormously from the nationalist extremism of twentieth-century wars, which also profoundly affected people throughout Asia, the Middle East, and other parts of the world.

It would, of course, be impossible to describe all of the twentieth-century nationalisms and nationalist conflicts that reshaped the modern world, but this chapter (and the next) will briefly examine how nationalisms and nation-states carried nineteenth-century ideas into the politics, cultures, and collective identities of later historical eras. Although there were few creative additions to the common themes of twentieth-century nationalist thought, the rapidly expanding movements for national sovereignty among colonized or suppressed peoples transformed long-developing, Western claims for national and human rights into new nationalist struggles *against* Western empires. There was also a growing emphasis (after 1945) on both the multicultural diversity within nations and the need for transnational collaborations, all of which began to reshape nationalism in the late twentieth century. These challenges to earlier nationalist ideas emerged partly from the belief that excessive nationalism had led to catastrophic world wars and partly from the global commerce and migrations that made national boundaries less relevant for modern economic and social life. At the same time, however, nation-states remained extremely powerful political and cultural forces, and modern individuals continued to fuse their personal or family identities with the collective identities of nations. When violence and economic changes threatened national communities, most people quickly rallied to nationalist ideologies and symbols—as one could see in the nationalist reactions to terrorism, foreign military occupations, globalizing economic systems, ethnic minorities, and immigrant workers. The last sections of this book will thus focus on a few events and nationalist movements that exemplify the remarkable continuities in modern nationalisms and also (in some cases) point toward the gradual emergence of transnational institutions or multicultural identities.

Nationalism before the First World War

Nationalism acquired greater public influence after 1870 in countries such as Germany and Italy, where well-developed cultural nationalisms achieved the long-sought political unification of previously fragmented territories and populations. Although some Germans and Italians remained outside the new German Empire and Italian monarchical state, the political aspirations of J. G. Fichte, Giuseppe Mazzini, and many other nationalist thinkers were finally achieved by new national governments that began to "nationalize" their people and assert their growing power within Europe or in the wider competition for global empires. The German emperor Wilhelm I and his prime minister Otto von Bismarck, for example, made aggressive efforts to expand Germany's international role after defeating the French in the Franco-Prussian War (1870) and gaining control over most of the population in the former French territories of Alsace and Lorraine. German anger over the earlier Napoleonic imperialism gave way to new French anger over Germany's imperial confiscation of French lands. French national writers such as Ernest Renan argued for a "voluntarist" rather than "ethnic" approach to national identity, stressing that people must have the right to choose their own national state; the broad political claim for national self-determination thus became as

popular in France as it had been in Germany and the other European countries that had once opposed the French Empire. Historians have often portrayed the political differences between France and Germany as partly a
debate between advocates of civic and ethnic conceptions of nationhood,
and it is certainly true that Germans claimed an ethnic link to Alsatians on
the basis of language, culture, history, and religious traditions. But there
were also ethnic themes in France's political, linguistic nationalism, and
the *ressentiment* of French nationalists after 1871 resembled in this respect
the contemporary nationalisms that were demanding territories from the
Austrian and Ottoman Empires in central or eastern Europe.[2]

The establishment of a new, expansive German Empire and the political
unification of Italy showed other nationalists that the struggle for national
political sovereignty could lead to a unified political state. Well-organized
nationalist groups in Poland, Hungary, and the Balkans continued to seek
the self-determination that Adam Mickiewicz and other central European
writers had advocated in earlier times, and new activists were recruited
because the achievement of national unity for some peoples reinforced
the desire for sovereign states among others. Meanwhile, the growing
centralization of national states contributed to the further development
of national monuments, education systems, historical narratives, and
newspapers in the older, unified "nation-states" of Britain and France as
well as the newly unified states of Germany and Italy. National languages
were imposed on remote provinces through new public schools, required
service in the national army, and transportation systems that gave central
governments better access to their own populations.[3]

The internal consolidation of increasingly powerful nation-states,
however, also intensified the external political and economic competition between sovereign governments. German and American industrial
expansion began to challenge the earlier dominance of the British and
French economies, creating a new global competition for markets and raw
materials. All of the most powerful modern states sought "spheres of influence" in Asia, Africa, or the Middle East, and each national government
was willing to use military force to protect its interests around the world.
By the beginning of the twentieth century, most of the leading national
states had joined an international arms race that produced large navies
and "peace-time" armies. There were no late nineteenth-century European military conflicts on the scale of the earlier Napoleonic wars, and
yet most Europeans believed that their nations were engaged in a long-
term, competitive struggle for limited resources, global territories, and

commercial wealth. Fear of foreign enemies remained a common theme in almost every national political culture because prominent writers and public leaders expected that conflicting national interests would eventually lead to war.[4]

European governments therefore began to enter into international alliance systems as part of a broader strategy to protect their national security and evolving economic needs. Germany joined with Austria-Hungary and Italy to form a "Triple Alliance," while republican France and tsarist Russia established an unlikely alliance that would gradually attract enough British support to become the "Triple Entente." New alliances thus emerged from the widely held nationalist beliefs that dangerous enemies threatened every sovereign state, that each nation must prepare for inevitable future wars, and that military alliances offered the best protection against foreign powers or the limited resources of one's own nation. The alliance system itself, however, would become a major cause of the Great War that destroyed the German, Austrian-Hungarian, Russian, and Ottoman Empires. Local conflicts between states such as Serbia and Austria-Hungary could quickly drag every major (allied) power into a general conflagration because all governments feared international isolation; and the complex alliances helped to produce many of the precise political outcomes that reciprocal military commitments were supposed to prevent.[5]

The nationalist account of inescapable imperial rivalries gained additional cultural force from the popular belief that each nation embodied a particular race. We have seen how this theory developed in the nineteenth-century writings of theorists such as Arthur de Gobineau, but the idea of "race" came to be linked with the Social Darwinian assumption that "racial nations" must also wage constant struggles for survival in which the "fittest" national population would ultimately prevail. As the English racial theorist Houston Steward Chamberlain (1855–1927) wrote in an influential summary of "racial" history, the "national union" of a people "fixes firmly the existing bond of blood and impels us to make it ever closer." The nation itself was much more than a government, in Chamberlain's view; it consisted of "common memory, common hope, [and a] common intellectual nourishment" that all derived from the shared racial character of a people.[6] Explicitly rejecting Renan's claim that nations were based on political will rather than on racial identities, Chamberlain and many others insisted that nationhood and national power depended on racial coherence. These allegedly scientific arguments portrayed the people of other nations as different races rather than as simply the citizens of another state, thereby providing biological justification for the build-up of military forces and even for warfare against alien "racial" groups.

The complex preconditions for Europe's catastrophic Great War had thus coalesced by 1914 in a powder keg of intersecting nationalist ideas and policies. This combustible mix of historical trends included centralizing nation-states; conflicts over territories and populations within Europe; imperial rivalries in Asia and Africa; rising expenditures for large armies and navies; opposing alliance systems and national pledges for mutual military support; ideological and "scientific" theories about race, nationality, or the "survival of the fittest"; and nationalized, educated populations who learned about "threats to the nation" in modern newspapers and through the agitations of popular political parties. Although the unification of new national states and the rapid industrialization in Germany had altered the earlier balance of power in Europe, many of the nationalist ideas that first emerged in the early nineteenth century remained influential in early twentieth-century national cultures. Romanticism evolved in most places toward new forms of political realism or "*Realpolitik*," and yet there was little change in the now-familiar emphasis on sovereign nations, dangerous national enemies, "manly" national service, and distinctive national languages or histories. The assassination of an heir to the throne in the Austrian-Hungarian Empire could therefore lead to a global war because nationalist ambitions and anxieties had steadily developed everywhere during the century after the Napoleonic wars. Conflicts that were once viewed as dynastic or religious disputes between powerful kings came to be seen as life-or-death struggles between national cultures, national populations, and sovereign national states.

The world war that exploded in 1914 thus gave violent expression to nationalist ideas that had become the "conventional wisdom" among prewar political elites, but the pervasive national and racial thinking of this era becomes even more apparent when one looks also at the ideas or aspirations of "marginalized" groups in various national cultures. The ideas of Zionism, for example, emerged as a distinctive (but also typical) late nineteenth-century national/ethnic analysis of the situation that Jewish communities faced in both eastern and western Europe. Theodor Herzl (1860–1904), the Austrian Jewish writer who became the early leader of the Zionist movement, responded to the vehement anti-Semitism of European, racial nationalisms (including the French hostility to Jews during the Dreyfus Affair in the 1890s) by describing the autonomous national identity of the Jewish people. He also extended his account of Jewish

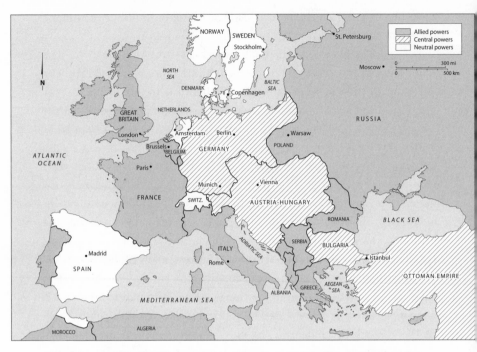

Europe in 1914. The major European states formed competing alliances to protect their political, military, and economic interests, but the alliances ultimately contributed to the Great War that destroyed four empires in eastern Europe and weakened other European empires in Africa and Asia. The continuing agitation for new national states in eastern Europe and the pervasive nationalism in modern European political cultures came together in 1914 and led to the unprecedented military casualties of the First World War.

national identity into the nationalist political claim that this collective community should have the right to control a particular geographical space, which could become the territory for a new Jewish state in modern Palestine. Noting that anti-Semitism developed within every nation that included a significant Jewish population, Herzl defended a unique, ancient Jewish identity and destiny with the modern language of ethnic nationality. "[T]he distinctive nationality of the Jews neither can, will, nor must be destroyed," he wrote in his influential book, *The Jewish State* (1896). "It cannot be destroyed, because external enemies consolidate it. It will not be destroyed; this is shown during two thousand years of appalling suffering."[7] Herzl thus drew on his historical conception of long-term continuities to develop a new national definition of the Chosen People—a people whose long national suffering showed why it was necessary to establish a

Jewish national state. His national narrative, however, also drew on the nineteenth-century political arguments and cultural assumptions that other disenfranchised peoples had used to justify the creation of new sovereign states on disputed territories.

The subsequent Zionist struggle to establish an autonomous modern state in the Middle East ultimately became a distinctive twentieth-century success among the many nationalist movements that sought to carve out new states on the lands of declining empires. Like the European Americans who established the United States after breaking from the British Empire and asserting God-given rights to displace Native Americans from the territories on which they had long lived, the Zionist settlers in Palestine would eventually create the new sovereign state of Israel (1948) after the departure of imperial powers (Ottoman and then British) and after claiming divinely ordained rights to occupy lands that other people had long controlled. The Zionist movement that Herzl launched in late nineteenth-century Europe therefore emerged in direct opposition to intolerant racial, anti-Semitic nationalisms, but Zionism also developed a typical nationalist emphasis on the destiny or mission of a unique people. Herzl and other Zionists, in short, adapted the pervasive cultural themes and political aspirations of modern nationalism to defend people whom many European nationalists were portraying as "dangers" to the imagined coherence of racial, ethnic, or religious nations. Reflecting the nationalist themes of that particular historical era, however, Zionism itself would soon repeat the pattern of other nationalisms as it developed its own criteria for an imagined religious and national coherence.

Meanwhile, the African American writer W. E. B. DuBois (1868–1963) was making similar arguments for a distinctive new cultural and "national" movement in America, where a wave of late nineteenth-century racist nationalism condemned and discriminated against black Americans in much the same way that nationalist anti-Semitism attacked European Jews. DuBois noted in "The Conservation of Races" (1897) that African Americans were "hated here, despised there, and pitied everywhere"; but he argued that this pervasive racism would force black people to recognize the ways in which "our one haven of refuge is ourselves." He therefore proposed the development of autonomous black academies, arts, and social organizations that could foster a self-reliant black community. Although this struggle for an independent social identity would necessarily evolve in America, it would also embody the universal mission that European writers such as Mickiewicz and Jules Michelet had earlier assigned to the Poles or the French. The new movement for racial self-respect "*must* be inspired with the Divine faith of our black mothers," DuBois wrote, and then "out of the blood and dust of battle will march a victorious host, a mighty nation, a peculiar people, to speak to the nations of earth a Divine truth that shall make them free."[8] The freedom and cultural achievements of African Americans, in other words, would also advance the freedom of other peoples. Guided by the faith of women (a common gendered theme of nationalist movements), the long-oppressed "mighty nation" of black Americans would promote historical progress for the whole world.

An emerging black nationalist movement in America thus began to describe its unique collective mission with the kind of quasi-religious terminology that had become common among nationalists who sought new states or defended repressed ethnic communities or simply reaffirmed the historical destiny of well-established national states. This emphasis on unique, divinely supported racial and national identities shows how identity-shaping nationalist discourses spread widely in the decades before 1914. Political leaders in the major modern states and imperial systems exercised far more global power than the advocates for vulnerable social, cultural, or racial minorities, but the common language of nationality, race, and collective mission resonated through otherwise diverse social and nationalist movements—most of which came to expect future conflicts rather than transnational cooperation.

Nationalism and Self-Determination
in the Era of the First World War

The war between great national powers, which so many had long anticipated, began in August 1914. It was set off by the Austrian-Hungarian Empire's demand that its security forces be allowed to enter Serbia and repress Bosnian terrorist groups that were linked to the assassination of the Austrian archduke Franz Ferdinand (killed on June 28, 1914)—a demand that the Serbs rejected. The Austrians gained firm support from their German ally, and the Serbs turned to Russia for aid against the Austrians, thereby pushing the entire European system of national alliances into action. Germany feared a dangerous French assault from the West if German armies went first into Russia, so the Germans immediately launched their carefully developed plan for a preemptive invasion of France through "neutral" Belgium. This violation of Belgian national

Unknown photographer, *Off to War*, 1914. The declarations of war in 1914 provoked an initial surge of popular nationalism as the various armies set out for a conflict that was expected to be brief and decisive. These German soldiers marched through city streets on a festive summer parade with patriotic women, none of whom could have imagined the deadly, grinding war that would decimate an entire generation of European men. (Hulton Archive/Getty Images)

sovereignty brought Britain into the war, and the allied forces of France, Britain, and Russia managed to halt the German armies on both the western and eastern fronts. Well-crafted strategies for military victory, in short, ran up against intractable realities on the ground.

The German and Austrian-Hungarian Empires were thus engaged in a "total war" with France, Britain, and Russia by September 1914, but the war soon engulfed even more people after the Ottoman Empire joined the German/Austrian alliance and Italy chose to pursue its national interests by joining France and England. When the war bogged down in a bloody stalemate, every government set out to increase the size of its armies, mobilize all of its economic resources, and develop more direct control over its own people. Earlier patterns of national centralization, which had been steadily expanding since the eighteenth century, now became even more pronounced as each national state conscripted millions of soldiers and organized its factories to produce essential weaponry and supplies.

The "rights of man" lost ground everywhere to the overarching demands for national security, national armies, and national goods.[9]

The military and economic crises contributed to the further ascendancy of nationalist ideologies, which were invoked constantly to justify the horrific loss of life and the repression of domestic dissent. Each government portrayed the war as a battle for the very survival of its national culture, political traditions, and way of life, so that an irrational "total war" appeared to be the only rational action for nations to pursue. The scale of casualties in the war's greatest battles—the Marne, the Somme, Verdun, Tannenberg, and others—went far beyond the largest battles of the Napoleonic wars, but there were also daily losses in the grinding trench warfare that produced an endless stream of casualties. By the end of the war, more than 10 million soldiers had been killed and more than 20 million wounded. The deaths of men from France (1.4 million), Germany (1.8 million), Britain (700,000), Italy (465,000), Austria-Hungary (1.2 million), and Russia (1.7 million) disrupted social institutions and devastated families throughout Europe. There were also extensive losses among the troops who were brought from British or French colonies and among the many others who were sent to the war from Australia, New Zealand, North America, and the Ottoman Empire.[10]

The First World War thus became a more deadly conflict than any previous war or revolution in the long history of modern nationalism. National leaders could only explain the vast human and economic costs by repeating that such sacrifices were required for defense of the nation's ultimate survival as an independent people. This claim led the European governments to unprecedented military conscriptions and expenditures, but the general argument for the self-determination of national populations may have received its most systematic statement after the United States entered the war in 1917. Seeking to explain why America's participation in the war was essential, President Woodrow Wilson defined the "Fourteen Points" or objectives that guided America's first military intervention in a European war. Wilson's American themes were also widely publicized in Europe, where they could be readily connected to the common nationalist belief that each national population must have its own sovereign national government—or what Wilson called the right to national self-determination. This familiar nineteenth-century nationalist idea presumed that nations had essential ethnic or linguistic components and that (as far as possible) the "national populations" in Poland, Hungary, Czechoslovakia, the Balkans, and elsewhere must have their own independent states.[11]

H. R. Hopps, designer, *Destroy This Mad Brute*, American war poster, ca. 1917.
National governments used every form of communication to sustain popular
support for the Great War and to build the largest possible armies. This military
recruitment poster provides a vivid, gendered message about a militaristic German
enemy who aggressively threatens America's freedom and families. Such images
helped to justify the sacrifices for a "total war," but they also impeded the processes
of rational peacemaking after 1918. (Hoover Institution Poster Collection, Stanford University)

Wilson therefore sought to combine the democratic political themes of the American and French Revolutions with the later cultural themes of romantic nationalism. "An independent Polish state should be erected," he explained in a concise summary of the national ideal (Point XIII of the Fourteen Points), "which should include the territories inhabited by indisputably Polish populations . . . and whose political and economic independence and territorial integrity should be guaranteed by international covenant."[12] Wilson's other "Points" advanced similar principles for Balkan nationalities, for Turks, for the French people of Alsace, and for many others, though in most cases the complex entanglements of languages and ethnic groups made it impossible to align the boundaries of culture, geography, and politics. The long-evolving aspiration to create independent national states for every significant ethnic or cultural nation nevertheless reached a kind of historical climax at the Versailles peace conference. The ideal was actually applied only in Europe, however, and only within the former empires of the defeated European powers (Germany, Austria-Hungary, Ottoman) and along the frontiers of the Russian Empire that had collapsed in the Russian Revolution of 1917.

Wilson interpreted the campaign for national "self-determination" as an outgrowth of national principles that America itself had established in its Revolutionary War and early national history. He thus urged the strongest possible American support for the Treaty of Versailles, arguing repeatedly that the new plans for independent nationhood in Europe simply confirmed that "people have a right to live their own lives under the governments which they themselves choose to set up. That is the American principle and I was glad to fight for it." Wilson envisioned autonomous political and cultural nationhood as an extension of America's own national ideas (a world "made safe for democracy"), and he assured the many American skeptics that the Treaty of Versailles was "shot through with the American principle of the choice of the governed."[13] Many Americans nevertheless feared that provisions for a new international "League of Nations" would threaten national sovereignty—the popular nationalist critique that prevailed when the U.S. Senate refused to ratify the treaty that Wilson had described as the embodiment of "American principles."

Wilson's Fourteen Points thus gained more immediate influence outside the United States than within his own political culture. The American president had reaffirmed the most popular political and cultural ideas of modern nationalism, raising nationalist expectations in many parts of the world. Germans, Austrians, and many Italians, for example, soon

Europe after the First World War. The peace settlements in 1919 brought Alsace/Lorraine back into France and established new national states in territories that had previously belonged to the Austrian-Hungarian, Russian, or Ottoman empires. Diplomats tried to create political borders along the geographical boundaries of ethnic and linguistic groups in central Europe, but ethnic minorities continued to live within each of the new nations. The postwar "nation-states" nevertheless represented the precarious culmination of a century-long struggle to make national "self-determination" the legitimating foundation for all modern European governments.

believed that the Treaty of Versailles itself had violated the principles of national self-determination in their societies, and new *ressentiments* quickly emerged among the groups that expressed these grievances. At the same time, people living in European-controlled colonies in Asia, Africa, and the Middle East saw that the Wilsonian theories of national "self-determination" would not be implemented outside of Europe. In one particularly notable Asian response to Wilson's ideas, the young Vietnamese nationalist Ho Chi Minh (then living in Paris) presented a petition to the American delegation at Versailles, asserting the need for basic human rights in the French colonies of Indochina: the right to a free press and free association, an amnesty for political prisoners, and various reforms in the colonial justice system. Although the petition was completely ignored at Versailles, it is significant that Ho used the language of modern nationalism to affirm the coming "self-determination" of the Vietnamese people (much like Herzl and DuBois had defined other struggles for the rights of oppressed peoples before 1914). "While waiting for the principle of national self-determination to pass from ideal to reality through the effective recognition of the sacred right of all peoples to decide their own destiny," Ho wrote in his petition, "the inhabitants of the ancient Empire of Annam, at the present time French Indochina, present to the noble governments of the Entente in general and the honorable French government the following humble claims."[14] The political-cultural links between human rights and national sovereignty, in other words, moved rapidly from a Euro-American context into global, anticolonial movements that Ho and others launched after the Great War. The campaigns against European empires in Asia and Africa would replicate and also transform most of the political themes that nationalist groups had developed during earlier struggles to create the new national states that broke away from the multinational empires in Europe.

The emergence of new anticolonial nationalisms, however, was also influenced by the Russian Bolshevik Party, whose leader, Vladimir Lenin, described national self-determination as an objective for twentieth-century Marxism. Lenin was already arguing by 1914 that the "self-determination of nations means the political separation of these nations from alien national bodies, and the formation of an independent national state." Challenging those who applied "self-determination" only to Europeans, Lenin insisted that this principle should apply everywhere in the world; and the struggles for national independence (as Lenin described them) could even lead Marxists to cooperate with "bourgeois" political groups—"*Insofar as* the bourgeoisie of the oppressed nation fights the oppressor." This new Marxist argument for anticolonial national movements helps to explain why the Bolshevik Revolution of 1917 attracted the attention of young nationalists such as Ho Chi Minh, who became a communist and moved on to Russia after his sojourn in Paris. Lenin's anticolonial, political-economic theories offered an alternative to Wilson's liberal approach to national self-determination, in part because Lenin claimed that the Bolsheviks were "always, in every case, and more strongly than anyone . . . the staunchest and the most consistent enemies of oppression."[15]

The First World War, the Russian Revolution, and the Treaty of Versailles thus contributed decisively to the reformulation and expansion of twentieth-century nationalism. The wartime crisis led to (and justified) more centralized, national control of public and private institutions, new forms of nationalist propaganda and censorship, and more systematic state management of national economies, but it also generated a new ideological insistence on the universal right of national self-determination. The conflicts between Wilson and Lenin or between the Western powers and the Soviet Union also added economic themes to other nationalist debates about empires, anticolonialism, and the global meaning of "national self-determination." The Soviet state's emergence from the ruins of the Russian Empire offered a model for new kinds of national, economic autonomy, thereby helping to connect numerous twentieth-century anticolonial nationalisms with a transnational communist critique of modern capitalism and a wider campaign for "socialist internationalism."

Meanwhile, the First World War also carried all national populations back to the traditional mourning for casualties of war. The traumatic losses of sons, brothers, fathers, and husbands were mourned everywhere, but people tried to make sense of the carnage by repeating emotionally charged narratives about the eternal life of the nation. Every nation created new war memorials that included elaborate tombs for "unknown soldiers" in national capitals and military cemeteries, as well as countless humble monuments that were constructed to honor deceased soldiers in even the smallest villages. Historians have described the "memorializing" of fallen soldiers after 1918 as a new kind of ritualized national grief that affirmed "collective identity through the rites of death and commemoration."[16] Dying in war came to symbolize both a virtuous individual life and the virtues or sacrifices of an entire nation. As one French senator noted in a typical commemorative speech, "We feel infinite gratitude to our heroic soldiers, the greatest on earth, to whom we owe victory, and whose sacrifice will allow us to end our days in a reconstituted France."[17] This kind of praise for military sacrifices could provide some consolation for the French because the deaths had helped to bring Alsace and Lorraine back to a "reconstituted France." But the memory of such deaths could also provoke new nationalist mobilizations among those who fervently believed that the nation must honor the lost lives through new struggles against national enemies. The mourning for national losses thus evolved into new political-military campaigns for the cause of self-determination or ethnic national identities, especially in those countries that seemed to gain little or nothing from the deaths

Unknown photographer, *French Remembrance Ceremony*, ca. 1927. National commemorations for those who died in World War I became well-publicized, nationalist rituals during the 1920s and 1930s. The French veterans in this parade marched past the tomb of an unknown soldier at the Arc de Triomphe in Paris, but there were comparable commemorations (often on 11 November) in every nation that had joined the "winning" or "losing" side of the recent war. (Archive Photos/Getty Images)

of their soldiers. A new surge of right-wing nationalism would therefore emerge after 1919 and shape the political context for another nationalist-inspired world war.

Nationalism, Fascism, and the Violence of the Second World War

Although all nations honored their deceased soldiers and struggled to reintegrate unemployed military veterans into postwar social and economic life, the Great War carried different meanings among populations who believed they had won or lost the war. People in "victorious" nations such as France, Britain, and the United States could link their personal mourning to national stories about the heroic sacrifices that had brought a new national triumph, but people in the defeated nations could not understand the human costs in the same way. Austria lost most of its prewar imperial territories, and Germany lost much of its international military and economic power as it struggled in the 1920s to pay huge financial reparations to its recent enemies. The principles of national self-determination seemed not to apply to the defeated powers. Many Italians also believed that they had not received the territorial or financial compensation that their victorious allies had promised in exchange for Italy's military support during the war. Millions of restless ex-soldiers struggled to find work or to fit into civilian institutions, and persistent economic insecurity made many unemployed veterans receptive to angry nationalist messages about the sufferings of the German, Austrian, or Italian nations. The postwar economic problems, social dislocation, national resentments, and bitter memories of military defeat thus began to fuel the development of Fascism in Italy and Nazism in Germany, both of which became militant advocates for a new kind of nationalism that was neither liberal nor conservative. Fascists and Nazis transformed the idea of national mobilizations from older French revolutionary traditions into profoundly undemocratic nationalist rallies. The national state was more important for Fascists than the individuals or social groups within the national population, and a single, supreme leader was supposed to express the voice of the entire nation: Benito Mussolini became the charismatic leader for all Italian Fascists, and Adolf Hitler became the *Führer* for all German Nazis.

Despite the Fascist tendency to redefine older forms of European nationalism, the Fascist parties clearly gained popular support through their manipulation of familiar national symbols at carefully staged political rallies and their nationalist uses of the modern mass media.[18] Fascists claimed to defend ancient national values against groups whom they portrayed as domestic or international threats to the survival of the nation (for example, communists and Jews), but their "defense" of the much-celebrated and imagined national traditions constantly violated traditional political and ethical constraints. Above all, the radical right-wing groups forcefully asserted their intention to revive national grandeur, overturn recent national humiliations, and reorganize government institutions that seemed unable to protect the nation from its internal or foreign enemies. Mussolini, for example, described these national state-centered aspirations in a book-length summary of his party's political goals. "Fascism sees . . . not only the individual but the nation and the country," he wrote, "individuals and generations bound together by a moral law, with common traditions and a mission." This national mission would ultimately be achieved when individuals set aside their own interests and rallied collectively to the overarching national destiny: "Anti-individualistic, the fascist conception of life stresses the importance of the state and accepts the individual only insofar as his interests coincide with those of the state. . . . The fascist conception of the state is all-embracing; outside of it no human or spiritual values can exist, much less have value."[19] The meaning of individual lives therefore fused with the shared identity of an entire national population whenever the national state took decisive action. More specifically, a single political party and national leader were said to embody the collective will of the people, thus giving the concept of national sovereignty an explicitly authoritarian structure.

Fascist control of the nation-state added new authoritarian themes to modern nationalism (Mussolini's Italian fascists took over the government in 1922), and yet right-wing nationalists continued to repeat familiar ideas about the unique destinies of nations and the national duty to honor the sacrifices of those who came before. The Nazis often reiterated such ideas in speeches and publications that also blamed Germany's defeat in the Great War on the betrayals of internal enemies. The Nazi theorist Alfred Rosenberg, among many others, developed the common narrative of German "blood" and dangerous domestic enemies in *The Myth of the Twentieth Century* (1930), which included a nationalist summary of Germany's postwar identity:

> Nameless sacrifices were demanded and made by all. We soon
> discovered that the demonic forces had triumphed over the god-
> like by striking the army in the back. . . . But at the same time in the
> bowed souls of the surviving kin of the dead warriors, that mythos
> of the blood for which the heroes died was renewed, deepened,
> comprehended and experienced. . . . *Volk* and personality, blood
> and honor. These virtues must triumph alone and uncompromis-
> ingly. . . . The German people demands that the two million dead
> heroes have not fallen in vain.[20]

Rosenberg's descriptions of sacrifice, deceased soldiers, German "blood," and "demonic" internal forces all exemplify the ways in which right-wing political parties used the long-evolving themes of nationalism to attract popular support in the 1930s. The virtues of dead soldiers must be honored by the living, whose respect for the dead would lead to a national "renewal" and rid the country of its dangerous enemies.

The emphasis on recent sacrifices also overlapped with the pseudo-scientific racism that had spread across Europe in the decades before the First World War. The new radical nationalism therefore fostered a racist, anti-Semitic suspicion of Jews and others who were deemed to lack the requisite "racial purity." Rosenberg's account of German identity repeated this kind of racism and portrayed "racial" struggles as the guiding force in every nation's ideas and actions. "Every race has its soul," Rosenberg wrote in the same work that praised godlike German soldiers, "and every soul [has] its race. . . . The real struggle of our times . . . concerns the preservation of the racial substance itself." The national task, Rosenberg went on to explain, was to "create a new, yet very old, type of German" who would be "conscious of soul, race and history."²¹ Nazi theorists thus came back to the racial essentialism that earlier writers such as Gobineau and Chamberlain had promoted among European elites, but the racial scapegoating took on new historical significance after 1933, when the Nazis gained absolute power in Germany. The Nazi ban on "interracial marriage" and the systematic removal of Jews from all positions in public life, as the historian Joep Leerssen notes, became "the militaristically organized implementation of notions dreamed up by tweed-clad, upper-middle-class philosophers of the previous generation."²² This emphasis on race, in turn, easily merged with other ideas about the national duty of women to produce the next generation of "Aryan" youth, so that women's work as "good mothers" was also linked to racism. "The development of a 'cult of motherhood,'" Matthew Stibbe explains in a concise account of women in Nazi Germany, "was . . . designed not to increase the number of births per se, but rather the number of 'racially desirable' births."²³ Such ideological connections with the history of gendered and racist nationalisms suggest why Nazism can be viewed as an extremist extension of earlier nationalist theories rather than as a radical break from late nineteenth-century nationalist thought.

Hitler's own emphasis on the racial meaning of nations repeated the racist and anti-Semitic views of radical theorists whose arguments now resonated with the economic fears and postwar resentments of alienated German nationalists. For many such militant nationalists, race theories seemed to explain the nation's most enduring dangers. "All great cultures of the past," Hitler argued in *Mein Kampf* (1926), "perished only because the originally creative race died out from blood poisoning." The German defeat in the Great War could thus be interpreted as historical evidence for Hitler's racist nationalism because (to quote his distorted theories again) among "all the causes of the German collapse [in 1918] . . . the ultimate

Ahrle, designer, *The National Socialist Party Ensures the People's Community*, German Nazi poster, ca. mid-1930s. The emphasis on a "racial nation" can be seen in this image of what the Nazi Party liked to portray as the ideal German family. The blond children, the happy maternal woman, and the strong man were represented as the gendered identities and racial essence of "true Germans" for a political movement that fused racism, militarism, and authoritarianism into a distinctive form of racialized nationalism. (Hoover Institution Poster Collection, Stanford University)

and most decisive remains the failure to recognize the racial problem and especially the Jewish menace." The "old Reich," as Hitler described it, thus began to collapse when it ignored "the racial foundations of the nation."[24] The Nazi Party linked this dangerous racist idea to the emotional components of German nationalism by claiming to embody German national traditions, honoring the deaths of soldiers in the Great War, defending the "racial essence" of the German nation, and promoting the historic destiny of the German people. Much like the Fascists in Italy, the Nazis portrayed their movement as the best defense against national enemies and the best advocate for the "self-determination" of all Germans. Indeed, Hitler justified his international actions throughout the 1930s with popular claims that the German people were simply asserting their fundamental rights for national self-determination as they remilitarized the German Rhineland (1936), incorporated Austria into the German Reich (1938), supported Sudeten Germans in Czechoslovakia (1938), and undertook other aggressive policies that overturned provisions of the Treaty of Versailles. Hitler could thus use Wilsonian theories of national sovereignty as skillfully as a liberal democrat whenever the concept served the particular goals of German expansionism.

All of the nationalist themes in the Fascist and Nazi movements came together after Germany's invasion of Poland launched the Second World War in 1939: the desire to avenge the outcome of the previous war, the racist conception of national identity, the belief in a superior historical destiny for the German nation, and the claim that this destiny included the incorporation of all German-speaking peoples into an expanding German Reich. Although the events of the Second World War extended well beyond the history of nationalism and the specific themes of this book, the long-evolving components of nationalist politics and cultures reappeared constantly in this vast conflict. Nationalist ideologies shaped the military aggression in both Europe and Asia, where the war expanded after Japan's imperial ambitions brought the United States, China, and many other countries into the most far-reaching conflagration in world history. Despite the extraordinary scale of violence and destruction, however, Hitler's plans for a German-controlled continental empire resembled some of Napoleon's earlier imperial aspirations for France, and the Nazi conquests, like the Napoleonic conquests, led to new forms of national resistance as well as new collaborations with an occupying military force.

German occupation policies in France and Russia, for example, provoked nationalist opposition as oppressed populations began to resist

Nazi armies and the systematic exploitation of local resources. Meanwhile, prominent national leaders of the complex alliance against the Fascist "Axis powers" all claimed to defend the enduring essence of their nations. Winston Churchill, Franklin Roosevelt, and Joseph Stalin constantly invoked British, American, and Russian nationalisms to rally popular support for difficult military campaigns or to mobilize every economic resource for the expansion of their national armies. This new global struggle became another "total war" for which national governments demanded exceptional sacrifices. The centralization of economic planning, the conscription of soldiers, and the systematic organization of national life advanced even more comprehensively than during the First World War; and nationalizing processes that had begun with the *levée en masse* during the French Revolution now reached their historical culmination in all the warring countries.[25]

Among the many appeals for national sacrifices, Charles de Gaulle's famous call to arms after France's ignominious surrender to the German *blitzkrieg* in 1940 offers one of the best examples of how the new war elicited the recurring themes of modern national warfare and identity. "It is quite true that we were, and still are, overwhelmed by enemy mechanized forces," de Gaulle conceded in a London radio address to his French compatriots on June 18, 1940. "But has the last word been said? Must we abandon all hope? Is our defeat final and irremediable? To those questions I answer—No! Speaking in full knowledge of the facts, I ask you to believe me when I say that the cause of France is not lost. . . . The destiny of the world is at stake." Using an optimistic argument to predict an eventual national revival in the wake of France's most crushing military defeat, de Gaulle strongly affirmed that the nation could not perish, that the sacrifices of his generation would not be in vain, and that "the flame of French resistance must not and shall not die."[26] His emphasis on the permanent "French resistance" (ironically) asserted the kind of enduring national identity that Fichte and others had expressed after Napoleon's French armies occupied Germany in 1806. A great European power's aggressive military campaigns, in short, again gave rise to nationalist resistance among people who refused to accept a foreign occupation of their national land or cities. The diverse national struggles against the German and Japanese occupations were all savagely repressed, but they merged finally with the massive military campaigns in which Russian, American, British, and other armed forces eventually destroyed the imperial systems and governing regimes of the Axis nations.

William Vandivert, photographer, *Residents Cleaning Bombed-Out Buildings in Berlin*, 1945.
The Second World War caused more deaths than any war in human history and destroyed
some of the most important cities in Europe and East Asia. This photograph of women
in the rubble of postwar Berlin suggests why many people came to question the militant
nationalist ideas that had helped to produce the twentieth-century's hugely destructive
world wars. The United Nations and other global institutions thus developed as part of
a post-1945 search for alternatives to unrestrained, violent nationalisms. (Time & Life
Pictures/Getty Images)

This second, nationalist-inspired world war became an even more deadly "total war" than the Napoleonic wars or the Great War of 1914–18. In addition to the millions of people who were killed in the bombings of cities, the brutal military campaigns, the forced labor of civilians, and the starvation of vulnerable urban populations, the Nazis organized a systematic genocidal assault on Jewish communities and other condemned "racial groups" who were sent to death camps in eastern Europe. More than 6 million Jews and others died in this genocidal crime that would soon be described as "the Holocaust" of the Second World War, and 50 to 70 million people died in all parts of the world before the war finally ended in 1945.[27] The racism, genocide, and "industrial organization" of the Holocaust far exceeded the systematic violence of previous nationalist wars, and yet some aspects of the Nazi ideology that justified this incomprehensible brutality could be linked to ideas that had also appeared in other modern nationalisms. The Nazis carried to unprecedented extremes the older cultural desires for purified, coherent national communities, the scapegoating of allegedly dangerous internal enemies, the racial and ethnic conceptions of nationhood, the belief in a superior mission for particular national cultures, the celebration of national wars as the most noble expression of the nation's will or virtues, and the repression of individual human rights for the higher cause of "national interests."

Although it would be wrong to blame the extraordinary violence of the two world wars entirely on the ideas or ambitions of modern nationalisms, these catastrophic events came to be seen in many places as the ultimate consequence of unrestrained nationalist passions and ideologies. Whatever else could be said about "total" wars or genocide, it was apparent that radical nationalism had helped to produce these appalling modern horrors. Critics of twentieth-century nationalism stressed that nationalist wars were destroying millions of people as well as the economies, cultures, and cities of the industrialized world. Responding to the unprecedented military violence, the Holocaust, and the terrifying atomic bombs that the United States had used to end the war in Japan, postwar political activists launched new campaigns to defend human rights and to challenge the racism that had often pervaded both nationalism and imperialism.[28]

This growing desire to mitigate the worst aspects of modern nationalism led directly to the postwar creation of new transnational organizations (for example, the United Nations) and the search for new forms of international cooperation.[29] Yet the most influential political leaders and organized political parties still insisted everywhere on national political sovereignty and on the essential differences of national cultures. The terrible costs of modern warfare may have discredited the most extreme ideas of late nineteenth-century nationalists, but the political and cultural desire for national independence (which had sustained the national resistance to German and Japanese imperialism) soon reappeared in the anticolonial movements of Asia, Africa, and the Middle East. Nationalism therefore remained a powerful historical force after 1945, even as people condemned the devastating violence of the world wars and lived in a new era of global politics, cultures, and economic exchanges.

CHAPTER EIGHT

Nationalism & Nation-States after 1945

The extraordinary violence of the twentieth-century world wars left much of Europe and Japan in ruins, but the horror of these wars also provoked the Europeans and the Japanese to move away from their earlier cycles of national warfare. European nations stopped preparing for wars against one another, and there were no further wars among the major powers in Europe—a transition that became one of the greatest changes in modern human history. The long-developing legacy of Western nationalisms nevertheless remained apparent in the European empires that still existed after 1945 and in the complex efforts to create new international institutions or economic exchanges. Nationalism also influenced numerous conflicts during the Cold War in the 1950s and 1960s, as the United States and the Soviet Union competed for influence in nations that emerged from the disintegrating political and economic systems of modern colonialism. If nationalism began to lose some of its former political influence within European societies, it gained new importance as a mobilizing force among the colonized peoples who now declared their independence from European empires.

Nationalist ideas that had shaped political conceptions of a national "mission" in imperialist countries thus evolved into new arguments for anti-imperialist movements in all parts of the world, much as early nineteenth-century European nationalists had transformed French ideas about "sovereign peoples" into resistance movements against the Napoleonic empire. Although anticolonialist activists challenged the European control of their societies, they often repeated familiar Western claims for the political sovereignty of independent nation-states. Asian political and intellectual elites, for example, drew constantly on what the historian Harry Gelber calls the "contagious" ideas of European nationalism to argue that every culture had "a natural right to political autonomy and . . . that the idea of the nation should be tied to that of the state."[1] Nationalism, in other words, provided attractive political and cultural ideas that could move quickly across territorial boundaries, creating a kind of transnational confidence in the significance of national identities. Every "new nation" also used nationalist themes in well-publicized campaigns to "catch up" with the national institutions and economies that had given so much power to the governments of "older nations."

This chapter therefore brings the history of modern nationalism toward the present era by noting briefly how post-1945 nationalisms replicated nineteenth-century nationalist movements and also began to transform older nationalist themes in a postcolonial world. The breakup of European empires in Asia and Africa helped to change both the populations and the traditional nationalist assumptions within European societies. Indeed, the collapse of global empires coincided with an emerging transnational movement for cooperation among the previously warring European nation-states and a new recognition of the diversity within national cultures. Older ideas about multicultural empires gradually gave way to new ideas about multicultural nations and a unified, multicultural Europe. The history of nationalism since the Second World War thus includes the continuing development of anticolonialism as well as the concurrent emergence of a new transnational collaboration or "internationalism" among the political elites of long-established European states. It is also true, however, that nationalism continued to pervade political and cultural life, so that nationalist ideas and emotions reappeared regularly in political responses to the collapse of communist states, to terrorism, to immigration, and to economic globalization. This overview of nationalism's post-1945 influence and evolution thus comes back finally to nationalist themes that remain important in the twenty-first-century political cultures of nations such as the United States and France.

Decolonization and the Global Struggles for National Independence

Woodrow Wilson's emphasis on national "self-determination" attracted much global attention at the end of the First World War, but, as noted in the previous chapter, nationalists such as Ho Chi Minh quickly recognized that this concept would not be applied to the European colonies in Asia or Africa. France and Great Britain actually expanded their imperial influence by dissolving Germany's overseas empire and receiving League of Nations "mandates" to govern most of the former Ottoman Empire in the Middle East. Ho Chi Minh's complaints about the European denial of national rights were therefore repeated far beyond Versailles and wherever intellectual elites had launched campaigns against Western imperialism. The Chinese nationalist Sun Yat-sen (1866–1925), for example, summarized this perspective in a typical nationalist argument in the "post-Wilsonian" context of the early 1920s. Although Sun stressed that the "great phrase, used by President Wilson and warmly received everywhere—'self-determination of peoples'"—seemed to promise a new era of national autonomy, he complained bitterly that Asians and Africans soon faced what he called "an oppression more terrible than before." To be sure, the idea of "self-determination" did not disappear, and yet the Western powers simply decided to ignore it in other regions of the world. New anti-imperial movements therefore "began independently and separately to carry out the principle of the 'self-determination of peoples,'" thereby taking action to resist Europe's global hegemony and to affirm the importance of autonomous national cultures. Sun described this evolving national consciousness in his own Chinese society as a pervasive determination "to revive China's lost nationalism and use the strength of our four hundred million to fight for mankind against injustice; this is our divine mission."[2]

Sun's arguments for Chinese autonomy, in short, drew on Wilson's themes to promote national political independence, but he also reiterated broader nationalist ideas to define China's "divine mission" in the modern human struggle for justice and national rights. This mission suggested international tasks in which Chinese nationalism could shine with "greater splendor," but the cosmopolitan destiny had to begin with national self-determination. "[W]e must talk nationalism first," Sun argued, "if we want to talk cosmopolitanism . . . [and] have some ground for discussing internationalism."[3] Nineteenth-century ideas about the "concert of nations" and transnational collaborations therefore reemerged in Asian accounts of distinctive national identities, which, as Sun insisted, could only fuse with internationalism *after* China and other nations gained their equal rights to "self-determination."

Sun's writings about the autonomous Chinese nation pointedly referred to Lenin as well as Wilson in arguing for an alternative to Western imperialism, but other Asian activists sought to define their national movements without depending on either Wilsonian or Leninist perspectives. Nobody made the case for an autonomous, non-Western political and cultural movement more forcefully than India's Mohandas Gandhi (1869–1948), an advocate for national independence who proposed a new kind of struggle (or "swaraj") for the Indian nation. As Gandhi described it, this struggle went beyond traditional political movements for independence to become a long-term moral campaign for a new national culture. "I long for freedom from the English yoke," he wrote in a 1928 account of the new anti-imperial movement. "Anything would be better than this living death of a whole [Indian] people. This satanic rule has well-nigh ruined this fair land materially, morally and spiritually." Yet his description of India's independence also insisted that a postcolonial Indian nation must provide a moral example for the whole world. In this respect, Gandhi's argument—despite the rigorous attempt to break with traditional nationalist ideas in the West—repeated familiar aspirations for a "model nation" whose own exceptional mission and national achievements would also benefit all other peoples. "My ambition is much higher than independence," Gandhi explained. "Through the deliverance of India, I seek to deliver the so-called weaker races of the earth from the crushing heels of Western exploitation in which England is the greatest partner. If India converts . . . Englishmen, it can become the predominant partner in a world commonwealth of which England can have the privilege of becoming a partner if she chooses. . . . India's coming into her own will mean every nation doing likewise."[4] Gandhi's claim for India's universal historical significance suggests how even the most self-conscious critics of powerful Western nations evoked common nationalist themes. As postcolonial critics have noted, traditional ideas about the universal significance of a particular national history or about the state's embodiment of nationhood often reappeared among anti-imperialist leaders who otherwise wanted to break away from Western cultural practices.[5] Cross-cultural borrowings helped to shape the political and cultural assumptions of all anticolonial nationalist movements, much as earlier Western nationalisms had adapted themes from other national cultures in the nineteenth century. Nationalisms always defined specific cultural traditions that created national identities, but they used transnational comparisons to describe the identities they affirmed. The identity-shaping definitions of nationhood always carried something from "outside" the nation to the "inside" of new national cultures.

Anticolonial nationalists typically sought to defend the "inner life" of their nations by describing a distinctive, non-Western cultural essence. National independence was thus portrayed as the best possible protection for this essential cultural spirit, even when national development or defense required the adoption of Western science and technology.

Mansell, photographer, *Gandhi Leading the "Salt March" to Protest British Policies in India,* 1930. The anticolonial nationalisms in twentieth-century Asia and Africa used diverse political strategies and affirmed different cultural traditions, but they all asserted modern nationalist claims for the rights of national sovereignty, political self-determination, and cultural autonomy. Mohandas Gandhi (shown here with a stick in hand and surrounded by other activists) led the distinctive, spiritually inflected anticolonial movement in India, which included this famous protest against British taxation policies and which eventually established an independent national state in 1947. (Time & Life Pictures/Getty Images)

Extending Gandhi's call for an autonomous Indian culture into a more pragmatic program for the independent Indian state, Jawaharlal Nehru (1889–1964) broke with his predecessor to argue (like other postcolonial national leaders) that India must borrow freely from Western technologies. "India, as well as China, must learn from the West, for the modern West has much to teach," Nehru insisted. "But the West is also obviously in need of learning much . . . [about] the deeper lessons of life, which have absorbed the minds of thinkers in all ages and in all countries."⁶ Nehru's summary of "Eastern" and "Western" nations thus returned to a theme that Slavic nationalists such as Adam Mickiewicz had developed in their earlier critiques of unified, industrial nation-states during the nineteenth century: "you" may have more advanced political institutions and technologies, but "our" spiritual strengths offer the foundation for an even more elevated national culture. Similar assertions of national superiority would become common in the many anticolonial movements that claimed to protect cultural traditions by also adapting modern sciences.

Nationalist attempts to fuse the "traditional" with the "modern," however, became one of the most enduring cultural challenges for postcolonial nations when they sought to "catch up" with ascendant or wealthier national states. As the historian Gregory Jusdanis explains in a discussion of these competing national ambitions, "nationalism constitutes an acknowledgement of and a reaction to the need to copy the institutions of hegemonic powers." This pattern of rejection and emulation appeared in most postcolonial national movements as well as in the earlier German or central European responses to the Napoleonic empire. Struggles to establish national autonomy have always faced a paradox because the successful defense of national difference requires the frequent appropriation of methods or knowledge from *other* national cultures. These inescapable processes of cultural borrowing confirm for Jusdanis and many historians that nationalism is also a "global discourse" because "nation building, like identity, is a synthetic process."[7] Decolonization therefore led to complex "nationalizing educations" that simultaneously required definitions of distinctive national missions or identities *and* an endless borrowing from other cultures.

Among the many anticolonial nationalist intellectuals who examined this process of cultural borrowings, Léopold Senghor (1906–2001), the first president of Senegal, became the best-known analyst and advocate of cultural hybridity in francophone Africa. Writing in the early 1960s, Senghor argued that European and African methods of attaining knowledge often differed insofar as "European reasoning" tended to be "analytical" or "discursive" and "African reasoning" tended to be more "intuitive" and communitarian. He insisted, however, that these methods of reasoning provided complementary approaches to truth because "every ethnic group possesses different aspects of reason and all the virtues of man." These connections between cultural particularities and universal human virtues meant that postcolonial African nations "must maintain the Negro-African method of knowledge, but integrate into it the methods Europe has used throughout her history—classical logic, Marxian dialectics, and that of the twentieth century." African nationalists, as Senghor described them, were thus developing distinctive national cultures that would also contribute to the "*civilization of the universal* yet to be built. The latter . . . will be a symbiosis of the most fecundating elements of all civilizations."[8]

This conception of postcolonial nationalism could be compared to the ideas of earlier romantic nationalists who envisioned the collaboration or "concert" of diverse national cultures, but Senghor and others extended the older multicultural themes far beyond Europe. Equally important, the proposals for a postcolonial cultural hybridity rejected, at least in theory, the racial or ethnic nationalisms that sought to remove "alien elements" from the national community. Senghor's ideal national movement drew on both European and African components, thereby contributing to a future global civilization that was "yet to be built." Recognizing that most new states in Africa could not represent the kind of coherent or unified national cultures that romantic nationalisms had *imagined*, Senghor stressed the multiple traditions and forms of knowledge that would have to coexist in multicultural African nations.

Senghor's interest in cultural hybridity, however, was only one of the cultural models for nationhood that emerged among anticolonial writers. In many places, the struggle to define an independent national culture led to more vehement critiques of imperial cultural oppression and to new historical claims for cultural differences—some of which resembled the earlier anti-Napoleonic writings of J. G. Fichte or Ernst Moritz Arndt. Like the nineteenth-century critics of the French Empire in Europe, the twentieth-century writers emphasized that imperial conquests endangered cultural traditions as well as the political and economic interests of everyone in the occupied territories. The French Caribbean poet and political theorist Aimé Césaire (1913–2008), for example, described European colonialism as the action of "a civilization that is morally diseased." Colonizing other peoples, Césaire wrote in his influential *Discourse on Colonialism* (1955), "dehumanizes even the most civilized man" because imperial systems lead inevitably to "contempt for the native." The colonial administrator comes to view the colonized person "as *an animal*," but this hierarchical, degrading treatment of others also forces the colonizer "to transform *himself* into an animal." Stark social and cultural dichotomies therefore separated the colonizers from the people they controlled, and the radical devaluation or destruction of autonomous cultural traditions produced an "inferiority complex" among all colonized peoples. "I am talking about societies drained of their essence," Césaire explained in one summary of the pattern, "cultures trampled underfoot, institutions undermined, lands confiscated, religions smashed, magnificent artistic creations destroyed, extraordinary *possibilities* wiped out."[9] Césaire's critique brought a post-1945, Afro-Caribbean perspective to the long-developing condemnation of both political and cultural imperialism. Expanding the arguments of earlier cultural nationalists in Europe (and moving beyond Senghor, with whom he had developed the concept of "Negritude" in Paris), Césaire assumed that all imperial occupations "drained" the cultural life from national populations and destroyed national memories. The writings of Césaire, in other words, pointed to a nearly universal response to modern imperialism: popular and ultimately irrepressible nationalist movements gradually emerged to oppose "foreign" powers wherever military, political, and cultural interventions denied the autonomy or self-determination of colonized peoples.

The twentieth-century responses to imperial systems therefore repeated many of the demands for political and cultural independence that American, German, Italian, Polish, and other nationalists had proclaimed during earlier campaigns against European empires. In contrast to the European-centered ideas of writers such as Fichte, Mickiewicz, and Giuseppe Mazzini, however, the best-known twentieth-century advocates for oppressed national cultures came mostly from Asia, Africa, and the Caribbean Islands. This modern pattern of nationalist writing and action, which we have seen in Ho Chi Minh, Sun Yat-sen, Gandhi, and Senghor, appears also in the life and work of Frantz Fanon (1925–61), who began his theoretical career as a student of Césaire in Martinique. Although he served in the French army at the end of the Second World War and studied medicine in France, Fanon joined the Algerian movement for independence from France in the late 1950s. His important anticolonial book, *The Wretched of the Earth* (1962), emphasized the imperialist threats to local cultures and reiterated themes that European nationalists had developed in their political and cultural critiques of the Napoleonic, Ottoman, and Habsburg Empires. Yet Fanon also went beyond his nineteenth-century predecessors in stressing the psychological alienation of colonized intellectuals and the traumas that resulted from a "colonial domination . . . [that] manages to disrupt in spectacular fashion the cultural life of a conquered people." Controlled by foreign powers, writers and artists could easily lose the creative and emotional resources that sustained imaginative cultural work, but Fanon argued that the alienating encounters with colonialism could also provoke nationalist intellectuals to "brush the cobwebs off national consciousness, to question oppression, and to open up the struggle for freedom."[10]

Indeed, Fanon's response to French forces in Algeria might be compared with Fichte's response to Napoleon's occupation of Berlin. In both cases, the nationalist theorist described French imperialism as the starting point for a new national movement in which intellectuals must align themselves with the national population. This convergence of politics and culture became possible because, to quote Fanon again, "it is only from that moment that we can speak of a national literature ... [or] a literature of combat, in the sense that it calls on the whole people to fight for their existence as a nation." Fanon's nationalist intellectuals—like Fichte's—thus joined the political struggle for independence when they contributed a new kind of nationalist writing that "molds the national consciousness, giving it form and contours and flinging open before it new and boundless horizons." According to Fanon, intellectuals did not create the national culture, but they expressed the "fight for national existence" in coherent narratives that set the "culture moving" and helped to mobilize a collective national identity. "The nation gathers together the various indispensable elements necessary for the creation of a culture," Fanon argued, "those elements which alone can give it credibility, validity, life, and creative power."[11]

Fanon repeatedly urged writers and political activists to establish an autonomous, decolonized national life, but he also assumed that this all-important defense of national culture and sovereignty was merely the prelude to new transnational collaborations in the postcolonial world. Nationalism, in short, opened the way to a new internationalism. "Far from keeping aloof from other nations," he wrote in *The Wretched of the Earth*, "it is national liberation which leads the nation to play its part on the stage of history. It is as the heart of national consciousness that international consciousness lives and grows."[12] Here, too, Fanon's theories echo the themes of nineteenth-century nationalists, connecting in this respect with those who saw national independence as the prelude to a new cooperation among equal, sovereign peoples.[13] Fanon shared the long-developing belief that free nations could only combine their political and cultural aspirations in wider international movements *after* all nations had achieved independence. Although Fanon died from leukemia before the end of the Algerian War, his political and psychological insistence on the rights of autonomous national states and cultures continued to provide an influential defense of postcolonial identities and to attract wide interest among critics of neocolonial hierarchies in the twenty-first century.

Despite the enduring inequalities among nations in the postcolonial world, the constantly expanding movements for national independence brought almost 700 million people into new national states between 1945

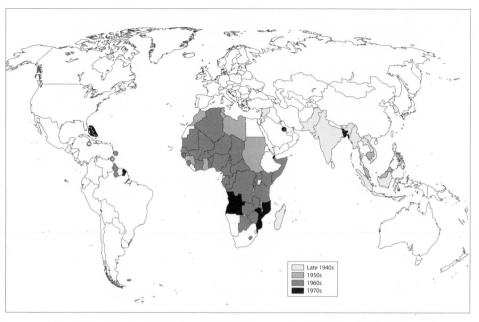

Decolonization and the Emergence of New Nations, 1945–1975. The pervasive themes of
modern nationalism shaped the worldwide movements for national independence, which
(as this map indicates) achieved their political objectives in formerly colonized societies from Southeast Asia to the Caribbean Islands during the three decades after 1945.
Although the newly independent national states faced constant challenges in the global
economy and struggled with internal conflicts, the rapid progress of decolonization confirmed that the long-developing theories of national sovereignty and national rights had
become the foundation for public life and human identities throughout the modern world.

and the late 1960s. These new states took control over some of the world's
largest "national" populations in places such as India, Pakistan, Indonesia,
the Philippines, Nigeria, Kenya, and Vietnam. Governments in all of these
large states set about the tasks of constructing coherent national identities
that would unite their diverse populations, but even the smaller new states
(for example, Singapore, Ghana, and Sri Lanka) faced the challenge of
merging multicultural diversity into "national" unity. Anticolonial movements everywhere evolved into "imagined communities" that carried
very different and often contested national meanings. The Zionist movement, for example, finally established an independent Jewish state in the
former British "mandate" of Palestine (1948), only to enter immediately
into new conflicts with competing Arab and Palestinian nationalisms and
new struggles to reconcile diverse populations within its own territorial

borders. Ethnic or religious rivalries also threatened the unity of almost every new "nation-state" in Africa. All nations raised a new national flag and then launched long campaigns to "nationalize" their populations through education, language training, military service, national holidays, national histories, new communication systems, and quasi-religious memorials to the deceased national heroes who had led the struggles for national independence.[14]

The traditional nationalist desires for a coherent culture, territory, and historical identity therefore faced major challenges in postcolonial nations, but all such nations resembled one another and also the longer-established "nation-states" by asserting their sovereign independence. They also followed familiar patterns of nation building as they emphasized the identity-shaping significance of national differences, created symbols and rituals to represent collective identities, and defined the national duties of men, women, and children. The underlying structures of postcolonial nationalisms and nation building would thus replicate the cultural processes in older "national" states, including the essential efforts to link personal identities with collective national identities. There were, of course, significant cultural differences among national states in various parts of the world, but modern nations everywhere ("old" and "new" alike) sought to unite their multicultural populations and to defend their national sovereignty within global economic systems that crossed all national boundaries.

Multicultural Nations and Transnational Systems

Nationalists have typically sought to define an enduring cultural essence for their nations, but this long-desired "cultural essentialism" has always collided with the inescapable reality of cultural differences within modern national boundaries. Recognizing these inevitable internal differences, some twentieth-century nationalists began to accept the multicultural diversity within nations and to connect national identities with political or economic institutions rather than with the (imagined) essences of race, language, or ethnicity. New strands of nationalist thought rejected earlier, univocal cultural themes and attracted growing support after 1945 as people reacted against the exclusionary racist policies of Nazism. Arguments for what would become a "multicultural" conception of nationhood had already emerged during the early twentieth century in the "cosmopolitan" nationalism of various anti-imperialist writers and among the critics of race-conscious, ethnic nationalisms. The Irish poet W. B. Yeats (1865–1939), for example, argued that "Ireland is not wholly Celtic any more than England is wholly Saxon, or wholly Catholic any more that England is wholly Protestant." The Indian poet Rabindranath Tagore (1861–1941) also rejected racial or religious definitions of India's national identity and stressed the value of internal diversity—themes that began to emerge at about the same time in the United States. Indeed, the American writer Randolph Bourne (1886–1918) proposed a multi-cultural nationalism for America at the end of the First World War, thus redefining the ideas of nationhood that Woodrow Wilson was then pro-moting in his Fourteen Points.[15]

Bourne challenged a popular American nationalism that expected immigrants to adopt a single cultural identity as they flowed through a "melting pot" that would fuse them into a unified "Anglo-Saxon" national heritage. According to Bourne, however, this imaginary cultural fusion should be rejected, so that the future of the United States could "be what the immigrant will have a hand in making it, and not what a ruling class, descendant of those British stocks which were the first permanent immigrants, decides that America shall be." The multicultural aspects of American society were thus for Bourne the most distinctive character-istics of the nation's identity, which meant (as he explained in an essay titled "Trans-national America" [1916]) that "what we emphatically do not want is that these diverse qualities [of immigrant cultures] should be washed out into a tasteless, colorless fluid of uniformity." Like other nationalists, Bourne envisioned a unique national mission for America, but the great task for this still-young nation was to lead the world toward a new kind of multicultural, national state. "In a world which has dreamed of internationalism," he wrote, "we find that we have all unawares been building up the first international nation.... America is already the world federation in miniature ... [filled with] the most heterogeneous peoples under the sun."[16]

The United States could therefore become a model for future multicul-tural nations that would lack a long-imagined ethnic or cultural "purity" but gain creative advantages from the "diverse qualities" of their con-stantly evolving immigrant populations. "America," Bourne concluded, "is coming to be, not a nationality but a trans-nationality, a weaving back and forth ... of many threads of all sizes and colors."[17] Although Bourne's own conception of cultural diversity focused mainly on European Ameri-cans, others would expand the theory of multiculturalism in the later twentieth century to encompass increasingly diverse racial and ethnic groups. This new emphasis on the value of internal diversity explicitly rejected the racial nationalism that theorists such as Arthur de Gobineau and Houston Steward Chamberlain had promoted in an earlier era. At the same time, the multicultural perspectives in the writings of Bourne, Tagore, and other "cosmopolitan" nationalists suggested that the Wilsonian support for "culturally coherent" nation-states could lead to dangerous ethnic distortions of modern nationhood.

The early twentieth-century arguments for culturally diverse national states may have emerged in colonial or postcolonial societies outside of Europe, but a similar interest in multicultural and transnational political systems would also gradually lead most Europeans away from radical ethnic and cultural nationalisms after 1945. National populations in many European "nation-states" became more multicultural in the postwar era as immigrants arrived from former colonies. Meanwhile, other nationalists in the centralized European states developed new appreciation for older, internal regional and cultural diversities that had survived the "nationalizing" policies of modern governments. The most assertive later twentieth-century European nationalisms often emerged in militant regional campaigns for the political or social autonomy of various cultural minorities within previously unified nations (for example, Scotland and Wales in Great Britain, Brittany and Corsica in France, the Basque region in Spain, among others). The new regionalism, however, coincided with a growing desire for the "unified nations" of Europe to collaborate in transnational political and economic systems that would control or even eliminate the traditional causes of recurring warfare. Europeans became aware of their need to weave together "many threads of all sizes and colors" (to extend Bourne's language into a different context); and this idea contributed directly to the creation of a new European Union, which would bring more than twenty-five nations into close economic, cultural, and political collaboration by the early twenty-first century.[18]

This new transnational cooperation took on particular significance in Germany and France because of the bitter wars that the two nations had fought between the early nineteenth century and 1945. People in both countries had come to view German-French conflicts as an almost inescapable component of their modern national histories, but the recurring wars had also disrupted the politics and economy of the whole European continent. The development of a new collaboration between these leading European powers thus became one of the major transitions in the history of modern nationalism. The cooperation developed first in the economic sphere when the two countries joined with four other smaller countries to create the European Coal and Steel Community (ECSC) in 1951. This economic partnership eliminated all tariffs and facilitated the free circulation of these basic industrial products among the member nations, but the economic alliance was viewed from the beginning as the model for a broader transnational system. As the German chancellor Konrad Adenauer explained in a later account of the ECSC treaty, Europeans increasingly recognized that the era of "exaggerated nationalism brought Europe to the edge of the abyss" and that Europe's future peace and prosperity would require new forms of "practical cooperation." The treaty that launched the new economic cooperation thus, in Adenauer's view, "put a solemn and irrevocable end to a past in which two people had again and again confronted each other with arms as a result of mistrust, rivalry and egotism."[19]

Europe's plan for economic collaboration therefore emerged as a self-conscious alternative to the militant nationalisms that had long stressed the radical differences of German and French national identities. "I was firmly convinced that . . . once six European countries had voluntarily and without coercion transferred a part of their sovereignty to a superior body," Adenauer wrote in his assessment of the ECSC, "that similar developments would occur in other fields and that nationalism, the cancer of Europe, would thereby be dealt a fatal blow."[20] Although Adenauer's view of nationalism's impending demise went beyond what most Europeans may have desired or expected, the German chancellor strongly supported a post-Nazi German elite that wanted to collaborate with the French rather than wage national wars. This collaborative approach found willing partners in France, where political leaders such as Robert Schuman (an architect of the ECSC agreement) and even Charles de Gaulle would seek to expand the French role in Europe's evolving "Common Market" during the 1950s and 1960s.

De Gaulle sought constantly to protect France's "national interests," but he recognized that transnational collaborations within Europe could help sustain France's international influence amid the Cold War conflicts of the Soviet Union and the United States. He therefore affirmed Adenauer's multinational conception of European social and economic interests and stressed what he began to call "the overriding importance of the union of Europe, a union which above all demanded the co-operation of Paris and Bonn." The modern task for France and Germany, as de Gaulle defined it in his *Memoirs*, was "to reverse the course of history by reconciling our two peoples and uniting their efforts and abilities." Although he would never endorse Adenauer's forward-looking proposals for an expansive *political* unity in Europe, de Gaulle met often with the German chancellor to develop plans for new transnational economic and cultural exchanges. His conversations with Adenauer at the cathedral in Rheims (1962) carried particular historical significance for de Gaulle because the "first Frenchman and the first German came together to pray that on either side of the Rhine the deeds of friendship might for ever supplant the miseries of war."[21]

This new era of French-German cooperation transformed the history of European nationalism by removing the perennial threat of warfare from the center of Europe. To be sure, de Gaulle continued to oppose Great Britain's admission to the Common Market, and the Gaullist defense of national autonomy often hindered transnational cooperation; but the emerging European institutions began to change the older system of unbending national sovereignty into a collaborative system that allowed the free movement of people across national borders, established a "European parliament," developed a common currency (the Euro), introduced continent-wide economic and budgetary regulations, created a European University Institute, and began to promote a common strategy for military defense.[22] Meanwhile, the painful human losses of Europe's twentieth-century wars were remembered at symbolic international ceremonies rather than at the kind of emotionally charged nationalist rituals that had been common in the 1920s and 1930s. French president François Mitterrand and German Chancellor Helmut Kohl came together for a commemorative reconciliation on the battlefield at Verdun (1984); and on Armistice Day in 2009, France's president Nikolas Sarkozy stood beside Germany's chancellor Angela Merkel at the Arc de Triomphe in Paris for a joint remembrance of the casualties on *both* sides of the Great War's deadly battlefields.[23] A permanent Franco-German collaboration had replaced the earlier nationalist call to arms against ancient enemies, so that war between the nations of western Europe had become unimaginable.

National identities did not disappear, of course, and the nationalism evident in European schools, mass media, political parties, and sporting events continued to shape collective and individual identities in this new era of multinational systems. There was still a rich European diversity of languages, literatures, foods, holidays, religions, and public rituals. Yet the leading themes in Europe's late twentieth-century national cultures

Unknown photographer, *François Mitterrand and Helmut Kohl at Verdun*, 1984. A new transnational system emerged in Europe when France and Germany moved away from their centuries-long cycle of national wars and embraced the concept of a European Union. This transnationalism led to new economic and cultural exchanges as well as a new political alliance, but it gained its more profound symbolic meaning when national leaders such as French president Mitterrand and German chancellor Kohl stood together on a historic battlefield for a joint homage to the deceased soldiers of both nations. (AFP/Getty Images)

moved steadily away from the nationalism that had fueled the German writings of Fichte and Arndt, or the French anger over the loss of Alsace and Lorraine, or the ideological arguments for "total" wars. As the steadily expanding European Union (EU) noted in a self-congratulatory twenty-first-century account of its political and economic achievements, "War between EU countries is now unthinkable, thanks to the unity that has been built up between them over the last fifty years." Older definitions of collective identity or "who could belong" evolved (in theory) from the specific ethnic or linguistic criteria of many earlier nationalisms toward the acceptance of multicultural civic and social principles. "Any European country can join," to cite once more the EU's self-portrait of international collaboration, "provided it has a stable democracy that guarantees the rule of law, human rights and the protection of minorities. It must also have a functioning market economy and a civil service capable of applying the EU's laws in practice."[24] Although this "civic" definition of the EU's collective identity faced repeated challenges as the union expanded into eastern Europe and debated the possible membership of Turkey, many Europeans came to see their continental system of transnational cooperation as a model for the modern world—much as earlier nationalists had often viewed their own national institutions as exemplary models for less-advanced modern nations. "The European Union shows how democratic countries can successfully pool economic and political resources in the common interest," the EU's official website explained, "serving as a possible model to be followed in other parts of the world."[25]

The end of the Cold War in the 1990s and the continuing development of global economic and cultural systems thus gave Europeans new reasons to extend the transnational collaboration that began after the Second World War. International cooperation and the acceptance of multicultural diversity became pragmatic strategies for defending "national interests" in a world where people, ideas, and money moved constantly across national borders. As the contemporary Dutch historian Joep Leerssen explained in a historical argument for "civic" rather than "ethnic" national identities, the older nationalist belief in coherent cultural nations had gradually lost credibility in the multicultural, democratic societies of contemporary Europe. Leerssen thus joined other Europeans in extending the earlier twentieth-century analysis of multicultural nations (for example, the themes of Bourne in the United States or Tagore in India) toward a more recent insistence on the inevitable diversity within all nation-states. "[W]hat binds citizens and fellow-nationals nowadays," Leerssen argues, "must be a communality of political responsibilities, a shared membership and participation in the same public sphere." In this era of multicultural societies, modern states could actually achieve the greatest coherence by affirming the cultural diversity within their territories and then stressing that these diverse groups shared a commitment to democratic political processes. Ignoring or repressing cultural diversity, in other words, destabilized modern nations. "Given the increasing multiculturalism and multi-ethnicity of our societies," Leerssen writes in his analysis of modern nationhood, "the state should . . . abandon its old reliance on nationality as its enabling principle, and revert from the outworn ideal of the nation-state to that of the *civic state*."[26] Although Leerssen and others never referred explicitly to Bourne's earlier conception of the "transnational" society, the contemporary European views of the national state increasingly overlapped with the ideas of "multicultural" nationalists in America. This multicultural, civic approach to modern nationalisms claimed that national coherence comes from what the nineteenth-century theorist Ernst Renan called the people's political will—a kind of ongoing plebiscite rather than an ethnic, racial, or religious essence.[27]

Despite the growing European support for multiculturalism and the new emphasis on transnational collaboration, however, the political ambitions and emotional passions of modern nationalisms continued to challenge international cooperation in much of the contemporary world. Indeed, powerful nations such as China, Russia, and the United States regularly resisted multinational attempts to limit their sovereign autonomy within global institutions that sought to regulate environmental pollution, defend human rights, or reduce nuclear armaments. Nationalism thus retained a political and emotional power that could overwhelm transnational or multicultural views of nationhood whenever people felt threatened or vulnerable.

The Enduring Power of Nationalisms and National Identities

The campaign for a transnational European Union began during the Cold War in the 1950s and continued to develop after the breakup of the Soviet Union in 1991. The end of the Cold War, however, also contributed to a new surge of nationalist movements and militant national identities, especially among groups who lived in the fifteen nations that emerged from the former Soviet Union or in the nations that emerged from the disintegrating Yugoslav state in the Balkans. There was wide international concern about new ethnic violence in southeastern Europe, in part because the nationalist conflicts that helped to precipitate the Great War in 1914 seemed to be returning in the 1990s. Serbs, Bosnians, Croats, and Kosovars all struggled to establish new states or extend their control over wider territories through the repression and forced removal of various ethnic communities. Although Europeans increasingly described their post-1945 political communities with the language of "civic" identities and international collaboration, the resurgent nationalisms in the post–Cold War Balkans stressed essential ethnic or religious identities, evoked memories of now-distant historical injustices, and pursued new national goals through a brutal "ethnic cleansing" that appeared to come from an earlier era of nationalist history.[28]

Political and cultural elites provided the all-important narratives of national memory and *ressentiment* that encouraged violent militia groups from Croatia and Serbia to assault civilians in Bosnia and Kosovo until international negotiators and military forces from the European-American NATO alliance intervened to stop the violence. The late twentieth-century nationalist conflicts in the Balkans therefore did not lead to the kind of wider war that erupted in 1914, mainly because new forms of international collaboration had replaced the earlier national alliance systems in Europe.[29] The resurgence of ethnic nationalisms became very deadly on the frontiers of the European Union, but such conflicts could no longer draw the major powers into a global war. International forces ended the violence, arrested the most radical nationalist leaders, and showed that the nationalist wars of smaller states could be at least partially controlled.

Nationalism and nationalist anxieties could nevertheless take many other nonmilitary forms, including hostility toward diverse immigrant communities that settled within wealthy countries such as France, Germany, Britain, Italy, and the United States. Although immigrants had become an essential part of the workforce in almost all industrialized countries during the later twentieth century, they were often viewed with suspicion because their religious beliefs, racial characteristics, or languages differed from what nationalists defined as the essence of their nation's historical identity. Immigrants who moved into Europe from Africa and the Middle East or into the United States from Latin America and Asia were condemned for their "illegal" status and for their alleged refusal to accept the cultural traditions of the societies in which they now lived. Vocal critics of multiculturalism appeared in every national political culture, and these broader cultural anxieties merged with more specific political concerns about international terrorism. The terrorist and illegal immigrant replaced earlier enemies in the always-evolving descriptions of the nation's most dangerous adversaries. National governments, like their predecessors, therefore responded to these new concerns with specific actions, such as the increased surveillance of Muslim religious groups, the construction of barriers to prevent Mexicans from entering the southwest United States, and the passage of a law that barred Muslim girls from wearing head scarves in French schools.[30]

Anxiety about outsiders has thus remained a common concern in most contemporary nationalisms, but the anxiety has been particularly notable in the United States and France because these nations have long accepted large numbers of immigrants and promoted civic or political conceptions of nationhood. Although cultural and religious nationalisms have also flourished in both countries, American and French nationalists have always stressed the political ideas of national sovereignty, the political symbolism of national rituals, and the political uses of cultural memories, all of which helped sustain coherent national identities. The popular twenty-first-century repetition of nationalist themes in the United States and France may therefore provide the best concluding examples for this brief overview of how nationalism has both changed and stayed the same in recent decades. We have seen that many of modern nationalism's ideas and institutions emerged in late eighteenth-century America and France, so the continuities in these national cultures point to the continuities in modern nationalist thought.

Nationalism may have remained more influential in the United States than in many European nations because American civilians never experienced the modern horrors of total war in their own cities; because both world wars were viewed as unambiguous American victories; or because the nation's extraordinary post-1945 political, economic, and cultural power seemed to confirm traditional American confidence in the nation's unique global mission. In any case, popular descriptions of the United States as the "greatest and most powerful nation in human history" continued to shape the national political culture and the military responses to the international challenges that great powers inevitably provoke. The continuities of American nationalism could be seen, for example, in the national response to the terrorist attacks by the radical Muslim group Al-Qaeda in New York and Washington on September 11, 2001. Reacting to the terrorists' use of hijacked airplanes to kill more than 3,000 people in American cities, President George W. Bush described the attacks as part of an assault on America's fundamental political and cultural traditions. He also drew on traditional nationalist themes to assert that the deaths of innocent Americans required new military actions, new sacrifices from the living generation, and new commemorations to ensure that the nation would always remember those who had died. National mourning, in short, was a prelude for unified national action, and the familiar themes of the American Revolution and the Gettysburg Address reappeared in the public interpretations of "September 11."[31]

Reiterating the national innocence that President Franklin Roosevelt had also invoked after the Japanese attack on Pearl Harbor in 1941 (an event that would "live in infamy"), President Bush repeated the classic themes of American nationalism to mourn the loss of innocent lives and to affirm the need for immediate state action. The presidential speech to Congress on 20 September 2001 could in fact be compared to President Wilson's arguments for American entry into the First World War or to President Roosevelt's arguments for a declaration of war in 1941. Bush, in other words, gave twenty-first-century expression to the earlier (and still popular) themes of America's national narratives. "We are a country awakened to danger and called to defend freedom," he declared in his account of the new national crisis. "Our grief has turned to anger, and anger to resolution." A new war was therefore beginning between America and dangerous national enemies who "hate our freedoms—our freedom of religion, our freedom of speech, our freedom to vote and assemble and disagree." The war to defend these values, however, was not merely America's struggle because "what is at stake is not just America's freedom. This is the world's fight. This is civilization's fight."[32]

Bush's description of America's special duty to defend a universal cause resembled the kind of national exceptionalism that Jules Michelet had claimed for nineteenth-century France or Mickiewicz had claimed for Poland, but the American president also referred to his own beliefs in the God-given tasks for the "chosen people" of the United States. Appealing to the familiar faith in the sanctity of the nation, Bush portrayed the American government as the protector of human lives and global freedom—thereby linking the national cause to a religious struggle for higher truths. "Freedom and fear, justice and cruelty, have always been at war," Bush continued, "and we know that God is not neutral between them." America's new conflict would therefore be difficult, but it was also clear that Americans could be "assured of the rightness of our cause, and confident of the victories to come." Bush's concluding assurance of future victories and divine support thus reaffirmed the nation's special destiny, repeating in this respect the national assurances of Franklin Roosevelt in 1941. "With confidence in our armed forces, with the unbounding determination of our people," Roosevelt had emphasized in his declaration of war against Japan, "we will gain the inevitable triumph. So help us God."[33] Every international conflict is different, of course, but the modern call to arms returns always to the same national themes.

Bush and other political leaders thus drew on America's most enduring nationalist ideas and identities as they launched new wars in Afghanistan (2001) and Iraq (2003). The initial public support for these wars showed how Bush had successfully linked his military policies with the traditional components of America's national identity (a nation of freedom, justice, and global duties). Indeed, public opinion polls in the fall of 2001 indicated that almost 90 percent of the American population supported his international actions, and a powerful surge of popular nationalism proclaimed America's national unity, shaped the "post-9/11" national mourning, and contributed to a new suspicion of Muslims both inside and outside the United States.[34]

America's nationalist response to the unprecedented terrorist attacks thus led to new wars, but the nationalist arguments for these conflicts were by no means unusual or uniquely American. Earlier chapters in this book have argued that the history of America's national identity and political culture resembles the history of nationalisms in other parts of the world, and these similarities could be seen again in the commemorations and public events after September 11. At the same time, however, the recent American wars also reaffirmed some of the more distinctive themes of America's national identity and history. Attempts to create a rigid ethnic definition of American identity, for example, could not gain broad popular support in a twentieth-century "nation of immigrants," which may explain why multiculturalism became an attractive modern idea for many of the diverse social groups within the United States.[35] The enduring political assumptions about America's global mission to promote freedom and democracy nevertheless remained as influential for George W. Bush as they had been for Abraham Lincoln and Woodrow Wilson. Although the specific tasks and enemies of this mission have changed over time, American leaders have evoked the nation's unique destiny to justify almost every complex or controversial policy. When the American war in Afghanistan continued inconclusively from the presidency of George Bush into the presidency of Barack Obama, the new commander in chief tried to rally public support for an expanded military campaign by developing a new summary of the cause—which he presented in the symbolic setting of the national military academy at West Point, New York in December 2009.

> Since the days of Franklin Roosevelt, and the service of our grandparents and great-grandparents, our country has borne a special burden in global affairs. We have spilled American blood in many countries. . . . [But] unlike the great powers of old, we have not sought world domination. . . . We do not seek to occupy other nations. We will not . . . target other peoples because their faith or ethnicity is different from ours. . . . As a country, we are not as young—and perhaps not as innocent—as we were when Roosevelt was president. Yet we are still heirs to a noble struggle for freedom. . . . I believe with every fiber of my being that we—as Americans—can still come together behind a common purpose. For our values are not simply words written into parchment—they are a creed that calls us together, and that has carried us through the darkest of storms as one nation, as one people. America—we are passing through a time of great trial. And the message we send in the midst of these storms must be clear: our cause is just, our resolve unwavering. We will go forward with the confidence that right makes might, and with the commitment to forge . . . a future that represents not the deepest of fears but the highest of hopes.[36]

No matter what the many foreign or domestic critics might say about the Afghan war, it had become for President Obama another "trial" for America's national unity, values, and "noble struggle for human freedom." And Obama's speech in 2009 (despite important, changing nuances) echoed the national themes of Thomas Paine in Philadelphia, Abraham Lincoln at Gettysburg, and Franklin Roosevelt on the radio.

The long-term continuities in American descriptions of the nation's mission and identity can perhaps be best compared with the nationalism in France, where belief in a universal mission has long formed a central theme of French republicanism. Like many twenty-first-century Americans, French nationalists feared that immigrants—especially Muslims from North Africa—were threatening their national culture. The French presidential elections in 2002 gave political force to these nationalist fears when the far-right National Front leader, Jean-Marie Le Pen, received almost as many votes as the incumbent president Jacques Chirac in the first round of voting. Although Chirac eventually won reelection,

Steve Hockstein, photographer, *Barack Obama Announces Strategy for Afghanistan*, 2009. American presidents, like the national leaders in other modern societies, typically evoked long-familiar nationalist symbols and themes whenever they launched new public actions or military campaigns. This image of President Obama suggests such continuities as he stands amid flags and soldiers at the U.S. Military Academy to announce his strategy for the war in Afghanistan (December 2009)—a strategy that would require the "common purpose" of "one people" in a nation that was passing "through a time of great trial." (Bloomberg via Getty Images)

nationalist anxieties about immigrant communities later contributed to the passage of laws that banned the wearing of Muslim head scarves in public schools (2004) and of Muslim burqas (full face veils) in all public places (2010). Such laws expressed a national insistence on "secularity" as a core value of French republicanism and suggested that some aspects of modern Islam were viewed as inherently "un-French." The conservative presidential candidate Nicholas Sarkozy played upon such nationalist ideas during the electoral campaign in 2007 and attracted support from some of the National Front voters who had previously voted for Le Pen. Indeed, Sarkozy may have won the election by stressing his respect for French national traditions—even though the opposing socialist candidate also emphasized her loyalty to the French flag and encouraged the singing of "La Marseillaise" at campaign events.[37]

Sarkozy expanded upon his electoral strategies with the creation of a new "Minister for Immigration and National Identity," thus suggesting that the assimilation of immigrant communities would be linked to a broader affirmation of French national identity. Many conservatives had become preoccupied with the meaning of citizenship in France, so they returned (unself-consciously) to the nationalizing themes of the French Revolution and to later debates about citizenship in the Third Republic or in the Vichy era. Seeking to launch a broad discussion of these issues in the contemporary public sphere, the French minister for "National Identity," Eric Besson, organized government-sponsored events at which the French people debated the meaning of French citizenship. All French *départements* and *arrondissements* were required to organize such events, but critics interpreted the new interest in "national identity" as part of a political campaign to placate conservative nationalists and to justify official (exclusionary) actions such as the bans on specific forms of Muslim clothing. The Sarkozy government defended its "identity debates" by arguing that the affirmation of French national identity simply carried forward the republican traditions of France's eighteenth-century revolution. Besson put forward his own ministerial view of "Frenchness" as a commitment to "the emancipation of people, [and] the republican idea of an enlightened, Cartesian citizen who believes in the Republic and in the three values of the phrase: Liberty, Equality, Fraternity."[38] Although the government-ordained debates about French identity may have been merely a brief episode of political theater, they clearly reflected wider nationalist fears about an evolving multicultural French society. The French "identity" debates also resembled the American war against terrorism in that neither campaign could lead to a decisive, final outcome. The French and American campaigns to define and defend specific national values nevertheless showed how two nations that helped to shape modern nationalism during their eighteenth-century revolutions still struggled to reaffirm or reconstruct their national cultures in an era of multicultural diversity, international terrorism, transnational economic systems, and religiously inflected debates about human rights. In the most general terms, the twenty-first-century political cultures in France and America repeated perennial nationalist claims for the distinctive traits that define a nation and separate it from other peoples and cultures.

Contemporary nationalisms thus carry numerous connections to the long history of nationalist movements and ideologies, even as nationalism has evolved since 1945. The demise of colonialism, the end of the Cold War, the diversity of multicultural nations, and the emergence of international organizations such as the European Union have all helped to transform earlier nationalist thought. The romantic aspiration for coherent nation-states that would embody the cultures of specific ethnic, linguistic, or religious groups, for example, seems far too narrow for complex, multicultural nations in which a shared commitment to civic values has gradually become the central component of nationhood. Equally important, there has been a decisive change since 1945 in the long-existing pattern of great wars between major national powers. Recent wars have become increasingly "asymmetrical" campaigns that powerful nations such as the United States and Great Britain wage against states lacking any comparable military power (Afghanistan, Iraq). Powerful nations still fight long wars, but they mostly fight nonstate enemies, guerrilla bands, or shadowy terrorist groups. The famous land battles that comparably equipped national armies fought in the Napoleonic era and the two world wars now seem almost as remote as battleships and horse-mounted cavalry brigades. Although national and local wars will surely continue to erupt in different regions of the world, new global wars between once-warring nations such as Britain, France, Germany, Japan, China, and the United States have become what the European Union calls "unthinkable."

The history of nationalism since 1945 therefore includes some of the most significant transitions of the modern era, and yet it is also obvious that nationalist politics, economic initiatives, cultural identities, and religious passions have not disappeared. Nationalism constantly arouses strong emotions and fosters violence in places that range from the Balkans, the Middle East, and South Asia to America, Africa, and Russia. People everywhere still learn history in national schools, hear the news through national media, seek political power in national states, and link their personal identities to the collective national identities of families, towns, and cultures. Nationalism, in other words, remains a dynamic, identity-shaping cultural force that constantly evokes the long-developing political and cultural ideas of previous generations. Contemporary nationalists have increasingly pushed many nationalist ideas toward broader, multicultural, or even transnational conceptions of nationhood, but nationalism still influences the daily life of almost everyone in the modern world.

Continuity & Change in the History of Nationalism

This book has ranged across more than two centuries of modern history and discussed numerous themes in nationalist thought, but it has also suggested why it would be impossible to write (or read) a complete, global history of nationalism's vast influence throughout the modern world. The study of nationalist ideologies and conflicts since the late eighteenth century can lead into virtually every sphere of modern politics, economics, culture, diplomacy, warfare, religion, and education. This historical survey has therefore focused only on the most common ideas and cultural assumptions of nationalist movements, stressing themes that have reappeared in many countries and in diverse historical contexts. Although nationalist thinkers and political leaders have emphasized different ideas in various times and places, it is the similarities and continuities among nationalist practices that give this "ism" its enduring historical significance.

These similarities include the overlapping cultural patterns in European and American nationalisms that clearly challenge traditional assumptions about "American exceptionalism." American nationalists have promoted at one time or another almost every nationalist concept that ever appeared in Europe. There are also long-term continuities that link eighteenth-century political revolutions to twentieth-century anticolonialism; and there are long-existing connections between so-called civic and ethnic nationalisms. The analytical dichotomies of "Western" and "Eastern" nationalisms quickly blur when one looks closely at the political goals of "ethnic" national movements or the ethnic themes in the early "civic" nationalisms of countries such as the United States and France. Multiple layers of nationalism constantly intersect in modern societies, so that it is difficult to separate nationalism into distinct political and cultural categories. The continuities in nationalist thought become especially conspicuous in times of international conflict—as we have seen, for example, in the reiterated themes that extend from America's earliest Fourth of July celebrations into contemporary presidential addresses. The claims for a unique national mission or destiny return in every national crisis.

Like all important "isms," of course, nationalism has continued to evolve, especially since the end of the Second World War. A new emphasis on the "multiculturalism" of national societies and the importance of transnational institutions has transformed some key aspects of earlier nationalist thought. Growing support for civic or cosmopolitan nationalisms in the contemporary world has helped to discredit the racist nationalisms of early twentieth-century imperialism and Nazism. The emotional identification with nationalist causes has also varied as people have lived through periods of war, peace, or social conflicts; and new global organizations have enhanced international cooperation. Yet there are also patterns of thought and action that shape nationalism's continuities across the centuries and cultures of modern history. This book has focused almost entirely on the nationalisms of Europe and the United States, but even a brief examination of modern anticolonial and postcolonial nationalisms has noted that the main themes of earlier Western nationalisms have often been repeated in nationalist movements and writings on other continents and in other times. Redefining and expanding the anti-imperial arguments that eighteenth-century Americans had used to justify their Revolutionary War against Great Britain, new anticolonial campaigns destroyed the empires of Western governments and created new national states in Asia, Africa, and the Middle East. Despite all the differences in these modern national movements, nationalist institutions have shown remarkable structural similarities in the cultural processes that construct and sustain national identities.

All nationalisms require narratives about the distinctive historical, cultural, and political traits that make the nation different from all other nations or societies. These narratives of national difference create the boundaries of national space, time, and culture within which people are able to define their national identities. Definitions of identity and difference thus recur in all specific nationalist conceptions of political and cultural independence—which means, ironically, that all nations and nationalisms are similar in that they claim to be different from others. Repeating the earlier political arguments of American and French revolutionaries, nationalists have always believed in the existence of a sovereign "people" whose will should be embodied in government institutions. Democratic and authoritarian political movements alike have typically defined their ideas as the authentic political voice of the "people" or the "true nation," and they have used the language of human rights to justify their demands for national independence and autonomy. The "right" of national sovereignty is seen as essential for the protection of other individual or collective rights and freedoms.

The independent national state has therefore become the universally recognized protection for the sovereignty of the "people," but this political definition of the distinctive national will has usually merged with other definitions of a distinctive national culture. All nationalisms have needed intellectuals who describe the meaning of the national history, language, literature, and art, and who also work to communicate this national narrative through schools, newspapers, and books. The story of national events, leaders, and traditions must always be retold, much as Jules Michelet told the story of France or George Bancroft told the story of America. Modern nationalists have also found effective new ways to narrate the national culture in museums, films, radio, television, Internet websites, and media spectacles.

National stories have often gained the greatest emotional power when they merged with traditional religious ideas about moral duties or reverence for the dead. Nationalists in Europe and North America borrowed from Judaism and Christianity to develop their descriptions of "Chosen Peoples" and "messianic" missions, but other nationalisms have been equally successful in drawing on Islam, Hinduism, Shintoism, and other religious traditions to give transcendent meanings to a national cause. Nationalisms have thus resembled the world's most enduring religions in explaining the essence of individual lives (linked to a transcendent national spirit), in creating a social community (the national "family" that supports and asks sacrifices from everyone), and in providing consolation for death (the nation is eternal). Nationalisms have become closely connected to the deepest human anxieties about life and death, in part because they promise a kind of immortality for the dead and in part because they promise a better life for the nation's children and future generations. Most nationalists have shown a strong interest in the continuing reproduction of the nation and have celebrated the national significance of "good families," "good mothers," and "good fathers." These biological preoccupations have sometimes led to "racial" nationalisms in modern Africa and Asia, which can be compared to theories about race or ethnicity in Europe and America, but even nationalists who ignore race have worried about the purity of families or the dangers of "abnormal" sex. A healthy, well-ordered domestic life becomes linked to a healthy, well-ordered public life in most nationalist definitions of virtuous national identities.

This linkage between the life (or reproduction) of the nation and the life (or death) of the individual gives nationalism much of its exceptional emotional power. Cultural identities and personal identities fuse in nationalist definitions of groups and individuals, which may help to explain why so many modern people have been willing to kill or die in the name of their national states and cultures. Nationalisms have provided crucial ideological justifications for major wars from the time of the French Revolution down to the twentieth-century world wars and the anticolonial wars after 1945. Narratives of national identity have connected the individual to a social community in times of war and peace, offering at least partial satisfaction to the deep human desires for status, immortality, power, freedom, and security. These desires draw strength from both the conscious and unconscious processes of individual psychology and cultural tradition, and they have by no means disappeared from our constantly changing history of political conflict, economic production, and technological innovation.

Although the diverse cultures of the world have become steadily more connected through trade and communications, the identity-shaping definitions of cultural difference continue to construct the meaning of national coherence and the desire for national unity in every modern society. National identities evolve across time, and nationalism may well take new forms over the course of the twenty-first century. The deep, overlapping structures of personal and cultural identity suggest, however, that emotionally charged nationalist identities and conflicts will remain powerful historical forces in the personal lives of modern people and the political cultures of all modern states.

Notes

CHAPTER ONE

1 Nathan Hale's last words appear in Henry Phelps Johnston, *Nathan Hale 1776: Biography and Memorials* (New Haven, 1914), p. 129. Quoted passages of "The Marseillaise" are from the translation in the *New Encyclopaedia Britannica*, 15th ed., vol. 7 (Chicago, 1993), p. 875. Johann Gottlieb Fichte, *Addresses to the German Nation*, trans. and ed. Gregory Moore, with introduction and notes (Cambridge, 2008), p. 186.

2 The historical interest in the premodern history of nations and national identities often stresses the "ethnosymbolic" continuities that are said to link modern nations to long-existing, even ancient collective identities in places such as early Mediterranean societies and the Middle East. See, for example, two books by Anthony D. Smith, *The Nation in History: Historiographical Debates about Ethnicity and Nationalism* (Hanover, N.H., 2000) and *The Antiquity of Nations* (Cambridge, 2004); an earlier study by John A. Armstrong, *Nations before Nationalism* (Chapel Hill, 1982); and the concise account in Stephen Grosby, *Nationalism: A Very Short Introduction* (Oxford, 2005). For a helpful overview of historical approaches to nationalism as well as the recent theoretical debates, see Paul Lawrence, *Nationalism: History and Theory* (Harlow, England, 2005).

3 Hans Kohn, *The Idea of Nationalism: A Study in Its Origins and Background* (New York, 1944), p. 10.

4 Liah Greenfeld, *Nationalism: Five Roads to Modernity* (Cambridge, Mass., 1992), p. 21. Ernest Gellner, by contrast, argues that nationalism emerged from modernization (rather than predating it), most notably in *Nations and Nationalism* (Ithaca, 1983); and Anthony D. Smith repeatedly questions most scholarly assumptions about the modernity of nationalism in a series of influential books, including *The Nation in History*, *The Antiquity of Nations*, and *The Cultural Foundations of Nations: Hierarchy, Covenant, and Republic* (Malden, Mass., and Oxford, 2008).

5 Anthony D. Smith, *Chosen Peoples* (Oxford, 2003), pp. 24–25.

6 Anthony D. Smith, "The Nation: Invented, Imagined, Reconstructed?," in *Reimagining the Nation*, ed. Marjorie Ringrose and Adam J. Lerner (Buckingham and Philadelphia, 1993), pp. 15–16. Similar themes reappear in the more detailed

arguments of Smith's many other books; for example, see *The Ethnic Origins of Nations* (Oxford, 1986) and *National Identity* (London, 1991).

7 Walker Connor, *Ethnonationalism: The Quest for Understanding* (Princeton, 1994), pp. xi, 202; Grosby, *Nationalism: A Very Short Introduction*, p. 14.

8 The American historian Robert H. Wiebe is much closer to the "modernist" than the "ethnosymbolist" view of nationalism, but he also emphasizes the influence of "ancestry" ideas in his concise definition: "Nationalism is the desire among people who believe they share a common ancestry and a common destiny to live under their own government on land sacred to their history." Robert H. Wiebe, *Who We Are: A History of Popular Nationalism* (Princeton, 2002), p. 5.

9 Gellner, *Nations and Nationalism*, pp. 35–39, 138–42 (quotations on pp. 35 and 39). Eric Hobsbawm also emphasizes the connections between nationalism and modernizing economies in *Nations and Nationalism since 1780: Programme, Myth, Reality* (Cambridge, 1990), pp. 9–10, 24–31.

10 David M. Potter, "The Historian's Use of Nationalism and Vice Versa," *American Historical Review* 67, no. 4 (July 1962): 932.

11 Peter Alter, *Nationalism*, 2nd ed. (London, 1994), p. 4.

12 Greenfeld, *Nationalism: Five Roads to Modernity*, pp. 15–16. Greenfeld also discusses these anxieties and the search for empowering "dignity" in a more recent book, *Nationalism and the Mind: Essays on Modern Culture* (Oxford, 2006); see especially chapter 4, "Nationalism and Modernity."

13 Greenfeld, *Nationalism: Five Roads to Modernity*, p. 490.

14 Stuart Hall, "Cultural Identity and Diaspora," in *Colonial Discourse and Post-Colonial Theory: A Reader,* ed. Patrick Williams and Laura Chrisman (New York, 1993), pp. 394–95, 401–2.

15 For examples of (and commentaries on) the evolving emphasis on the role of language in historical experience and cultural identities, see Hayden V. White, *Tropics of Discourse: Essays in Cultural Criticism* (Baltimore, 1978); Dominick LaCapra and Steven L. Kaplan, eds., *Modern European Intellectual History: Reappraisals and New Perspectives* (Ithaca, 1982); Lynn Hunt, ed., *The New Cultural History* (Berkeley, 1989); Frank Ankersmit and Hans Kellner, eds., *A New Philosophy of History* (London, 1995); Donald Kelley, *The Descent of Ideas: The History of Intellectual History* (Burlington, Vt., 2002); Keith Jenkins, *Re-Thinking History* (London, 2003); Elizabeth A. Clark, *History, Theory, Text: Historians and the Linguistic Turn* (Cambridge, Mass., 2004); and Simon Gunn, *History and Cultural Theory* (Harlow, England, 2006).

16 In addition to the helpful survey in Lawrence, *Nationalism: History and Theory,* there are valuable accounts of nationalist thought, institutions, and conflicts in numerous edited collections. See, for example, Geoff Eley and Ronald Grigor Suny, eds., *Becoming National: A Reader* (New York, 1996); Guntram H. Herb and David H. Kaplan, eds., *Nations and Nationalism: A Global Historical Overview,* 4 vols. (Santa Barbara, 2008); Athena S. Leoussi and Steven Grosby, eds., *Nationalism and Ethnosymbolism: History, Culture and Ethnicity in the Formation of Nations* (Edinburgh, 2007); and Stefan Berger and Chris Lorenz, eds., *The*

Contested Nation: Ethnicity, Class, Religion and Gender in National Histories (Basingstoke, England, and New York, 2008). Athena S. Leoussi, ed., *Encyclopaedia of Nationalism* (New Brunswick and London, 2001) is also helpful and provides short, lucid articles on various theories and components of nationalism.

17 Benedict Anderson, *Imagined Communities: Reflections on the Origin and Spread of Nationalism*, 2nd rev. ed. (London and New York, 2006), pp. 6–7.

18 Critics who stress the influence of premodern ethnic communities and memories predictably question Anderson's assumptions about the modern construction of nationalism; see, for example, the respectful critique of Anderson's neglect of "pre-existent ethnic ties" in Anthony D. Smith, *The Antiquity of Nations*, pp. 92–94. Among the many works that address the omission of gender in Anderson's analysis are Andrew Parker, Mary Russo, Doris Sommer, and Patricia Yaeger, eds., *Nationalisms and Sexualities* (New York, 1992); and Ida Blom, Karen Hagemann, and Catherine Hall, eds., *Gendered Nations: Nationalisms and Gender Order in the Long Nineteenth Century* (Oxford and New York, 2000).

19 Eric Hobsbawm, "Introduction: Inventing Traditions," in *The Invention of Tradition*, ed. Eric Hobsbawm and Terence Ranger (Cambridge, 1983), pp. 2, 13–14. Hobsbawm also develops his views on the "inventions" of nationalist history in his later book, *Nations and Nationalism since 1780*.

20 Homi K. Bhabha, "DissemiNation: Time, Narrative, and the Margins of the Modern Nation," in *Nation and Narration*, ed. Homi K. Bhabha (London, 1990), pp. 297, 299–300.

21 Peter Sahlins, *Boundaries: The Making of France and Spain in the Pyrenees* (Berkeley and Los Angeles, 1989), p. 270.

22 Anthony W. Marx, *Faith in Nation: Exclusionary Origins of Nationalism* (Oxford, 2003), pp. 73–112. Although I focus on political transitions that accompanied the later eighteenth-century emphasis on national sovereignty, I think it is also true (as Marx argues) that the early modern exclusions of religious minorities created illiberal social-political patterns that continued to influence nationalism long after modern states had become more democratic.

23 Joep Leerssen, *National Thought in Europe: A Cultural History* (Amsterdam, 2006), p. 17.

24 Paul Lawrence discusses the tendency of historians to express their own nationalist and political assumptions in ostensibly "objective" comparisons of nations and nationalisms; see Lawrence, *Nationalism: History and Theory*, especially chapters 2, 3, and 4.

25 Greenfeld stresses such distinctions in *Nationalism: Five Roads to Modernity*, pp. 11–12, and returns to them often throughout her book. For other discussions of distinctions that have long served to differentiate nationalisms, see Alter, *Nationalism*, pp. 19–20, 26–27; Gregory Jusdanis, *The Necessary Nation* (Princeton, 2001), pp. 134–65; Philip Spencer and Howard Wollman, *Nationalism: A Critical Introduction* (Thousand Oaks, Calif., and London, 2002), pp. 94–120; Hans Kohn, *Prelude to Nation-States: The French and German Experience, 1789–1815* (Princeton, 1967); Louis Dumont, *German Ideology: From France to Germany and*

Back (Chicago, 1994); Rogers Brubaker, *Citizenship and Nationhood in France and Germany* (Cambridge, Mass., 1992) and *Nationalism Reframed: Nationhood and the National Question in the New Europe* (Cambridge, 1996); Friedrich Meinecke, *Cosmopolitanism and the National State*, trans. Robert B. Kimer (Princeton, 1970); and John Plamenatz, "Two Types of Nationalism," in *Nationalism: The Nature and Evolution of the Idea*, ed. Eugene Kamenka (New York, 1976), pp. 22–36.

26 See, for example, the analysis of nationalism's evolving "place" on the left/right spectrum of modern political cultures in Alter, *Nationalism*, pp. 24–54; Benedict Anderson, *Imagined Communities*, pp. 67–111; and Hobsbawm, *Nations and Nationalism since 1780*, pp. 101–30.

27 Jusdanis, *The Necessary Nation*, pp. 89–93 (quotation on p. 162). For another analysis of how nationalisms develop cross-cultural comparisons and evoke anxieties about the dangers of "lagging behind," see Christopher L. Hill, *National History and the World of Nations: Capital, State, and the Rhetoric of History in Japan, France, and the United States* (Durham, N.C., 2008), especially pp. 1–81.

28 A concise discussion of derivative nationalisms can be found in Plamenatz, "Two Types of Nationalism," pp. 29–34; and a critique of the European themes in this concept appears in Partha Chatterjee, *Nationalist Thought and the Colonial World: A Derivative Discourse?* (London, 1986), pp. 1–30. See also the analysis of Euro-centered approaches to nationalism in Dipesh Chakrabarty, *Provincializing Europe: Postcolonial Thought and Historical Difference* (Princeton, 2000); see especially chapter 6, "Nation and Imagination."

29 Leerssen, *National Thought in Europe*, p. 20.

30 Important accounts of how these rapidly spreading political ideas transformed Western political cultures include the synthetic work of R. R. Palmer, *The Age of the Democratic Revolution: A Political History of Europe and America, 1760–1800*, 2 vols. (Princeton, 1959, 1964); the analysis of the French Revolution and new conceptions of human rights in Lynn Hunt, *Politics, Culture, and Class in the French Revolution* (Berkeley, 1984) and *Inventing Human Rights: A History* (New York, 2007); the useful, concise work by Jeremy D. Popkin, *A Short History of the French Revolution*, 5th ed. (Boston, 2010); and Gordon S. Wood, *The Radicalism of the American Revolution: How a Revolution Transformed a Monarchical Society into a Democratic One Unlike Any That Had Ever Existed* (New York, 1991). Wim Klooster's recent account of the revolutionary era, *Revolutions in the Atlantic World: A Comparative History* (New York, 2009), is a more superficial survey, but it extends the earlier work of Palmer and Wood by including the Haitian and Latin American revolutions and discussing social groups that were excluded from "democratizing," national political cultures in this era.

CHAPTER TWO

1 Jane Burbank and Frederick Cooper argue in an important recent book that the ancient Roman Empire and other premodern imperial governments wanted

people to imagine themselves as part of a larger imperial community. An "imperial imaginary" thus contributed to collective identities before the modern era; indeed, the authors suggest that the imperial management of cultural differences might still have some relevance for the organization of multicultural, modern nations (though contemporary nation-states are much more democratic). See Jane Burbank and Frederick Cooper, *Empires in World History: Power and the Politics of Difference* (Princeton, 2010), pp. 1–22, 443–59.

2 On the development of nationalist themes among social elites in early modern England and France, see Liah Greenfeld, *Nationalism: Five Roads to Modernity* (Cambridge, Mass., 1992), pp. 44–70, 145–72. For discussions of early nationalist themes that emerged and evolved in America and France before the late eighteenth-century revolutions, see Jon Butler, *Becoming America: The Revolution before 1776* (Cambridge, Mass., 2000); and David A. Bell, *The Cult of the Nation in France: Inventing Nationalism, 1680–1800* (Cambridge, Mass., 2001), pp. 1–139. Accounts of how the French Revolution redefined the political meaning of nations can be found in Brian Jenkins, *Nationalism in France: Class and Nation since 1789* (London, 1990), pp. 11–22; and Chimène I. Keitner, *The Paradoxes of Nationalism: The French Revolution and Its Meaning for Contemporary Nation Building* (Albany, N.Y., 2007), pp. 23–119.

3 Hans Kohn, *The Idea of Nationalism: A Study in Its Origins and Background* (New York, 1944), p. 237. For a more recent critical analysis of the links (and tensions) between "national" sovereignty and the emergence of postmonarchical, democratic political institutions, see Philip Spencer and Howard Wollman, *Nationalism: A Critical Introduction* (Thousand Oaks, Calif., and London, 2002), pp. 121–31.

4 Jean-Jacques Rousseau, *On the Social Contract*, trans. Donald A. Cress and introduction by Peter Gay (Indianapolis, 1987), pp. 24, 29. On the subsequent history of the political themes that connect nationalisms to modern states, see John Breuilly, *Nationalism and the State*, 2nd ed. (Manchester, England, 1993).

5 Louis Dumont, *German Ideology: From France to Germany and Back* (Chicago, 1994), pp. 7–8. For an insightful cultural history of the ways in which sentimental literature and epistolary novels extended and popularized the emerging legal theories of individual rights, see Lynn Hunt, *Inventing Human Rights: A History* (New York, 2007), pp. 35–112. As Hunt notes in her discussion of the terminology, the common eighteenth-century words were "natural rights" or "rights of man." In the revolutionary era, these terms came to convey legal and political meanings that we now describe as "human rights." I use the term "human rights" (like Hunt) to designate conceptions of individual rights and legal equality that began to accompany the claims for national sovereignty. For an alternative view of when and how the modern idea of universal human rights developed (stressing the concept's emergence and redeployment after the 1960s), see the provocative work of Samuel Moyn, *The Last Utopia: Human Rights in History* (Cambridge, Mass., 2010), especially pp. 1–43. Moyn's argument for the late twentieth-century emergence of ideas about "universal human rights" is unpersuasive. European critics of slavery in the Americas, for example, were already affirming a belief

in transnational, universal rights before 1800. Late eighteenth-century political activists also assumed, however, that the free exercise of individual rights would need the protecting power of independent national governments—which is the only aspect of the earlier era's "rights language" that Moyn recognizes.

6 Rousseau, *Social Contract,* pp. 26, 34.

7 Kohn, *The Idea of Nationalism,* p. 226.

8 For more on nationalism's role in the social and economic transitions to nineteenth-century liberal societies, see Eric Hobsbawm, *Nations and Nationalism since 1780: Programme, Myth, Reality* (Cambridge, 1990), pp. 14–45.

9 Benedict Anderson, *Imagined Communities: Reflections on the Origin and Spread of Nationalism,* 2nd rev. ed. (London and New York, 2006), p. 191. Although I focus here on the political movement in English-speaking North America, it should be stressed that new national movements and identities also emerged in various forms throughout the New World. For perceptive, well-informed descriptions of the distinctive "Americano" identities that evolved during revolutionary struggles against imperial Spain, see John Chasteen, *Americanos: Latin America's Struggle for Independence* (Oxford and New York, 2008). Chasteen and others have challenged or revised much of Anderson's account of early nationalism in Latin America; see, for example, the essays in Sara Castro-Klarén and John Charles Chasteen, eds., *Beyond Imagined Communities: Reading and Writing the Nation in Nineteenth-Century Latin America* (Washington, D.C., and Baltimore, 2003).

10 Thomas Jefferson, "The Declaration of Independence, As Amended by the Committee and by Congress," in *The Papers of Thomas Jefferson,* ed. Julian P. Boyd and others (Princeton, 1950), 1:429, 432.

11 Thomas Paine, "Common Sense," in *Collected Writings,* ed. Eric Foner (New York, 1995), pp. 5–6, 36.

12 David Ramsay, "An Oration on the Advantages of American Independence," in *David Ramsay, 1749–1815: Selections from His Writings,* ed. Robert L. Brunhouse (Transactions of the American Philosophical Society, vol. 55, pt. 4 [Philadelphia, 1965]), pp. 188, 190. Ramsay served in the South Carolina legislature during the revolutionary era, and his oration on freedom (like Jefferson's Declaration of Independence) ignored the obvious contradictions of the slave system in American society.

13 Philip Freneau, "POEM on . . . gallant capt. Paul Jones," in *The Newspaper Verse of Philip Freneau,* ed. Judith R. Hiltner (Troy, N.Y., 1986), pp. 80–81.

14 For a succinct, insightful account of the material objects that helped to diffuse America's new national narrative and identity, see Leora Auslander, *Cultural Revolutions: Everyday Life and Politics in Britain, North America, and France* (Berkeley and Los Angeles, 2009), pp. 81–111. Perceptive descriptions of early American national festivals can be found in David Waldstreicher, *In the Midst of Perpetual Fetes: The Making of American Nationalism, 1776–1820* (Chapel Hill, 1997).

15 Philip Freneau, "[The Popularity of the French Cause]," *National Gazette,* May 22, 1793, in *The Prose of Philip Freneau,* ed. Philip M. Marsh (New Brunswick, N.J., 1955), p. 299. For examples of Freneau's poetic commentary on the

French-American connections, see "On the Fourteenth of July" in *Newspaper Verse*, pp. 498–99.

16 Thomas Paine, *Rights of Man*, in *Collected Writings*, ed. Foner, pp. 549, 555–56.

17 The priest was a Jesuit named Augustin Barruel, who believed that a vast conspiracy of radical freethinkers was responsible for the French Revolution. He denounced *"nationalisme"* in his book *Mémoires pour servir à l'histoire du Jacobinisme* (Memoirs Illustrating the History of Jacobinism) (1798). Herder began to refer to "Nationalismus" at about this same time. For more on the history of the word "nationalism," see Eugene Kamenka, "Political Nationalism—the Evolution of the Idea," in *Nationalism: The Nature and Evolution of the Idea*, ed. Eugene Kamenka (New York, 1976), pp. 8–9; and Jacques Godechot, "The New Concept of the Nation and Its Diffusion in Europe," in *Nationalism in the Age of the French Revolution*, ed. Otto Dann and John Dinwiddy (London, 1988), pp. 13–16.

18 Greenfeld, *Nationalism: Five Roads to Modernity*, pp. 91–188. See also the accounts of prerevolutionary patriotism in Bell, *Cult of the Nation*, pp. 50–106; and Jay M. Smith, *Nobility Reimagined: The Patriotic Nation in Eighteenth-Century France* (Ithaca and London, 2005).

19 Lynn Hunt, *Politics, Culture, and Class in the French Revolution* (Berkeley, 1984), pp. 213–36 (quotation on p. 214). An excellent survey of the complex events, conflicts, and ideas of the French Revolution is available in Jeremy D. Popkin, *A Short History of the French Revolution*, 5th ed. (Boston, 2010).

20 "Declaration of the Rights of Man and Citizen," in *The French Revolution and Human Rights: A Brief Documentary History*, ed. and trans. Lynn Hunt (New York, 1996), p. 78.

21 On the expanding production of pamphlets and the new, popular press during the French Revolution, see Wim Klooster, *Revolutions in the Atlantic World: A Comparative History* (New York, 2009), pp. 48–49; and Jeremy D. Popkin, *Revolutionary News: The Press in France, 1789–1799* (Durham, N.C., 1990).

22 Abbé Sieyès, "What Is the Third Estate?," in *The French Revolution and Human Rights*, ed. and trans. Hunt, pp. 67–69.

23 For analysis of the French Revolution's political exclusion of women and (paradoxical) use of female symbols to represent the republic, see Joan B. Landes, *Visualizing the Nation: Gender, Representation, and Revolution in Eighteenth-Century France* (Ithaca and London, 2001), pp. 1–21; and Joan Wallach Scott, *Only Paradoxes to Offer: French Feminists and the Rights of Man* (Cambridge, Mass., 1996), pp. 19–56. Despite the political barriers, women gained new rights to divorce and equal inheritances, as Suzanne Desan explains in *The Family on Trial in Revolutionary France* (Berkeley and Los Angeles, 2004), pp. 93–177.

24 "Instruction Concerning the Era of the Republic and the Division of the Year, Decreed by the National Convention," in *A Documentary Survey of the French Revolution*, ed. John Hall Stewart (New York, 1951), p. 513. The decree was issued in October 1793.

25 Historians have given much recent attention to the political and cultural activities that converged in revolutionary campaigns to create a new, republican

nation. See, for example, Auslander, *Cultural Revolutions*, pp. 113–48; and Hunt, *Politics, Culture, and Class*, pp. 19–119. Music and the "theater" of politics are examined in Laura Mason, *Singing the French Revolution: Popular Culture and Politics, 1787–1799* (Ithaca and London, 1996); and Paul Friedland, *Political Actors: Representative Bodies and Theatricality in the Age of the French Revolution* (Ithaca and London, 2002).

26 "Statement of French Foreign Policy" (April 14, 1792) and "Circular from the Paris Jacobins to Local Branches of the Club" (April 5, 1793), in *Documentary Survey of the French Revolution*, ed. Stewart, pp. 285, 287, 428. For discussion of local responses to the Jacobin policies in Paris, see Alan Forrest, *Paris, the Provinces and the French Revolution* (London, 2004).

27 *Chant du départ* quoted in John A. Lynn, *The Bayonets of the Republic: Motivation and Tactics in the Army of Revolutionary France, 1791–94* (Urbana, Ill., 1984), p. 148.

28 Political messages circulated constantly in the popular (and fast-evolving) "songs in the street" as well as in the more enduring military songs, such as "The Marseillaise"; see Mason, *Singing the French Revolution*, pp. 34–60, 93–103.

29 "Decree Establishing the Levy *en masse*," in *Documentary Survey of the French Revolution*, ed. Stewart, p. 473.

30 Although the mobilization never reached the ideal "*levée en masse*" that later French republicans imagined, the revolutionary idea of an entire "nation in arms" gained new power whenever modern nations waged "total war" against their enemies. See Alan Forrest, *The Legacy of the French Revolutionary Wars: The Nation-in-Arms in French Republican Memory* (Cambridge, 2009); and David A. Bell, *The First Total War: Napoleon's Europe and the Birth of Warfare as We Know It* (New York, 2007), pp. 84–153.

31 For an informative summary of the revolutionary French state's use and abuse of foreigners, see Michael Rapport, *Nationality and Citizenship in Revolutionary France: The Treatment of Foreigners, 1789–1799* (Oxford, 2000), pp. 327–44.

32 Rousseau, *Social Contract*, pp. 96–102; Hunt, *Politics, Culture, and Class*, pp. 87–119; and Maurice Agulhon, *Marianne into Battle: Republican Imagery and Symbolism in France, 1789–1880*, trans. Janet Lloyd (Cambridge, 1981), pp. 30–36.

33 S. Sherlock, *Opinion sur la necessité de rendre l'instruction publique commune à tous les enfants des Français* (Year VII [1799]), quoted in Mona Ozouf, *Festivals and the French Revolution*, trans. Alan Sheridan (Cambridge, Mass., 1988), p. 200.

34 François de Neufchâteau, *Hymn to Liberty*, quoted in Emmet Kennedy, *A Cultural History of the French Revolution* (New Haven, 1989), p. 281.

35 On this Bonapartist transition within and beyond France, see Jenkins, *Nationalism in France*, pp. 31–42; Godechot, "The New Concept of the Nation," pp. 16–26; and Bell, *First Total War*, pp. 186–301.

36 Napoleon's empire disrupted political institutions and social hierarchies throughout Europe, thereby attracting local supporters who challenged traditional elites. French imperialism thus had a major impact on both the political conflicts and nationalist cultural movements *within* almost every European nation. For examples of how historians interpret this critical era in various countries, see Philip

G. Dwyer and Alan Forrest, eds., *Napoleon and His Empire: Europe, 1804–1814* (London and New York, 2007); Charles J. Esdaile, ed., *Popular Resistance in the French Wars: Patriots, Partisans and Land Pirates* (London and New York, 2005); and Michael Broers, *The Napoleonic Empire in Italy, 1796–1814: Cultural Imperialism in a European Context?* (London and New York, 2005).

37 For discussion of both the British mobilization and its possible effects on the nation's political culture, see Linda Colley, *Britons: Forging the Nation, 1707–1837* (New Haven, 1992), pp. 283–319, 371–72 (quotation on p. 303). Although the national army and navy grew steadily during the wars with France, Britain's government did not resort to military conscription.

38 Edmund Burke, *Reflections on the Revolution in France*, ed. J. G. A. Pocock (Indianapolis, 1987), pp. 27–28, 75–76. On the conservative themes in English national responses to the French Revolution, see John Dinwiddy, "England," in *Nationalism in the Age of the French Revolution*, pp. 53–70. The popularity of Paine's writings, however, showed that other nationalists wanted to bring "French" ideas into Britain.

39 Friedrich von Gentz to Christian Garve, December 5, 1790, quoted in Hans Kohn, *Prelude to Nation-States: The French and German Experience, 1789–1815* (Princeton, 1967), pp. 133–34.

40 Franz Dumont, "The Rhineland," in *Nationalism in the Age of the French Revolution*, pp. 157–70. Older but still helpful accounts of both the German and British responses to France's revolutionary influence appear in R. R. Palmer, *The Age of the Democratic Revolution: A Political History of Europe and America, 1760–1800* (Princeton, 1959, 1964), 2:425–505.

41 On the admiration for France and liberal forms of nationalism in Germany, see Kohn, *Prelude to Nation-States*, pp. 144–57; Dumont, *German Ideology*, pp. 90–134; and Peter Alter, "Nationalism and Liberalism in Modern German History," in *Nationality, Patriotism and Nationalism in Liberal Democratic Societies*, ed. Roger Michener (St. Paul, Minn., 1993), pp. 81–87. For a summary of how Prussian reformers drew lessons from their French enemy throughout the Napoleonic wars, see Matthew Levinger, "The Prussian Reform Movement and the Rise of Enlightened Nationalism," in *The Rise of Prussia, 1700–1830*, ed. Philip G. Dwyer (Harlow, England, 2000), pp. 259–77.

42 Friedrich Gentz, *The French and American Revolutions Compared*, trans. John Quincy Adams, in Stefan T. Possony, *Three Revolutions* (Chicago, 1959), pp. 67, 86.

43 Johann Gottfried von Herder, *Reflections on the Philosophy of the History of Mankind*, trans. T. O. Churchill and ed. Frank E. Manuel (Chicago, 1968), p. 7.

44 Johann Gottlieb Fichte, *Addresses to the German Nation*, trans. and ed. Gregory Moore, with introduction and notes (Cambridge, 2008), pp. 184, 187. For analysis of Fichte's philosophical responses to the French Revolution (which were initially very positive), see the insightful study by Anthony J. LaVopa, *Fichte: The Self and the Calling of Philosophy, 1762–1799* (Cambridge, 2001), pp. 100–130.

45 Ernst Moritz Arndt, *Geist der Zeit*, pt. 3 (1814), quoted in Hagen Schulze, *The Course of German Nationalism: From Frederick the Great to Bismarck, 1763–1867*,

trans. Sarah Hansbury-Tension (Cambridge, 1991), p. 50; Josef Görres, in the *Rheinischer Merkur* (May 11, 1815), quoted in Kohn, *Prelude to Nation-States*, p. 293. Such views express what David Bell calls the "apocalyptic" language of modern warfare; see Bell's commentary on Germany in *First Total War*, pp. 293–301, and the helpful survey of Prussian literary culture in Otto W. Johnston, *The Myth of a Nation: Literature and Politics in Prussia under Napoleon* (Columbia, S.C., 1989).

CHAPTER THREE

1 R. J. B. Bosworth, *Nationalism* (Harlow, England, 2007), p. 2. Anthony Smith examines the concept of "sacred homelands" in *Chosen Peoples* (Oxford, 2003), pp. 131–65.

2 Johann Gottfried von Herder, *Reflections on the Philosophy of the History of Mankind*, trans. T. O. Churchill and ed. Frank E. Manuel (Chicago, 1968), pp. 8, 10, 12.

3 Johann Gottlieb Fichte, *Addresses to the German Nation*, trans. and ed. Gregory Moore, with introduction and notes (Cambridge, 2008), pp. 48–49.

4 Joseph Mazzini, *The Duties of Man and Other Essays*, (London, 1907), pp. 53, 55. The introduction to a recent translation of Mazzini's writings rightly stresses his interest in collaboration among nations, but the passages from *Duties of Man* in this translation do not include his comments on Italian lands. See Giuseppe Mazzini, *A Cosmopolitanism of Nations: Giuseppe Mazzini's Writings on Democracy, Nation Building, and International Relations*, ed. Stefano Recchia and Nadia Urbinati, introduction by Recchia and Urbinati, and trans. Recchia (Princeton, 2009). For recent analysis of land, the "frontier," and "manifest destiny" in American nationalism, see Christopher L. Hill, *National History and the World of Nations: Capital, State, and the Rhetoric of History in Japan, France, and the United States* (Durham, N.C., 2008), pp. 82–118; and for an insightful discussion of "land" in a later era of British nationalism, see Paul Readman, *Land and Nation in England: Patriotism, National Identity, and the Politics of Land, 1880–1914* (Woodbridge, England, and Rochester, N.Y., 2008).

5 Herder, *Reflections on the Philosophy*, p. 7; Fichte, *Addresses*, p. 161.

6 H. H. Cludius, excerpt from *Musterpredigten über alle Evangelien und Episteln des Jahres, so wie über freie Texte und Casualfälle . . .*, vol. 9 (1819), p. 327; quoted in Arlie J. Hoover, *The Gospel of Nationalism: German Patriotic Preaching from Napoleon to Versailles* (Stuttgart, 1986), p. 60.

7 Fichte, *Addresses*, pp. 166–67.

8 For an introduction to the "communicative acts" that link politics to language, see Michael Townson, *Mother-Tongue and Fatherland: Language and Politics in German* (Manchester, England, 1992), pp. 6–33. For examples of the cultural diffusion of nationalist ideas, see George L. Mosse, *The Nationalization of the Masses: Political Symbolism and Mass Movements in Germany from the Napoleonic Wars through the Third Reich* (New York, 1975).

9 Grégoire's report to the National Convention appears in Michel de Certeau, Dominique Julia, and Jacques Revel, *Une politique de la langue: la Révolution*

française et les patois, l'enquête de Grégoire (Paris, 1975), pp. 300–317. For a useful analysis of the complex campaign for a "national language" in revolutionary France, see David A. Bell, *The Cult of the Nation in France: Inventing Nationalism, 1680–1800* (Cambridge, Mass., 2001), pp. 169–97.

10 Johann Georg Breidenstein, *Predigt am Dank- und Befreiungsfeste zu Homburg vor der Höhe den achten Mai 1814* (1814); quoted in Hoover, *Gospel of Nationalism*, p. 60. Fichte, *Addresses*, p. 67.

11 Adam Mickiewicz, *Les Slaves: Cours professé au Collège de France (1842–1844)* (Paris, 1914), pp. 323–24. On the problem of creating pure national cultures, see Homi Bhabha's introduction and concluding essay ("DissemiNation: Time, Narrative, and the Margins of the Modern Nation") in *Nation and Narration*, ed. Homi K. Bhabha (London, 1990), pp. 1–7, 291–322.

12 Grégoire, "Sur la necessité et les moyens d'anéantir les patois...," in *Une politique de la langue*, p. 303.

13 Bertrand Barère, "Rapport du Comité de Salut Public sur les idiomes," in *Une politique de la langue*, p. 295. For more on how the linguistic debates and policies of the French Revolution might be compared to religious missions in earlier eras, see David A. Bell, "Lingua Populi, Lingua Dei: Language, Religion, and the Origins of French Revolutionary Nationalism," *American Historical Review* 100, no. 5 (December 1995): 1403–37.

14 Fichte, *Addresses*, p. 19.

15 Mazzini, *Duties of Man*, p. 87. The essays in this book were originally published in the 1840s and 1850s. For the history of how other exiled Italian nationalists sought to educate their compatriots, see Maurizio Isabella, *Risorgimento in Exile: Italian Émigrés and the Liberal International in the Post-Napoleonic Era* (New York and Oxford, 2009).

16 On the general diffusion of nationalist ideas and languages in education, see Ernest Gellner, *Nations and Nationalism* (Ithaca, 1983), pp. 19–62. For examples of education policies in specific national contexts, see R. R. Palmer, *The Improvement of Humanity: Education and the French Revolution* (Princeton, 1985) (data on government expenditures, pp. 334–35); and (for a later period) Eric Hobsbawm, "Mass-Producing Traditions: Europe, 1870–1914," in *The Invention of Tradition* (Cambridge, 1983), ed. Eric Hobsbawm and Terence Ranger, pp. 263–307. On the enduring role of schools and the army in shaping national identities, see Alan Forrest, *The Legacy of French Revolutionary Wars: The Nation-in-Arms in French Republican Memory* (Cambridge, 2009), pp. 155–95; and Eugen Weber, *Peasants into Frenchmen: The Modernization of Rural France, 1870–1914* (Stanford, Calif., 1976), pp. 292–338.

17 Benedict Anderson, *Imagined Communities: Reflections on the Origin and Spread of Nationalism*, 2nd rev. ed. (London and New York, 2006), p. 46. On the role of communications in nationalism, see Karl W. Deutsch, *Nationalism and Social Communication: An Inquiry into the Foundations of Nationality* (New York, 1953), pp. 71–78.

18 Fichte, *Addresses*, p. 161.

19 Ralph Waldo Emerson, "The American Scholar," in *Selected Essays*, ed. Larzer Ziff (New York, 1982), pp. 103–5.

20 For examples of such arguments, see Elie Kedourie, *Nationalism*, 4th ed. (Oxford, 1993), pp. 33–43; and Liah Greenfeld, *Nationalism: Five Roads to Modernity* (Cambridge, Mass., 1992), pp. 293–352.

21 Joep Leerssen, *National Thought in Europe: A Cultural History* (Amsterdam, 2006), p. 195.

22 Benedict Anderson, *Imagined Communities*, pp. 24–36. On the importance of novels in the shaping of national identities, see also the essays by Timothy Brennan ("The National Longing for Form") and Doris Sommer ("Irresistible Romance: The Foundational Fictions of Latin America") in *Nation and Narration*, ed. Bhabha, pp. 44–98. Sommer has extended her analysis of novels and nationalism in *Foundational Fictions: The National Romances of Latin America* (Berkeley, 1991), stressing the literary themes of romance, desire, and memory that Christopher Hill also examines in the national literatures of Japan and America in *National History*, pp. 163–208.

23 On the political significance of Jacob Grimm and other German philologists, see Townson, *Mother-Tongue and Fatherland*, pp. 80–110; and Leerssen, *National Thought in Europe*, pp. 179–85.

24 Fichte, *Addresses*, pp. 64–65, 97.

25 Mickiewicz, *Les Slaves*, pp. 4, 12, 21–23. For a detailed study of Mickiewicz's literary work, politics, and romantic contributions to Polish nationalism, see Roman Koropeckyj, *Adam Mickiewicz: The Life of a Romantic* (Ithaca and London, 2008).

26 Emerson, "The Poet," in *Selected Essays*, pp. 261, 263, 271, 281. It might be argued that Walt Whitman would soon claim the role of Emerson's "American poet." See, for example, David Simpson, "Destiny Made Manifest: The Styles of Whitman's Poetry," in *Nation and Narration*, ed. Bhabha, pp. 177–96.

27 Ernest Renan, "What Is a Nation?" (1882), trans. Martin Thom; in *Nation and Narration*, ed. Bhabha, p. 11.

28 Ibid., p. 19.

29 For an introduction to this era's contribution to a new "historical-mindedness," see Stephen Bann, *Romanticism and the Rise of History* (New York, 1995), pp. 3–29. Also see various essays in Stefan Berger, Mark Donovan, and Kevin Passmore, eds., *Writing National Histories: Western Europe since 1800* (London and New York, 1999); Stefan Berger, ed., *Writing the Nation: A Global Perspective* (Basingstoke, England, and New York, 2007); and Stefan Berger and Chris Lorentz, eds., *The Contested Nation: Ethnicity, Class, Religion and Gender in National Histories* (Basingstoke, England, and New York, 2008).

30 Fichte, *Addresses*, p. 193.

31 Leopold von Ranke, "On the Relation of and Distinction between History and Politics" (1836), in *The Secret of World History: Selected Writings on the Art and Science of History*, ed. and trans. Roger Wines (New York, 1981), pp. 110, 112.

32 Leopold von Ranke, "The Great Powers" (1833), in *The Secret of World History*, ed. and trans. Wines, pp. 142–43.

33 Jules Michelet, *History of the French Revolution*, trans. Charles Cocks and ed. Gordon Wright (Chicago, 1967), pp. 3, 13.

34 Ibid., p. 449.

35 Jules Michelet, *The People*, trans. John P. McKay (Urbana, Ill., 1973), p. 9.

36 Ibid., pp. 19, 183, 188, 199. Michelet's historical claim to speak for the deceased "people" of France suggests how nationalists sought to fuse selfhood with a collective identity of nationhood. For analysis of this complex historical fusion, see Vivian Kogan, *The "I" of History: Self-Fashioning and National Consciousness in Jules Michelet* (Chapel Hill, 2006).

CHAPTER FOUR

1 For a discussion of the religious components of modern national identities, see the essays in Peter van der Veer and Hartmut Lehmann, eds., *Nation and Religion: Perspectives on Europe and Asia* (Princeton, 1999); and the wide-ranging analysis in Anthony D. Smith, *Chosen Peoples* (Oxford, 2003). Other valuable accounts of nations and religions can be found in Mary Anne Perkins, *Nation and Word, 1770–1850: Religious and Metaphysical Language in European National Consciousness* (Aldershot, England, 1999), esp. pp. 113–88; and Philip W. Barker, *Religious Nationalism in Modern Europe: If God Be for Us* (London and New York, 2009).

2 Carlton J. H. Hayes, "Nationalism as a Religion," in *Essays on Nationalism* (New York, 1966), pp. 93–125 (quotations on pp. 95–96).

3 For analysis of various overlapping themes in nationalism and religion, see Conor Cruise O'Brien, *God Land: Reflections on Religion and Nationalism* (Cambridge, Mass., 1988); and the essays in William R. Hutchison and Hartmut Lehmann, eds., *Many Are Chosen: Divine Election and Western Nationalism* (Minneapolis, 1984). Religious themes became especially prominent in early American nationalism, as Nicholas Guyatt shows with persuasive examples in *Providence and the Invention of the United States, 1607–1876* (Cambridge, 2007).

4 For a succinct discussion of how anxieties about death might contribute to nationalism, see Joshua Searle-White, *The Psychology of Nationalism* (New York, 2001), pp. 67–77.

5 Anthony D. Smith, *Chosen Peoples*, p. 15.

6 Jules Michelet, *The People*, trans. John P. McKay (Urbana, Ill., 1973), pp. 180–81.

7 Joseph Mazzini, *The Duties of Man and Other Essays*, (London, 1907), p. 29. The quotation comes from a section in *Duties* entitled "God," which was first published in 1844.

8 For a discussion of the Protestant national feeling in Britain, see Liah Greenfeld, *Nationalism: Five Roads to Modernity* (Cambridge, Mass., 1992), pp. 53–66; Linda Colley, *Britons: Forging the Nation, 1707–1837* (New Haven, 1992), pp. 11–54; and Hugh McLeod, "Protestantism and British National Identity, 1815–1945," in *Nation and Religion*, ed. van der Veer and Lehmann, pp. 44–70. On Protestantism and American nationalism, see O'Brien, *God Land*, pp. 52–63; James H.

Moorhead, "The American Israel: Protestant Tribalism and Universal Mission," in *Many Are Chosen*, ed. Hutchison and Lehmann, pp. 145–66; Ernest Lee Tuveson, *Redeemer Nation: The Idea of America's Millennial Role* (Chicago, 1968); and Patrice Higonnet, *Attendant Cruelties: Nation and Nationalism in American History* (New York, 2007), pp. xx–xxxix, 5–15.

9 Guyatt, *Providence and the Invention of the United States*, p. 4. Anthony Smith examines the long-developing, religious conceptions of "chosen peoples" and collective "covenants" in *Chosen Peoples*, pp. 44–65; and Stephen Grosby stresses the ancient Jewish origins of these ideas in *Nationalism: A Very Short Introduction* (Oxford, 2005), especially pp. 97–101.

10 Friedrich Schleiermacher to Baron von Stein, November 24, 1809 (?), quoted in Hans Kohn, *Prelude to Nation-States: The French and German Experience, 1789–1815* (Princeton, 1967), p. 249.

11 Adam Mickiewicz, *Les Slaves: Cours professé au Collège de France (1842–1844)* (Paris, 1914), pp. 49, 120.

12 Mazzini, *Duties of Man*, pp. 54–56.

13 Ibid., pp. 58–59.

14 Adam Mickiewicz, *The Books of the Polish Nation and Pilgrims* (1832), in *Poems by Adam Mickiewicz*, ed. and trans. George R. Noyes (New York, 1944), p. 380. For more examples of Messianic nationalism in nineteenth-century Europe, see Perkins, *Nation and Word*, pp. 175–88, and Alan Davies, *The Crucified Nation: A Motif in Modern Nationalism* (Brighton, England, and Portland, Oregon, 2008).

15 Mazzini, *Duties of Man*, p. 57.

16 Johann Dräseke, *Vaterlandsfreude: Eine Dankpredigt zur Feier des Tages von Leipzig* (1815), p. 24; quoted in Arlie J. Hoover, *The Gospel of Nationalism: German Patriotic Preaching from Napoleon to Versailles* (Stuttgart, 1986), p. 73.

17 Hayes, "Nationalism as a Religion," pp. 104–25. Hayes sometimes suggested that nationalism had replaced traditional religion, but he also referred to the intersection of nationalist and religious practices as a "syncretism." See also the still-useful analysis in Salo Wittmayer Baron, *Modern Nationalism and Religion* (New York, 1947).

18 For a perceptive analysis of America's early Independence Day celebrations, see David Waldstreicher, *In the Midst of Perpetual Fetes: The Making of American Nationalism. 1776–1820* (Chapel Hill, 1997), pp. 1–173.

19 Johann Gottlieb Fichte, *Addresses to the German Nation*, trans. and ed. Gregory Moore, with introduction and notes (Cambridge, 2008), pp. 75–76.

20 Mazzini, "Faith and the Future," in *Duties of Man*, p. 183; Mazzini wrote this essay in 1835.

21 For more on the role of national monuments in nationalist ideologies, see George L. Mosse, *The Nationalization of the Masses: Political Symbolism and Mass Movements in Germany from the Napoleonic Wars through the Third Reich* (New York, 1975), pp. 47–72; and Adam J. Lerner, "The Nineteenth-Century Monument and the Embodiment of National Time," in *Reimagining the Nation*, ed. Marjorie Ringrose and Adam J. Lerner (Buckingham and Philadelphia, 1993), pp. 176–96.

The later history of French monuments and memorials for deceased soldiers is analyzed with excellent examples and insights in Daniel J. Sherman, *The Construction of Memory in Interwar France* (Chicago, 1999).

22 Abraham Keteltas, *God Arising and Pleading His People's Cause . . . a sermon preached October 5, 1777 in . . . Newburyport* (1777), in *Nationalism and Religion in America: Concepts of American Identity and Mission*, ed. Winthrop S. Hudson (New York, 1970), pp. 49, 52–53. For an extended discussion of the religious themes in America's revolutionary war, see Guyatt, *Providence and the Invention of the United States*, pp. 95–133.

23 Diverse examples of the fusing tendencies in national and religious thought are discussed in van der Veer and Lehmann, eds., *Nation and Religion*. As the editors note in their introduction (p. 7), "Death and the afterlife form the stuff of which both religion and nationalism are made." Historians have also become increasingly interested in the ways that entire national populations as well as individuals may be affected by the trauma of violence and the wartime deaths of soldiers and civilians. See, for example, the discussion of such issues in Dominick LaCapra, *Writing History, Writing Trauma* (Baltimore, 2001), and also LaCapra's discussion of "trauma studies" in *History in Transit: Experience, Identity, Critical Theory* (Ithaca, 2004), pp. 106–43.

24 Ernst Moritz Arndt, *Geist der Zeit*, part 3 (1813), quoted in Kohn, *Prelude to Nation-States*, p. 261.

25 Fichte, *Addresses*, pp. 103–4.

26 Ibid., p. 108.

27 Mazzini, *Duties of Man*, p. 55.

28 Quoted passages of "The Marseillaise" are from the translation in the *New Encyclopaedia Britannica*, 15th ed., vol. 7 (Chicago, 1993), p. 875. For a more detailed account of the military themes in national anthems, see George L. Mosse's essay "National Anthems: The Nation Militant" in his book *Confronting the Nation: Jewish and Western Nationalism* (Hanover, N.H., 1993), pp. 13–26. On the theme of sacrifice and nationalist thought, see Jean Bethke Elshtain, "Sovereignty, Identity, Sacrifice," in *Reimagining the Nation*, ed. Ringrose and Lerner, pp. 159–75.

29 Anthony D. Smith, *Chosen Peoples*, p. 42.

CHAPTER FIVE

1 For examples of such "anti-essentialist" views of gender, race, and nationality, see the following essays in Geoff Eley and Ronald Grigor Suny, eds., *Becoming National: A Reader* (New York and Oxford, 1996): Anne McClintock, "'No Longer in a Future Heaven': Nationalism, Gender and Race," pp. 260–84; Stuart Hall, "Ethnicity: Identity and Difference," pp. 339–49; and Paul Gilroy, "One Nation under a Groove: The Cultural Politics of 'Race' and Racism in Britain," pp. 352–69. Other critiques of assumptions about the "natural" reality of gender, ethnicity, or nationality appear in Ida Blom, Karen Hagemann, and Catherine Hall, eds., *Gendered Nations: Nationalisms and Gender Order in the Long Nineteenth*

Century (Oxford and New York, 2000); Stefan Berger and Chris Lorenz, eds., *The Contested Nation: Ethnicity, Class, Religion and Gender in National Histories* (Basingstoke, England, and New York, 2008); Nira Yuval-Davis, *Gender and Nation* (London and Thousand Oaks, Calif., 1997); and Joan Wallach Scott, *Gender and the Politics of History*, rev. ed. (New York, 1999), esp. pp. 28–50.

2 Linda Colley, *Britons: Forging the Nation, 1707–1837* (New Haven, 1992), p. 252.

3 Maurice Agulhon, *Marianne into Battle: Republican Imagery and Symbolism in France, 1789–1880*, trans. Janet Lloyd (Cambridge, 1981), p. 129.

4 Michael D. Biddiss, ed., *Gobineau: Selected Political Writings* (New York, 1970), p. 89. This passage comes from Gobineau's *Essay on the Inequality of the Races* (1853–55).

5 Ralph Waldo Emerson, *The Collected Works of Ralph Waldo Emerson*, vol. 5, *English Traits*, with historical introduction by Philip Nicoloff, notes by Robert E. Burkholder, and textual introduction by Douglas Emery Wilson (Cambridge, Mass., 1994), pp. 36–37, 132. *English Notes* was first published in 1856.

6 Ida Blom, "Gender and Nation in International Comparison," in *Gendered Nations*, ed. Blom, Hagemann, and Hall, p. 8.

7 Joseph Mazzini, *The Duties of Man and Other Essays*, (London, 1907), pp. 54–55. The quotation comes from a chapter entitled "Duties to Country," which Mazzini first published in 1858; it has been republished in a slightly revised translation in Giuseppe Mazzini, *A Cosmopolitanism of Nations: Giuseppe Mazzini's Writings on Democracy, Nation Building, and International Relations*, ed. Stefano Recchia and Nadia Urbinati, introduction by Recchia and Urbinati, and trans. Recchia (Princeton, 2009), pp. 92–96.

8 George L. Mosse, *Nationalism and Sexuality: Middle-Class Morality and Sexual Norms in Modern Europe* (Madison, Wisc., 1985), pp. 9, 13. For more on the fusion of ideas about gender, sexual behavior, and nations, see the essays in Andrew Parker, Mary Russo, Doris Sommer, and Patricia Yaeger, eds., *Nationalisms and Sexualities* (New York, 1992); and specific French views are analyzed in Judith Surkis, *Sexing the Citizen: Morality and Masculinity in France, 1870–1920* (Ithaca, 2006).

9 Mosse, *Nationalism and Sexuality*, pp. 64, 98. Images of women were also used to represent the abstract meanings of both republicanism and liberty during the French Revolution; see, for example, Joan B. Landes, *Visualizing the Nation: Gender, Representation, and Revolution in Eighteenth-Century France* (Ithaca and London, 2001), pp. 24–80.

10 Adam Mickiewicz, *Les Slaves: Cours professé au Collège de France (1842–1844)* (Paris, 1914), p. 338.

11 Ibid.

12 Mazzini, *Duties of Man*, p. 61.

13 Jules Michelet, *The People*, trans. John P. McKay (Urbana, Ill., 1973), pp. 57, 167.

14 Mazzini, *Duties of Man*, p. 61. For more discussion of how nationalists have defined women's roles in both the biological and cultural reproduction of nations, see Yuval-Davis, *Gender and Nation*, pp. 26–67.

15 Johann Gottlieb Fichte, *Addresses to the German Nation*, trans. and ed. Gregory Moore, with introduction and notes (Cambridge, 2008), pp. 101–2, 108. Fichte himself had one son, who also became a philosopher.

16 Michelet, *The People*, pp. 120, 209.

17 Mazzini, *Duties of Man*, pp. 61–62, 65–66. All of these passages appeared in a chapter called "Duties to the Family," which was first published in 1858. For an excellent analysis of how families shape the national identities of individuals, see Etienne Balibar, "The Nation Form: History and Ideology," in *Becoming National*, ed. Eley and Suny, pp. 132–49.

18 George Mosse describes the nationalist anxiety about "nonproductive" sexual behavior in *Nationalism and Sexuality*, pp. 23–40.

19 Michelet, *The People*, p. 168. For information on the enduring French anxiety about birth rates, see Karen Offen, "Depopulation, Nationalism, and Feminism in Fin-de-Siècle France," *American Historical Review* 89, no. 3 (June 1984): 648–76.

20 For more on "captivity narratives" and early American national identity, see Carroll Smith-Rosenberg, "Captured Subjects/Savage Others: Violently Engendering the New American," *Gender and History* 5, no. 2 (June 1993): 177–95. Anxieties about captivity, gender, and nationality also appeared in English novels; see Nancy Armstrong, "Captivity and Cultural Capital in the English Novel," in *Revolutionary Histories: Transatlantic Cultural Nationalism, 1775–1815*, ed. W. M. Verhoeven (Basingstoke, England, and New York, 2002), pp. 104–21.

21 The French anxiety about sexual assaults from German soldiers is discussed in Ouriel Reshef, *Guerre, Mythes et Caricature: au berceau d'une mentalité française* (Paris, 1984), pp. 37–87, 153–207; on the French view of German sexual threats at the time of World War I, see Ruth Harris, "The 'Child of the Barbarian': Rape, Race and Nationalism in France during the First World War," *Past and Present* 141 (November 1993): 170–206.

22 Fichte, *Addresses*, pp. 47, 55–56, 58–59, 60, 96–97.

23 Friedrich Meinecke, *Cosmopolitanism and the National State*, trans. Robert B. Kimer (Princeton, 1970), p. 9.

24 Robert Knox, *The Races of Men: A Fragment* (Philadelphia, 1850; repr., 1969), pp. 43, 46, 48, 221.

25 Ibid., p. 49.

26 Emerson, *English Traits*, pp. 24–28, 75–76, 155, 177. It should be noted that the word "race" was often used in the nineteenth century somewhat like "nation" is used in modern languages, but Emerson's view of Americans as a modern extension of the British "race" also suggested themes of racial essentialism.

27 George Bancroft, *History of the United States, from the Discovery of the American Continent* (Boston, 1834–75), 1:180–82, 2:452.

28 Ibid., 3:302.

29 The later nineteenth-century American historical emphasis on a national "Anglo-Saxon" racial identity is discussed in Christopher L. Hill, *National History and the World of Nations: Capital, State, and the Rhetoric of History in Japan,*

France, and the United States (Durham, N.C., 2008), pp. 196–201, 208–14; and for an overview of how race has continued to shape American views of history, see James D. Anderson, "How We Learn about Race through History," in *Learning History in America: Schools, Cultures, and Politics*, ed. Lloyd Kramer, Donald Reid, and William L. Barney (Minneapolis, 1994), pp. 87–106.

30 Biddiss, ed., *Gobineau*, p. 59.

31 Ibid., pp. 65, 68; see also pp. 90, 162.

32 Ibid., pp. 136–40 (first quotation on p. 140), 172–73. For more on the growing significance of racist theories in nineteenth-century European nationalisms, see Joep Leerssen, *National Thought in Europe: A Cultural History* (Amsterdam, 2006), pp. 204–18; and Hugo Frey and Stefan Jordan, "National Historians and the Discourse of the Other: France and Germany," in *The Contested Nation*, ed. Berger and Lorenz, pp. 200–230.

33 Fichte, *Addresses*, pp. 195–96.

34 Michelet, *The People*, pp. 192–93, 209.

35 Ibid., p. 210.

36 Albert J. Beveridge, "On the Mission of the American Race," speech in the U.S. Senate, January 9, 1900, excerpted in Louis L. Snyder, *The Idea of Racialism: Its Meaning and History* (Princeton, 1962), p. 168.

CHAPTER SIX

1 For a historical analysis of the religious themes in American nationalism, see Ernest Lee Tuveson, *Redeemer Nation: The Idea of America's Millennial Role* (Chicago, 1968); Conor Cruise O'Brien, *God Land: Reflections on Religion and Nationalism* (Cambridge, Mass., 1988); Nicholas Guyatt, *Providence and the Invention of the United States, 1607–1876* (Cambridge, 2007); Paul C. Nagel, *This Sacred Trust: American Nationality, 1798–1898* (Oxford and New York, 1971); and the early American texts in Winthrop S. Hudson, ed., *Nationalism and Religion in America: Concepts of American Identity and Mission* (New York, 1970). Patrice Higonnet offers a somewhat polemical analysis/critique of America's long-developing religious nationalism in *Attendant Cruelties: Nation and Nationalism in American History* (New York, 2007), pp. xv–1, 3–76; and for more on the American conceptions of national uniqueness, see Seymour Martin Lipset, *American Exceptionalism: A Double-Edged Sword* (New York, 1996).

2 [John L. O'Sullivan], "The Great Nation of Futurity," *United States Magazine and Democratic Review* 6 (November 1839): 427.

3 [John L. O'Sullivan], "Annexation," *United States Magazine and Democratic Review* 17 (July/August 1845): 5. Guyatt offers perceptive analysis of the religious components of "manifest destiny" in *Providence and the Invention of the United States*, pp. 216–30.

4 Herman Melville, *White-Jacket; or, The World in a Man-of-War*, ed. A. R. Humphreys (Oxford, 1966), p. 158. For insightful discussions of Melville's view of

America's national identity, see Andrew Delbanco, *Melville: His World and Work* (New York, 2005), pp. 3–16, 101–6.

5 Richard M. Johnson, Speech in Congress, December 11, 1811, in Rebecca Brooks Gruver, *American Nationalism, 1783–1830: A Self-Portrait* (New York, 1970), p. 205. This book provides an excellent, edited collection of early American texts.

6 *Richmond Enquirer*, February 22, 1815, in Gruver, *American Nationalism* (New York, 1970), p. 224.

7 [John L. O'Sullivan], "Great Nation of Futurity," p. 426.

8 Timothy Flint, *Indian Wars of the West* (1833), in Gruver, *American Nationalism*, pp. 151–52.

9 For more information on Freneau's life and work, see Mary Weatherspoon Bowden, *Philip Freneau* (Boston, 1976); Lewis Leary, *That Rascal Freneau: A Study in Literary Failure* (New Brunswick, N.J., 1941); and Jacob Axelrad, *Philip Freneau: Champion of Democracy* (Austin, Tex., and London, 1967).

10 Philip Freneau, "To His Excellency George Washington" (September 1781), in *The Newspaper Verse of Philip Freneau*, ed. Judith R. Hiltner (Troy, N.Y., 1986), p. 83. All quotations from Freneau use his own spelling.

11 Philip Freneau, "Stanzas, Occasioned by the Death of General George Washington" (January 1800), in *The Newspaper Verse of Philip Freneau*, ed. Hiltner, p. 629.

12 Ibid., p. 630. Freneau's praise for other "Founding Fathers" appears in "Stanzas, Occasioned by the Death of Dr. Franklin" (April 1790) and "Lines Addressed to Mr. Jefferson, on his approaching retirement from the presidency of the United States" (March 1809), both in *The Newspaper Verse of Philip Freneau*, ed. Hiltner, pp. 387, 662–65.

13 Philip Freneau, "Lines occasioned by reading Mr. Paine's RIGHTS OF MAN" (May 1791), in *The Newspaper Verse of Philip Freneau*, ed. Hiltner, p. 457. The prose quotations are from Freneau's article "Women's Influence on Men and Politics—The Importance of Free Opinion," *National Gazette*, December 26, 1792, in *The Prose of Philip Freneau*, ed. Philip M. Marsh (New Brunswick, N.J., 1955), pp. 293–94. Freneau's assertions of American political superiority expressed a common American view of how the United States would become a republican, constitutional model for the whole world. See the discussion of this early confidence in the "American model" in George Athan Billias, *American Constitutionalism Heard Round the World, 1776–1989: A Global Perspective* (New York, 2009), pp. 15–104, 357–59.

14 Philip Freneau, "Independence" (July 1792), in *The Newspaper Verse of Philip Freneau*, ed. Hiltner, p. 497.

15 Philip Freneau, "Stanzas on the Emigration to America, and Peopling the Western Country" (1785), in *The Newspaper Verse of Philip Freneau*, ed. Hiltner, p. 230.

16 Philip Freneau, "The Republic and Liberty" (June 1798), in *The Newspaper Verse of Philip Freneau*, ed. Hiltner, p. 618.

17 Philip Freneau, ["The Greatness of America"], *The Miscellaneous Works of Philip Freneau* (1788), in *Prose of Freneau*, ed. Marsh, pp. 227–28. It should be noted that

Freneau's linkage of freedom and manliness ascribed America's superior political characteristics to a specific gender identity—the common pattern also in European nationalisms.

18 Philip Freneau, "On the American and French Revolutions" (March 1790), in *The Newspaper Verse of Philip Freneau*, ed. Hiltner, p. 368.

19 Philip Freneau, "To the Memory of the brave, accomplished and patriotic Col. JOHN LAURENS" (October 1787), in *The Newspaper Verse of Philip Freneau*, ed. Hiltner, p. 311; see also Freneau, "To the memory of the brave Americans . . . who fell in the action of September 8, 1781" (1786) and "Reflections, on walking . . . where many Americans were interred from the Prison Ships . . ." (April 1803), both in *The Newspaper Verse of Philip Freneau*, ed. Hiltner, pp. 96, 653 (earlier quotation on p. 653).

20 Philip Freneau, "The Infamy of Kings—and the Virtue of American Farmers," *Letters on Various Interesting and Important Subjects* (1799), in *Prose of Freneau*, ed. Marsh, pp. 401–2; see also Freneau, ["Royal Dangers in the American Stage"], *National Gazette*, March 6, 1793, in *Prose of Freneau*, ed. Marsh, pp. 295–96.

21 Philip Freneau, "Reflections on my Journey from the Tallassee Towns to the settlements on the river Hudson. By OPAY MICO . . . ," *New York Daily Advertiser*, August 31, 1790, in *Prose of Freneau*, ed. Marsh, pp. 256–57.

22 Philip Freneau, "Description of NEW YORK one-hundred and fifty years hence . . . ," *New York Daily Advertiser*, June 12 and 14, 1790, in *Prose of Freneau*, ed. Marsh, pp. 240–43.

23 For more information on Bancroft's life and work, see Russel B. Nye, *George Bancroft* (New York, 1964); and Lilian Handlin, *George Bancroft: The Intellectual as Democrat* (New York, 1984).

24 George Bancroft, *History of the United States, from the Discovery of the American Continent* (Boston, 1834–75), 7:400.

25 Ibid., 4:13.

26 Ibid., p. 12.

27 Ibid., 1:1, 3.

28 Ibid., 7:22–23.

29 Ibid., 1:2–3; also ibid., 8:473 and 10:592. Bancroft's view of the Declaration of Independence stressed its global significance in ways that more recent historians have also emphasized. See, for example, David Armitage, *The Declaration of Independence: A Global History* (Cambridge, Mass., and London, 2007), pp. 63–144. Armitage identifies more than 100 such declarations in all parts of the world since 1776 (see pp. 146–55).

30 Bancroft, *History*, 1:4. Also ibid., 5:4–5, 30–31, 320; 4:154; and 7:21. See also, George Bancroft, *Literary and Historical Miscellanies* (New York, 1855), pp. 424–25. This view of the political consequences of Protestantism also appeared among nineteenth-century liberals in European nations. For French examples, see Helena Rosenblatt, *Liberal Values: Benjamin Constant and the Politics of Religion* (Cambridge, 2008).

31 Bancroft, *History*, 7:295–96.

32 Ibid., pp. 290–91.

33 Ibid., p. 55.

34 Ibid., 3:406, 408.

35 Ibid., 4:456–57.

36 This Memorial Address appeared in numerous editions; see, for example, George Bancroft, *Abraham Lincoln: A Tribute* (New York, 1908), pp. 25, 66–69.

37 Abraham Lincoln, *The Collected Works of Abraham Lincoln*, vol. 7, ed. Roy P. Basler, Marion Dolores Pratt, and Lloyd A. Dunlap (New Brunswick, N.J., 1953), p. 23. For an insightful analysis of Lincoln's contribution to American national culture and identity, see Garry Wills, *Lincoln at Gettysburg: The Words That Remade America* (New York, 1992).

CHAPTER SEVEN

1 This number includes the deaths of over 30 million combatants in the two world wars. Historians estimate that well over 50 million civilians also died during these wars (mostly in the period between the late 1930s and 1945). At least 20 million people were wounded in the First World War and roughly 48 million in the Second World War; many of the wounded died prematurely or never fully recovered. Millions of other people died in smaller wars or during twentieth-century revolutions in countries such as Russia and China, where nationalist and communist forces fought long civil wars. For data on war casualties, see John Ellis and Michael Cox, *The World War I Databook* (London, 2001), pp. 269–81; and Alan Axelrod, *Encyclopedia of World War II* (New York, 2007), 1:213–15.

2 Joep Leerssen discusses the "voluntarist" and "ethnic determinist" views in a concise analysis of Renan's ideas in *National Thought in Europe: A Cultural History* (Amsterdam, 2006), pp. 227–31. For discussions of German and French descriptions of nationality, see Rogers Brubaker, *Citizenship and Nationhood in France and Germany* (Cambridge, Mass., 1992), which stresses contrasting views of citizenship; and the analysis of national similarities in Dieter Gosewinkel, "Citizenship in Germany and France at the Turn of the Twentieth Century: Some New Observations on an Old Comparison," in *Citizenship and National Identity in Twentieth-Century Germany*, ed. Geoff Eley and Jan Plamowski (Stanford, Calif., 2008), pp. 27–39. See also K. Steven Vincent, "National Consciousness, Nationalism, and Exclusion: Reflections on the French Case," *Historical Reflections/Réflexions Historiques* 19, no. 3 (Fall 1993): 433–49; and the analysis of German conceptions of ethnic nationality in Eric Kurlander, *The Price of Exclusion: Ethnicity, National Identity, and the Decline of German Liberalism, 1898–1933* (New York, 2006).

3 See the insightful account of these nationalizing processes in George L. Mosse, *The Nationalization of the Masses: Political Symbolism and Mass Movements in Germany from the Napoleonic Wars through the Third Reich* (New York, 1975). Other discussions of nationalization can be found in Oliver Zimmer, *Nationalism in Europe, 1890–1940* (Basingstoke, England, and New York, 2003), pp. 27–49; and

the classic study of France by Eugen Weber, *Peasants into Frenchmen: The Modernization of Rural France, 1870–1914* (Stanford, Calif., 1976).

4 For more on the European expectations and preparations for war in this era, see the excellent analysis in James J. Sheehan, *Where Have All the Soldiers Gone? The Transformation of Modern Europe* (Boston and New York, 2008), pp. 3–65.

5 The political and diplomatic assumptions of European national leaders are examined in the valuable books of Hew Strachan, *The Outbreak of the First World War* (Oxford, 2004); and David Stevenson, *The Outbreak of the First World War: 1914 in Perspective* (Basingstoke, England, and New York, 1997), which also summarizes the historical debates about this era.

6 Houston Stewart Chamberlain, "The Nation," in *Foundations of the Nineteenth Century*, trans. John Lees and introduction by George L. Mosse (New York, 1968), 1:293–94, 297. For the history of Social Darwinism (and its relation to racism), see the excellent analysis in Mike Hawkins, *Social Darwinism in European and American Thought, 1860–1945: Nature as Model and Nature as Threat* (Cambridge, 1997).

7 Theodor Herzl, *The Jewish State: An Attempt at a Modern Solution to the Jewish Question*, trans. Jacob W. Alkow (New York, 1946), pp. 79–80. For well-informed discussions of Zionism and its relation to European nationalisms, see Michael Brenner, *Zionism: A Brief History*, trans. Shelley L. Frisch (Princeton, 2003); Shlomo Sand, *The Invention of the Jewish People*, trans. Yael Lotan (London and New York, 2009); Shlomo Avineri, *The Making of Modern Zionism: The Intellectual Origins of the Jewish State* (New York, 1981); and Anthony D. Smith, *Chosen Peoples* (Oxford, 2003), pp. 85–94.

8 W. E. B. DuBois, "The Conservation of Races," in *African-American Philosophy: Selected Readings*, ed. Tommy L. Lott (Upper Saddle River, N.J., 2002), pp. 145–46. For a comprehensive analysis of DuBois and his role in defining a new African American cultural identity, see David Levering Lewis, *W. E. B. DuBois: Biography of a Race* (New York, 1993).

9 The literature on the Great War is voluminous, but for informative, recent accounts of the war's multilayered military, political, economic, and diplomatic history, see David Stevenson, *Cataclysm: The First World War as Political Tragedy* (New York, 2004); Hew Strachan, *The First World War* (New York, 2004); and Eric Dorn Brose, *A History of the Great War: World War One and the International Crisis of the Early Twentieth Century* (Oxford, 2010). For an excellent overview of how various governments used propaganda to sustain public support for the war, see Peter Paret, Beth Irwin Lewis, and Paul Paret, *Persuasive Images: Posters of War and Revolution from the Hoover Institution Archives* (Princeton, 1992).

10 Casualty figures are drawn from Anthony Bruce, *An Illustrated Companion to the First World War* (London, 1989), p. 86; and Ellis and Cox, *World War I Databook*, pp. 269–70. The *Databook* also provides detailed information on the armaments production and the huge shipping losses of the belligerent nations (pp. 278–88).

11 Wilson first described the "Fourteen Points" as America's war objectives in a speech to a joint session of Congress on January 18, 1918. Republished around

the world, this famous proposal for national self-determination can be found (among many other places) in Woodrow Wilson, *Essential Writings and Speeches of the Scholar-President*, ed. and introduced by Mario R. DiNunzio (New York, 2006), pp. 403–7.

12 Ibid., p. 406; other references to national territories appear on pp. 404–5.

13 Wilson tried to gain American support for the Treaty of Versailles and the League of Nations by traveling across the United States in the fall of 1919. The quoted passages here—from a speech in Columbus, Ohio, on September 4, 1919— are in Arthur Link and others, eds., *The Papers of Woodrow Wilson* (Princeton, 1966–94): 63:11, 14. Although Wilson failed to gain American ratification of the treaty, his views of America's exemplary (and increasingly assertive) national role in global politics continued to influence American foreign policy, even in the twenty-first century. For more on Wilson's influential themes, see Lloyd E. Ambrosius, *Wilsonianism: Woodrow Wilson and His Legacy in American Foreign Relations* (Basingstoke, England, and New York, 2002).

14 Ho Chi Minh, writing under the alias Nguyen Ai Quoc, submitted the petition in a letter to the American secretary of state Robert Lansing (dated June 18, 1919), which can be found in a collection of documents on the website of the journal *World History Connected*, <http://worldhistoryconnected.press.illinois.edu/2.2/gilbert_II.html> (14 January 2010). The specific points of the petition have also been published in Peter A. De Caro, *Rhetoric of Revolt: Ho Chi Minh's Discourse for Revolution* (Westport, Conn., and London, 2003), p. 101.

15 V. I. Lenin, *National Liberation, Socialism and Imperialism: Selected Writings* (New York, 1968), pp. 47, 61–62. In other commentaries on "Imperialism, Socialism and the Liberation of Oppressed Nations" (ibid., p. 110), Lenin wrote that "victorious socialism must . . . realize the right of the oppressed nations to self-determination." For more on the Bolsheviks' own attempts to organize, mobilize, and respond to nationalism in the Soviet Union, see David Brandenberger, *National Bolshevism: Stalinist Mass Culture and the Formation of Modern Russian National Identity, 1931–1956* (Cambridge, Mass., 2002); and Ronald Gregor Suny and Terry Martin, eds., *A State of Nations: Empire and Nation-Making in the Age of Lenin and Stalin* (Oxford, 2001).

16 Anthony D. Smith, *Chosen Peoples*, p. 246. See also Jay Winter, *Remembering War: The Great War between Memory and History in the Twentieth Century* (New Haven and London, 2006); Mosse, *Nationalization of the Masses*, pp. 47–72; and the discussion of how nations describe the virtues of deceased soldiers in Benedict R. Anderson, "The Goodness of Nations," in *Nation and Religion: Perspectives on Europe and Asia*, ed. Peter van der Veer and Hartmut Lehmann (Princeton, 1999), pp. 197–203.

17 Speech by Senator Magny, September 29, 1919, in French Senate's parliamentary debates; quoted in Daniel J. Sherman, *The Construction of Memory in Interwar France* (Chicago, 1999), p. 107.

18 Historians continue to debate the ways in which Fascism resembled or differed from traditional nationalism; see, for example, the summary of these debates in

Zimmer, *Nationalism in Europe*, pp. 80–106. Mosse's *Nationalization of the Masses* (pp. 1–20, 183–206) notes both continuities and changes in the ways that Fascists and Nazis used nationalist traditions. Fascist innovations receive more emphasis in the important work of Robert Paxton, though he also argues that traditional conservative support was essential for Fascist groups that actually gained power. Robert O. Paxton, *The Anatomy of Fascism* (New York, 2004).

19 Benito Mussolini, *Fascism: Doctrine and Institutions* (New York, 1968), pp. 8, 10–11. For insightful accounts of twentieth-century Italian nationalism and the Italian development of a Fascist state, see Emilio Gentile, *The Origins of Fascist Ideology, 1918–1925* (New York, 2005); Gentile, *La Grande Italia: The Myth of the Nation in the 20th Century*, trans. Suzanne Dingee and Jennifer Pudney (Madison, Wisc., 2009); and R. J. B. Bosworth, *Mussolini's Italy: Life under the Dictatorship, 1915–1945* (New York, 2006).

20 Alfred Rosenberg, *The Myth of the Twentieth Century*, trans. Vivian Bird (Newport Beach, Calif., 1982), p. 441. For a provocative study of the ways in which Nazi racism was used to define national identity in German politics and culture, see Claudia Koonz, *The Nazi Conscience* (Cambridge, Mass., 2003).

21 Rosenberg, *Myth of the Twentieth Century*, pp. 63, 65.

22 Leerssen, *National Thought in Europe*, p. 214.

23 Matthew Stibbe, *Women in the Third Reich* (London, 2003), p. 41.

24 Adolf Hitler, *Mein Kampf*, trans. Ralph Manheim (Boston and New York, 1999), pp. 289, 327. Among the countless studies of how Hitler and the Nazi movement came to power in Germany and set out to implement their racist-nationalist ideas, see the comprehensive study by Ian Kershaw, *Hitler* (London and New York, 2008), and Kershaw's much shorter book, also titled *Hitler* (Edinburgh and London, 2001). There is a concise analysis of nationalist racism in Montserrat Guibernau, *Nationalisms: The Nation-State and Nationalism in the Twentieth Century* (Cambridge, 1996), pp. 85–99.

25 For a wide-ranging, informative history of the Second World War, see Gerhard L. Weinberg, *A World at Arms: A Global History of World War II*, 2nd ed. (Cambridge, 2005). Weinberg has also written another valuable book on the ways in which various national leaders envisioned their nations' roles in the postwar world; see Weinberg, *Visions of Victory: The Hopes of Eight World War II Leaders* (Cambridge, 2005).

26 Charles de Gaulle, *The Complete War Memoirs of Charles de Gaulle*, trans. Jonathan Griffin and Richard Howard (New York, 1964), pp. 83–84. An insightful analysis of de Gaulle's role in redefining and asserting modern French interests and national identity can be found in Julian Jackson, *Charles de Gaulle* (London, 2003).

27 The estimates for total military casualties (over 20 million deaths) include 8.6 million Russians, 2.2 million Chinese, 3.25 million Germans, 2.5 million Japanese, 400,000 Americans, 400,000 British, and millions of others in numerous other countries (ranging from France to Italy and Australia). Estimates for civilian casualties vary between 30 and 55 million, including up to 12 million in the

Soviet Union, 5.6 million Poles, and unknown millions of Chinese. The Holocaust took the most lives in eastern European countries such as the Soviet Union and Poland (at least 3 million Polish Jews were killed), but the Nazis gathered Jews from all parts of Europe for transport to death camps such as Auschwitz in Poland. A list of military and civilian casualties in all the warring nations can be found in Axelrod, *Encyclopedia of World War II*, 1:214–15. For well-informed, comprehensive accounts of the Holocaust, see Christopher Browning, *The Origins of the Final Solution: The Evolution of Nazi Jewish Policy, September 1939–March 1942* (Lincoln, Neb., and Jerusalem, 2004); and Raul Hilberg, *The Destruction of the European Jews*, 3 vols., 3rd ed. (New Haven, 2003).

28 For discussions of the postwar interest in human rights, see Lynn Hunt, *Inventing Human Rights: A History* (New York), pp. 200–208; Samuel Moyn, *The Last Utopia: Human Rights in History* (Cambridge, Mass., 2010), pp. 44–83, 120–75; and Jack Donnelly, *International Human Rights*, 3rd ed. (Boulder, Colo., 2007). On the search for alternatives to national wars after 1945, see Sheehan, *Where Have All the Soldiers Gone?*, pp. 147–97. Although racist nationalisms were generally discredited after 1945, they did not entirely disappear. The Republic of South Africa, for example, enacted new Apartheid laws (1948), which explicitly defined the rights of South African citizenship in a racist, "whites only" system that would persist down to the early 1990s.

29 On the ideas and complex international negotiations that produced the postwar United Nations, see Stephen C. Schlesinger, *Act of Creation: The Founding of the United Nations* (Boulder, Colo., 2003).

CHAPTER EIGHT

1 Harry G. Gelber, *Nations out of Empires: European Nationalism and the Transformation of Asia* (Basingstoke, England, and New York, 2001), p. 159.

2 Sun Yat-Sen, "The Three Principles of the People [1924]," in *Nationalism in Asia and Africa*, ed. Elie Kedourie, with an introduction by Kedourie (New York, 1970), pp. 307–8, 311. Kedourie's long introduction to this volume (pp. 1–152) offers a provocative analysis of how European nationalism influenced the emergence of nationalist thought in other parts of the world.

3 Ibid., p. 317. For more on Sun's nationalism, his political actions after the overthrow of the Qing dynasty, and his contributions to anticolonial politics, see Audrey Wells, *The Political Thought of Sun Yat-Sen: Development and Impact* (Basingstoke, England, and New York, 2001); and David B. Gordon, *Sun Yatsen: Seeking a Newer China* (Upper Saddle River, N.J., 2010).

4 Mohandas Gandhi, "Independence vs. Swaraj," in *The Penguin Gandhi Reader*, ed. Rudrangshu Mukherjee (New York and London, 1993), p. 74. For analysis of Gandhi's complex approach to nationalism, see Manfred B. Steger, *Gandhi's Dilemma: Nonviolent Principles and Nationalist Power* (New York, 2000).

5 Historians of postcolonial thought have noted that anticolonial nationalists (including Gandhi) and postcolonial leaders often fluctuated between critiques

of European materialist traditions and a deep interest in European science or "modernization." See, for example, Partha Chatterjee, *Nationalist Thought and the Colonial World: A Derivative Discourse?* (London, 1986), pp. 1–53; Dipesh Chakrabarty, *Provincializing Europe: Postcolonial Thought and Historical Difference* (Princeton, 2000), pp. 3–46; Prasenjit Duara, "Postcolonial History," in *A Companion to Western Historical Thought,* ed. Lloyd Kramer and Sarah Maza (Oxford and Malden, Mass., 2002), pp. 417–31; Thomas Blom Hansen, *The Saffron Wave: Democracy and Hindu Nationalism in Modern India* (Princeton, 1999); and the analytical essays in Christopher J. Lee, ed., *Making a World after Empire: The Bandung Moment and Its Political Afterlives* (Athens, Ohio, 2010).

6 Jawaharlal Nehru, *The Discovery of India,* ed. Robert I. Crane (Garden City, N.Y., 1960), p. 386.

7 Gregory Jusdanis, *The Necessary Nation* (Princeton, 2001), pp. 89–133 (quotations on p. 92).

8 Léopold Sédar Senghor, *On African Socialism,* trans. Mercer Cook, with an introduction by Cook (New York and London, 1964), pp. 74–75, 83. Senghor's account of "symbiosis" stressed the idea of "Negritude," by which he meant a distinctive African racial-cultural identity that would interact with European identities; but critics noted that his descriptions of such identities drifted toward "essentialism"—despite his praise for cultural exchanges and a universal civilization. For more on Senghor's ideas, see Janet G. Vaillant, *Black, French, and African: A Life of Léopold Sédar Senghor* (Cambridge, Mass., 1990), pp. 243–71.

9 Aimé Césaire, *Discourse on Colonialism,* trans. Joan Pinkham, introduction by Robin D. G. Kelley (New York, 1972, 2000), pp. 39, 41, 43. Kelley's introduction, "A Poetics of Anticolonialism" (pp. 7–28), offers a helpful, brief overview of Césaire's ideas.

10 Frantz Fanon, *The Wretched of the Earth,* trans. Constance Farrington, preface by Jean-Paul Sartre (New York, 1966), p. 191.

11 Ibid., pp. 193, 197.

12 Ibid., p. 199.

13 Nineteenth-century nationalists (as noted in chapter 4) often argued that a new "concert of nations" would develop after all peoples achieved national self-determination. See, for example, the introductory essay by Stefano Recchia and Naida Urbinati titled "Giuseppe Mazzini's International Political Thought" in their edited collection of Mazzini's writings, *A Cosmopolitanism of Nations: Giuseppe Mazzini's Writings on Democracy, Nation Building, and International Relations,* trans. Stefano Recchia (Princeton, 2009), pp. 1–30. For an insightful account of Fanon's enduring importance for postcolonial theorists, see Nigel C. Gibson, *Fanon: The Postcolonial Imagination* (Cambridge, 2003).

14 For an overview of the anticolonial movements and the rise of postcolonial states, see Raymond F. Betts, *Decolonization,* rev. ed. (New York and London, 2004).

15 The quotation from Yeats appeared in an article, "Professor Dowden and Irish Literature—II" (1895), in W. B. Yeats, *Uncollected Prose by W. B. Yeats,* vol. 1, *First*

Reviews and Articles, 1886–1896, ed. John P. Frayne (New York, 1970), p. 352; quoted in Louise Blakeney Williams, "Overcoming the 'Contagion of Mimicry': The Cosmopolitan Nationalism and Modernist History of Rabindranath Tagore and W. B. Yeats," *American Historical Review* 112, no. 1 (February 2007): 69–100 (quotation on p. 84). Williams offers an excellent comparative account of the "cosmopolitan" nationalist views that Tagore and Yeats developed from their specific positions within the British Empire. For more on cosmopolitan conceptions of the nation, see the essays in Steven Vertovec and Robin Cohen, eds., *Conceiving Cosmopolitanism: Theory, Context, Practice* (Oxford, 2002).

16 Randolph Bourne, "Trans-National America," in *In Search of a Democratic America: The Writings of Randolph S. Bourne*, ed. Martin S. Sheffer (Lanham, Md., 2002), pp. 56, 59, 62–63. The essay was first published in the *Atlantic Monthly* in 1916.

17 Ibid., p. 66. For more on the evolving conception of American national identity in this era, see Jonathan Hansen, *The Lost Promise of Patriotism: Debating American Identity, 1890–1920* (Chicago, 2003); and David Hollinger, "Ethnic Diversity, Cosmopolitanism, and the Emergence of the Liberal Intelligentsia," in *In the American Province: Studies in the History and Historiography of Ideas* (Bloomington, Ind., 1985), pp. 56–73.

18 For a comprehensive account of the European Union's history and institutions, see Desmond Dinan, *Ever Closer Union: An Introduction to European Integration*, 3rd ed. (Boulder, Colo., 2005). Other useful discussions of Europe's evolving national identities and regional movements appear in Brian Jenkins and Spyros A. Sofos, eds., *Nation and Identity in Contemporary Europe* (London and New York, 1996); and Ireneusz Pawel Karoleski and Andrzej Marcin Suszycki, eds., *Multiplicity of Nationalism in Contemporary Europe* (Lanham, Md., 2010). For ongoing developments in the European Union, see the EU website at <http://europa.eu/index_en.htm> (4 February 2010). The twenty-seven member nations of the EU in 2010 were Austria, Belgium, Bulgaria, Cyprus, Czech Republic, Denmark, Estonia, Finland, France, Germany, Greece, Hungary, Ireland, Italy, Latvia, Lithuania, Luxembourg, Malta, Netherlands, Poland, Portugal, Romania, Slovakia, Slovenia, Spain, Sweden, and the United Kingdom.

19 Konrad Adenauer, *Memoirs 1945–53*, trans. Beate Ruhm von Oppen (Chicago, 1966), pp. 329–30.

20 Ibid., p. 331. For an excellent analysis of how Germans redefined their post-1945 nation, see Konrad H. Jarausch, *After Hitler: Recivilizing Germans, 1945–1995*, trans. Brandon Hunziker (Oxford, 2006).

21 Charles de Gaulle, *Memoirs of Hope: Renewal and Endeavor*, trans. Terence Kilmartin (New York, 1971), pp. 175, 180. De Gaulle also stressed his continuing commitment to French political autonomy in this same book (pp. 177–78, 194).

22 For detailed information on all of these "integrating" developments, see Dinan, *Ever Closer Union*, pp. 259–88, 387–517, 559–607.

23 French-German commemoration events were widely reported in the international press. See, for example, "Mitterrand and Kohl Honor Dead of Verdun,"

New York Times, September 23, 1984; and Alan Cowell and Steven Erlanger, "France and Germany Use the Remembrance of a War to Promote Reconciliation," *New York Times*, 12 November 2009. For more on the postwar history of French-German relations, see Julius W. Friend, *The Linchpin: French-German Relations, 1950–1990* (New York, 1991); and Frédérico Bozo, *Mitterrand, the End of the Cold War, and German Unification*, trans. Susan Emanuel (New York and Oxford, 2005).

24 The quotations come from descriptions of the European Union on the EU website: <http://europa.eu/abc/panorama/whatdoes/index_en.htm> (4 February 2010).

25 Ibid.

26 Joep Leerssen, *National Thought in Europe: A Cultural History* (Amsterdam, 2006), pp. 241, 249, 251.

27 Leerssen discusses Renan's themes in ibid., pp. 227–35. Renan's famous essay, "What Is a Nation?," appears in English translation in *Becoming National: A Reader*, ed. Geoff Eley and Ronald Grigor Suny (New York, 1996), pp. 42–55.

28 For discussions of ethnic identities and violence in the Balkans, see Cathie Carmichael, *Ethnic Cleansing in the Balkans: Nationalism and the Destruction of Tradition* (London, 2002); and Klejda Mulaj, *Politics of Ethnic Cleansing: Nation-State Building and Provision of In/Security in Twentieth-Century Balkans* (Lanham, Md., 2008). For a critical reevaluation of "ethnic identities," see Rogers Brubaker, *Ethnicity without Groups* (Cambridge, Mass., 2004), pp. 7–27.

29 European and international responses to the late twentieth-century conflicts in the Balkans are examined in the well-informed work of Tom Gallagher, *The Balkans in the New Millennium: In the Shadow of War and Peace* (London and New York, 2005).

30 For introductions to the twenty-first-century debates about national immigration policies and the rights of immigrant communities, see the wide-ranging essays in Terri E. Givens, Gary P. Preeman, and David L. Leal, eds., *Immigration Policy and Security: U.S., European, and Commonwealth Perspectives* (New York, 2009). Also see Reed Karaim, "America's Border Fence: Will It Stem the Flow of Illegal Immigrants?," in *Issues in Race, Ethnicity, Gender and Class: Selections from the CQ Researcher* (Los Angeles, 2010), pp. 141–63; and Joan Wallach Scott, *The Politics of the Veil* (Princeton, 2007).

31 Bush developed these themes in numerous public statements after 9/11, but the fullest statement can be found in his speech to a joint session of the U.S. Congress on 20 September 2001. For the complete text of that address, see the *New York Times*, 21 September 2001. Analysis of the American responses to the terrorist attacks appears in Matthew J. Morgan, ed., *The Impact of 9/11 on Politics and War: The Day That Changed Everything?* (New York, 2009); and Daniel J. Sherman and Terry Nardin, eds., *Terror, Culture, Politics: Rethinking 9/11* (Bloomington, Ind., 2006). Sherman's own essay in this collection, "Naming and the Violence of Place" (pp. 121–45), focuses on the complexity of national commemoration.

32 Bush, "Address to Congress" (transcript of speech), *New York Times*, 21 September 2001.

33 Ibid. The quotations from Franklin Roosevelt's "War Message to Congress" (December 8, 1941) appear in *The Roosevelt Reader: Selected Speeches, Messages, Press Conferences, and Letters of Franklin D. Roosevelt*, ed. Basil Rauch (New York, 1957), pp. 300–301.

34 See, for example, the report on President Bush's approval ratings in the Gallup poll in the *New York Times*, 23 September 2001. For discussion of American views of Muslims, see Idean Salehyan, "U.S. Asylum and Refugee Policy towards Muslim Nations since 9/11," in *Immigration Policy and Security*, ed. Givens, Preeman, and Leal, pp. 52–65.

35 For an engaging discussion of how multiculturalism may be evolving toward a "postethnic" or "cosmopolitan" American national identity, see David A. Hollinger, *Postethnic America: Beyond Multiculturalism* (New York, 1995, 2000). Hollinger notes (p. 14) that the "post-ethnic perspective on American nationality emphasizes the civic character of the American nation-state"—a theme that resembles views of the nations among contemporary European historians such as Joep Leerssen. It is worth noting, however, that some American nationalists claimed that American president Barack Obama could not be a "true American" because his father was Kenyan or because, despite clear evidence, his "American birth" had not been proven; see, for example, Jeff Zeleny, "Persistent 'Birthers' Fringe Disorients Strategists," *New York Times*, 5 August 2009.

36 Barack Obama, "Address on the War in Afghanistan," (delivered at West Point, New York, 1 December 2009); complete text in the *New York Times*, 2 December 2009.

37 For accounts of the 2002 French elections, see John Gaffney, ed., *The French Presidential Elections of 2002* (Alsdershot, England, and Burlington, Vermont, 2004). And a concise, insightful analysis of the 2007 French election can be found in William Pfaff, "In Sarkoland," *New York Review of Books* 54 (14 June 2007).

38 Eric Besson's definition of French "national identity" appears in Jean-Baptiste de Montvalon, "Identité nationale: les Français voient la manoeuvre, mais approuvent le débat," *Le Monde*, 7 November 2009. For examples of critical responses to France's "national identity" debates, see "L'inquiétant M. Besson," *Le Nouvel Observateur* (10–16 Décembre 2009), pp. 8–15.

Selected Bibliography

The published materials and scholarly works on nationalism are so numerous that no single bibliography could possibly include everything. The following selections therefore refer to the printed sources and scholarly studies that have been used to prepare this book and that can lead readers to further information or analysis on major themes and events in the history of nationalism. A few of the works cited in the notes are not listed here. A brief summary of useful websites comprises the final section of the bibliography.

SOURCE MATERIALS FOR THE STUDY OF NATIONALIST THOUGHT

Adenauer, Konrad. *Memoirs 1945–53*. Translated by Beate Ruhm von Oppen. Chicago, 1966.

Bancroft, George. *Abraham Lincoln: A Tribute*. New York, 1908.

———. *History of the United States, from the Discovery of the American Continent*. 10 vols. Boston, 1834–75.

———. *Literary and Historical Miscellanies*. New York, 1855.

Biddiss, Michael D., ed. *Gobineau: Selected Political Writings*. New York, 1970.

Bourne, Randolph. "Trans-National America." In *In Search of a Democratic America: The Writings of Randolph S. Bourne*. Edited by Martin S. Sheffer, pp. 55–68. Lanham, Md., 2002.

Burke, Edmund. *Reflections on the Revolution in France*. Edited by J. G. A. Pocock. Indianapolis, 1987.

Césaire, Aimé. *Discourse on Colonialism*. Translated by Joan Pinkham and with an introduction by Robin D. G. Kelley. New York, 1972, 2000.

Chamberlain, Houston Stewart. *Foundations of the Nineteenth Century*. 2 vols. Translated by John Lees and with an introduction by George L. Mosse. New York, 1968.

Dahbour, Omar, and Micheline R. Ishay. *The Nationalism Reader*. Atlantic Highlands, N.J., 1995.

De Gaulle, Charles. *The Complete War Memoirs of Charles de Gaulle*. Translated by Jonathan Griffin and Richard Howard. New York, 1964.

————. *Memoirs of Hope: Renewal and Endeavor.* Translated by Terence Kilmartin. New York, 1971.

DuBois, W. E. B. "The Conservation of Races." In *African-American Philosophy: Selected Readings,* edited by Tommy L. Lott, pp. 141–47. Upper Saddle River, N.J., 2002.

Emerson, Ralph Waldo. *English Traits.* In *The Collected Works of Ralph Waldo Emerson,* vol. 5. Historical introduction by Philip Nicoloff, notes by Robert E. Burkholder, and textual introduction by Douglas Emery Wilson. Cambridge, Mass., 1994.

————. *Selected Essays.* Edited by Larzer Ziff. New York, 1982.

Fanon, Frantz. *The Wretched of the Earth.* Translated by Constance Farrington and with a preface by Jean-Paul Sartre. New York, 1966.

Fichte, Johann Gottlieb. *Addresses to the German Nation.* Translated and edited with an introduction and notes by Gregory Moore. Cambridge, 2008.

Gandhi, Mohandas. *The Penguin Gandhi Reader.* Edited by Rudrangshu Mukherjee. New York and London, 1993.

Gentz, Friedrich. *The French and American Revolutions Compared.* Translated by John Quincy Adams. In *Three Revolutions,* by Stefan T. Possony. Chicago, 1959.

Gruver, Rebecca Brooks. *American Nationalism, 1783–1830: A Self-Portrait.* New York, 1970.

Herder, Johann Gottfried von. *Reflections on the Philosophy of the History of Mankind.* Translated by T. O. Churchill and edited by Frank E. Manuel. Chicago, 1968.

Herzl, Theodor. *The Jewish State: An Attempt at a Modern Solution to the Jewish Question.* Translated by Jacob W. Alkow. New York, 1946.

Hiltner, Judith R., ed. *The Newspaper Verse of Philip Freneau.* Troy, N.Y., 1986.

Hitler, Adolf. *Mein Kampf.* Translated by Ralph Manheim. Boston and New York, 1999.

Hudson, Winthrop S., ed. *Nationalism and Religion in America: Concepts of American Identity and Mission.* New York, 1970.

Hunt, Lynn, ed. and trans. *The French Revolution and Human Rights: A Brief Documentary History.* New York, 1996.

Jefferson, Thomas. "The Declaration of Independence, As Amended by the Committee and by Congress." In *The Papers of Thomas Jefferson.* 36 vols. to date. Edited by Julian P. Boyd, Charles T. Cullen, John Catanzariti, and others. Princeton, 1950–.

Knox, Robert. *The Races of Men: A Fragment.* Philadelphia, 1850; repr. Miami, 1969.

Lenin, V. I. *National Liberation, Socialism and Imperialism: Selected Writings.* New York, 1968.

Lincoln, Abraham. *The Collected Works of Abraham Lincoln.* 8 vols. Edited by Roy P. Basler, Marion Dolores Pratt, and Lloyd A. Dunlap. New Brunswick, N.J., 1953.

Link, Arthur, and others, eds. *The Papers of Woodrow Wilson.* 69 vols. Princeton, 1966–94.

Marsh, Philip M., ed. *The Prose of Philip Freneau.* New Brunswick, N.J., 1955.

Mazzini, Giuseppe. *A Cosmopolitanism of Nations: Giuseppe Mazzini's Writings on Democracy, Nation Building, and International Relations.* Edited and with an introduction by Stefano Recchia and Nadia Urbinati. Translated by Stefano Recchia. Princeton, 2009.

Mazzini, Joseph. *The Duties of Man and Other Essays*. London, 1907.

Michelet, Jules. *History of the French Revolution*. Translated by Charles Cocks and edited by Gordon Wright. Chicago, 1967.

————. *The People*. Translated by John P. McKay. Urbana, Ill., 1973.

Mickiewicz, Adam. *Poems by Adam Mickiewicz*. Edited and translated by George R. Noyes. New York, 1944.

————. *Les Slaves: Cours professé au Collège de France (1842–1844)*. Paris, 1914.

Mussolini, Benito. *Fascism: Doctrine and Institutions*. New York, 1968.

Nehru, Jawaharlal. *The Discovery of India*. Edited by Robert I. Crane. Garden City, N.Y., 1960.

Paine, Thomas. *Collected Writings*. Edited by Eric Foner. New York, 1995.

Pecora, Vincent P. *Nations and Identities: Classic Readings*. Malden, Mass., and Oxford, 2001.

Ramsay, David. *David Ramsay, 1749–1815: Selections from His Writings*. Edited by Robert L. Brunhouse. Transactions of the American Philosophical Society, vol. 55, pt. 4. Philadelphia, 1965.

Ranke, Leopold von. *The Secret of World History: Selected Writings on the Art and Science of History*. Edited and translated by Roger Wines. New York, 1981.

Renan, Ernest. "What Is a Nation?" (1882). Translated by Martin Thom. In *Nation and Narration*, edited by Homi Bhabha, pp. 8–22. London, 1990.

Roosevelt, Franklin D. *The Roosevelt Reader: Selected Speeches, Messages, Press Conferences, and Letters of Franklin D. Roosevelt*. Edited by Basil Rauch. New York, 1957.

Rosenberg, Alfred. *The Myth of the Twentieth Century*. Translated by Vivian Bird. Newport Beach, Calif., 1982.

Rousseau, Jean Jacques. *On the Social Contract*. Translated by Donald A. Cress and with an introduction by Peter Gay. Indianapolis, 1987.

Senghor, Léopold Sédar. *On African Socialism*. Translated and with an introduction by Mercer Cook. New York and London, 1964.

Stewart, John Hall, ed. *A Documentary Survey of the French Revolution*. New York, 1951.

Sun Yat-Sen. "The Three Principles of the People." Excerpt in *Nationalism in Asia and Africa*, edited and with an introduction by Elie Kedourie, pp. 304–17. New York, 1970.

Wilson, Woodrow. *Essential Writings and Speeches of the Scholar-President*. Edited and with an introduction by Mario R. DiNunzio. New York, 2006.

SCHOLARLY WORKS ON THE HISTORY OF NATIONALISM: BOOKS

Agulhon, Maurice. *Marianne into Battle: Republican Imagery and Symbolism in France, 1789–1880*. Translated by Janet Lloyd. Cambridge, 1981.

Alter, Peter. *Nationalism*. 2nd ed. London, 1994.

Ambrosius, Lloyd E. *Wilsonianism: Woodrow Wilson and His Legacy in American Foreign Relations*. Basingstoke, England, and New York, 2002.

Anderson, Benedict. *Imagined Communities: Reflections on the Origin and Spread of Nationalism*. 2nd rev. ed. London and New York, 2006.

Armitage, David. *The Declaration of Independence: A Global History*. Cambridge, Mass., and London, 2007.

Armstrong, John A. *Nations before Nationalism*. Chapel Hill, 1982.

Auslander, Leora. *Cultural Revolutions: Everyday Life and Politics in Britain, North America, and France*. Berkeley and Los Angeles, 2009.

Avineri, Shlomo. *The Making of Modern Zionism: The Intellectual Origins of the Jewish State*. New York, 1981.

Axelrad, Jacob. *Philip Freneau: Champion of Democracy*. Austin, Tex., and London, 1967.

Axelrod, Alan. *Encyclopedia of World War II*. 2 vols. New York, 2007.

Bann, Stephen. *Romanticism and the Rise of History*. New York, 1995.

Barker, Philip W. *Religious Nationalism in Modern Europe: If God Be for Us*. London and New York, 2009.

Baron, Salo Wittmayer. *Modern Nationalism and Religion*. New York, 1947.

Bell, David A. *The Cult of the Nation in France: Inventing Nationalism, 1680–1800*. Cambridge, Mass., 2001.

———. *The First Total War: Napoleon's Europe and the Birth of Warfare as We Know It*. New York, 2007.

Berger, Stefan, ed. *Writing the Nation: A Global Perspective*. Basingstoke, England, and New York, 2007.

Berger, Stefan, Mark Donovan, and Kevin Passmore, eds. *Writing National Histories: Western Europe since 1800*. London and New York, 1999.

Berger, Stefan, and Chris Lorenz, eds. *The Contested Nation: Ethnicity, Class, Religion and Gender in National Histories*. Basingstoke, England, and New York, 2008.

Betts, Raymond F. *Decolonization*. Rev. ed. New York and London, 2004.

Bhabha, Homi K., ed. *Nation and Narration*. London, 1990.

Billias, George Athan. *American Constitutionalism Heard Round the World, 1776–1989: A Global Perspective*. New York, 2009.

Blom, Ida, Karen Hagemann, and Catherine Hall, eds. *Gendered Nations: Nationalisms and Gender Order in the Long Nineteenth Century*. Oxford and New York, 2000.

Bosworth, R. J. B. *Mussolini's Italy: Life under the Dictatorship, 1915–1945*. New York, 2006.

———. *Nationalism*. Harlow, England, 2007.

Bowden, Mary Weatherspoon. *Philip Freneau*. Boston, 1976.

Bozo, Frédérico. *Mitterrand, the End of the Cold War, and German Unification*. Translated by Susan Emanuel. New York and Oxford, 2005.

Brandenberger, David. *National Bolshevism: Stalinist Mass Culture and the Formation of Modern Russian National Identity, 1931–1956*. Cambridge, Mass., 2002.

Brenner, Michael. *Zionism: A Brief History*. Translated by Shelley L. Frisch. Princeton, 2003.

Breuilly, John. *Nationalism and the State*. 2nd ed. Manchester, 1993.

Broers, Michael. *The Napoleonic Empire in Italy, 1796–1814: Cultural Imperialism in a European Context?* London and New York, 2005.

Brose, Eric Dorn. *A History of the Great War: World War One and the International Crisis of the Early Twentieth Century*. Oxford, 2010.

Browning, Christopher R. *The Origins of the Final Solution: The Evolution of Nazi Jewish Policy, September 1939–March 1942*. Lincoln, Neb., and Jerusalem, 2004.

Brubaker, Rogers. *Citizenship and Nationhood in France and Germany*. Cambridge, Mass., 1992.

———. *Ethnicity without Groups*. Cambridge, Mass., 2004.

———. *Nationalism Reframed: Nationhood and the National Question in the New Europe*. Cambridge, 1996.

Burbank, Jane, and Frederick Cooper. *Empires in World History: Power and the Politics of Difference*. Princeton, 2010.

Butler, Jon. *Becoming America: The Revolution before 1776*. Cambridge, Mass., 2000.

Carmichael, Cathie. *Ethnic Cleansing in the Balkans: Nationalism and the Destruction of Tradition*. London, 2002.

Castro-Klarén, Sara, and John Charles Chasteen, eds. *Beyond Imagined Communities: Reading and Writing the Nation in Nineteenth-Century Latin America*. Washington, D.C., and Baltimore, 2003.

Certeau, Michel de, Dominque Julia, and Jacques Revel. *Une politique de la langue: La révolution française et les patois, l'enquête de Grégoire*. Paris, 1975.

Chakrabarty, Dipesh. *Provincializing Europe: Postcolonial Thought and Historical Difference*. Princeton, 2000.

Chasteen, John. *Americanos: Latin America's Struggle for Independence*. Oxford and New York, 2008.

Chatterjee, Partha. *Nationalist Thought and the Colonial World: A Derivative Discourse?* London, 1986.

Colley, Linda. *Britons: Forging the Nation, 1707–1837*. New Haven, 1992.

Connor, Walker. *Ethnonationalism: The Quest for Understanding*. Princeton, 1994.

Davies, Alan. *The Crucified Nation: A Motif in Modern Nationalism*. Brighton, England, and Portland, Ore., 2008.

De Caro, Peter A. *Rhetoric of Revolt: Ho Chi Minh's Discourse for Revolution*. Westport, Conn., and London, 2003.

Delbanco, Andrew. *Melville: His World and Work*. New York, 2005.

Desan, Suzanne. *The Family on Trial in Revolutionary France*. Berkeley and Los Angeles, 2004.

Deutsch, Karl W. *Nationalism and Social Communication: An Inquiry into the Foundations of Nationality*. New York, 1953.

Dinan, Desmond. *Ever Closer Union: An Introduction to European Integration*. 3rd ed. Boulder, Colo., 2005.

Donnelly, Jack. *International Human Rights*. 3rd ed. Boulder, Colo., 2007.

Dumont, Louis. *German Ideology: From France to Germany and Back.* Chicago, 1994.

Dwyer, Philip G., and Alan Forrest, eds. *Napoleon and His Empire: Europe, 1804–1814.* London and New York, 2007.

Eley, Geoff, and Ronald Grigor Suny, eds. *Becoming National: A Reader.* New York, 1996.

Ellis, John, and Michael Cox. *The World War I Databook.* London, 2001.

Esdaile, Charles J., ed. *Popular Resistance in the French Wars: Patriots, Partisans and Land Pirates.* London and New York, 2005.

Forrest, Alan. *The Legacy of the French Revolutionary Wars: The Nation-in-Arms in French Republican Memory.* Cambridge, 2009.

———. *Paris, the Provinces and the French Revolution.* London, 2004.

Friedland, Paul. *Political Actors: Representative Bodies and Theatricality in the Age of the French Revolution.* Ithaca and London, 2002.

Friend, Julius W. *The Linchpin: French-German Relations, 1950–1990.* New York, 1991.

Gaffney, John, ed. *The French Presidential Elections of 2002.* Aldershot, England, and Burlington, Vt., 2004.

Gallagher, Tom. *The Balkans in the New Millennium: In the Shadow of War and Peace.* London and New York, 2005.

Gelber, Harry G. *Nations out of Empires: European Nationalism and the Transformation of Asia.* Basingstoke, England, and New York, 2001.

Gellner, Ernest. *Nations and Nationalism.* Ithaca, 1983.

Gentile, Emilio. *La Grande Italia: The Myth of the Nation in the Twentieth Century.* Translated by Suzanne Dingee and Jennifer Pudney. Madison, Wisc., 2009.

———. *The Origins of Fascist Ideology, 1918–1925.* New York, 2005.

Gibson, Nigel C. *Fanon: The Postcolonial Imagination.* Cambridge, 2003.

Givens, Terri E., Gary P. Preeman, and David L. Leal, eds. *Immigration Policy and Security: U.S., European, and Commonwealth Perspectives.* New York, 2009.

Gordon, David B. *Sun Yatsen: Seeking a Newer China.* Upper Saddle River, N.J., 2010.

Greenfeld, Liah. *Nationalism: Five Roads to Modernity.* Cambridge, Mass., 1992.

———. *Nationalism and the Mind: Essays on Modern Culture.* Oxford, 2006.

Grosby, Stephen. *Nationalism: A Very Short Introduction.* Oxford, 2005.

Guibernau, Montserrat. *Nationalisms: The Nation-State and Nationalism in the Twentieth Century.* Cambridge, 1996.

Guyatt, Nicholas. *Providence and the Invention of the United States, 1607–1876.* Cambridge, 2007.

Handlin, Lilian. *George Bancroft: The Intellectual as Democrat.* New York, 1984.

Hansen, Jonathan. *The Lost Promise of Patriotism: Debating American Identity, 1890–1920.* Chicago, 2003.

Hansen, Thomas Blom. *The Saffron Wave: Democracy and Hindu Nationalism in Modern India.* Princeton, 1999.

Hawkins, Mike. *Social Darwinism in European and American Thought, 1860–1945: Nature as Model and Nature as Threat.* Cambridge, 1997.

Hayes, Carlton J. H. *Essays on Nationalism.* New York, 1966.

Herb, Guntram H., and David H. Kaplan, eds. *Nations and Nationalism: A Global Historical Overview.* 4 vols. Santa Barbara, 2008.

Higonnet, Patrice. *Attendant Cruelties: Nation and Nationalism in American History.* New York, 2007.

Hilberg, Raul. *The Destruction of the European Jews.* 3 vols. 3rd ed. New Haven, 2003.

Hill, Christopher L. *National History and the World of Nations: Capital, State, and the Rhetoric of History in Japan, France, and the United States.* Durham, N.C., 2008.

Hobsbawm, Eric. *Nations and Nationalism since 1780: Programme, Myth, Reality.* Cambridge, 1990.

Hobsbawm, Eric, and Terence Ranger, eds. *The Invention of Tradition.* Cambridge, 1983.

Hollinger, David. *In the American Province: Studies in the History and Historiography of Ideas.* Bloomington, Ind., 1985.

———. *Postethnic America: Beyond Multiculturalism.* New York, 1995, 2000.

Hoover, Arlie J. *The Gospel of Nationalism: German Patriotic Preaching from Napoleon to Versailles.* Stuttgart, 1986.

Hunt, Lynn. *Inventing Human Rights: A History.* New York, 2007.

———. *Politics, Culture, and Class in the French Revolution.* Berkeley, 1984.

Hutchison, William R., and Hartmut Lehmann, eds. *Many Are Chosen: Divine Election and Western Nationalism.* Minneapolis, 1984.

Isabella, Maurizio. *Risorgimento in Exile: Italian Émigrés and the Liberal International in the Post-Napoleonic Era.* New York and Oxford, 2009.

Jackson, Julian. *Charles de Gaulle.* London, 2003.

Jarausch, Konrad H. *After Hitler: Recivilizing Germans, 1945–1995.* Translated by Brandon Hunziker. Oxford, 2006.

Jenkins, Brian. *Nationalism in France: Class and Nation since 1789.* London, 1990.

Jenkins, Brian, and Spyros A. Sofos, eds. *Nation and Identity in Contemporary Europe.* London and New York, 1996.

Johnston, Otto W. *The Myth of a Nation: Literature and Politics in Prussia under Napoleon.* Columbia, S.C., 1989.

Jusdanis, Gregory. *The Necessary Nation.* Princeton, 2001.

Kammen, Michael. *A Season of Youth: The American Revolution and the Historical Imagination.* New York, 1978.

Karoleski, Ireneusz Pawel, and Andrzej Marcin Suszycki, eds. *Multiplicity of Nationalism in Contemporary Europe.* Lanham, Md., 2010.

Kedourie, Elie. *Nationalism.* 4th ed. Oxford, 1993.

Keitner, Chimène I. *The Paradoxes of Nationalism: The French Revolution and Its Meaning for Contemporary Nation Building.* Albany, 2007.

Kennedy, Emmet. *A Cultural History of the French Revolution.* New Haven, 1989.

Kershaw, Ian. *Hitler.* Edinburgh and London, 2001.

———. *Hitler.* London and New York, 2008.

Klooster, Wim. *Revolutions in the Atlantic World: A Comparative History.* New York, 2009.

Kogan, Vivian. *The "I" of History: Self-Fashioning and National Consciousness in Jules Michelet*. Chapel Hill, 2006.

Kohn, Hans. *The Idea of Nationalism: A Study in Its Origins and Background*. New York, 1944.

———. *Prelude to Nation-States: The French and German Experience, 1789–1815*. Princeton, 1967.

Koonz, Claudia. *The Nazi Conscience*. Cambridge, Mass., 2003.

Koropeckyj, Roman. *Adam Mickiewicz: The Life of a Romantic*. Ithaca and London, 2008.

Kurlander, Eric. *The Price of Exclusion: Ethnicity, National Identity, and the Decline of German Liberalism, 1898–1933*. New York, 2006.

LaCapra, Dominick. *Writing History, Writing Trauma*. Baltimore, 2001.

Landes, Joan B. *Visualizing the Nation: Gender, Representation, and Revolution in Eighteenth-Century France*. Ithaca and London, 2001.

LaVopa, Anthony J. *Fichte: The Self and the Calling of Philosophy, 1762–1799*. Cambridge, 2001.

Lawrence, Paul. *Nationalism: History and Theory*. Harlow, England, 2005.

Leary, Lewis. *That Rascal Freneau: A Study in Literary Failure*. New Brunswick, N.J., 1941.

Lee, Christopher J., ed. *Making a World after Empire: The Bandung Moment and Its Political Afterlives* (Athens, Ohio, 2010).

Leerssen, Joep. *National Thought in Europe: A Cultural History*. Amsterdam, 2006.

Leoussi, Anthena S., ed. *Encyclopaedia of Nationalism*. New Brunswick, N.J., and London, 2001.

Leoussi, Anthena S., and Steven Grosby, eds. *Nationalism and Ethnosymbolism: History, Culture and Ethnicity in the Formation of Nations*. Edinburgh, 2007.

Lewis, David Levering. *W. E. B. DuBois: Biography of a Race*. New York, 1993.

Lipset, Seymour Martin. *American Exceptionalism: A Double-Edged Sword*. New York, 1996.

Lynn, John A. *The Bayonets of the Republic: Motivation and Tactics in the Army of Revolutionary France, 1791–94*. Urbana, Ill., 1984.

Marx, Anthony W. *Faith in Nation: Exclusionary Origins of Nationalism*. Oxford, 2003.

Mason, Laura. *Singing the French Revolution: Popular Culture and Politics, 1787–1799*. Ithaca and London, 1996.

Meinecke, Friedrich. *Cosmopolitanism and the National State*. Translated by Robert B. Kimer. Princeton, 1970.

Morgan, Matthew J., ed. *The Impact of 9/11 on Politics and War: The Day That Changed Everything?* New York, 2009.

Mosse, George L. *Confronting the Nation: Jewish and Western Nationalism*. Hanover, N.H., 1993.

———. *Nationalism and Sexuality: Middle-Class Morality and Sexual Norms in Modern Europe*. Madison, Wisc., 1985.

———. *The Nationalization of the Masses: Political Symbolism and Mass Movements in Germany from the Napoleonic Wars through the Third Reich*. New York, 1975.

Moyn, Samuel. *The Last Utopia: Human Rights in History*. Cambridge, Mass., 2010.

Mulaj, Klejda. *Politics of Ethnic Cleansing: Nation-State Building and Provision of In/Security in Twentieth-Century Balkans*. Lanham, Md., 2008.

Nagel, Paul C. *This Sacred Trust: American Nationality, 1798–1898*. Oxford and New York, 1971.

Nye, Russel B. *George Bancroft*. New York, 1964.

O'Brien, Conor Cruise. *God Land: Reflections on Religion and Nationalism*. Cambridge, Mass., 1988.

Ozouf, Mona. *Festivals and the French Revolution*. Translated by Alan Sheridan. Cambridge, Mass., 1988.

Palmer, R. R. *The Age of the Democratic Revolution: A Political History of Europe and America, 1760–1800*. 2 vols. Princeton, 1959, 1964.

———. *The Improvement of Humanity: Education and the French Revolution*. Princeton, 1985.

Paret, Peter, Beth Irwin Lewis, and Paul Paret. *Persuasive Images: Posters of War and Revolution from the Hoover Institution Archives*. Princeton, 1992.

Parker, Andrew, Mary Russo, Doris Sommer, and Patricia Yaeger, eds. *Nationalisms and Sexualities*. New York, 1992.

Paxton, Robert O. *The Anatomy of Fascism*. New York, 2004.

Perkins, Mary Anne. *Nation and Word, 1770–1850: Religious and Metaphysical Language in European National Consciousness*. Aldershot, England, 1999.

Popkin, Jeremy. *Revolutionary News: The Press in France, 1789–1799*. Durham, N.C., 1990.

———. *A Short History of the French Revolution*. 5th ed. Boston, 2010.

Rapport, Michael. *Nationality and Citizenship in Revolutionary France: The Treatment of Foreigners, 1789–1799*. Oxford, 2000.

Readman, Paul. *Land and Nation in England: Patriotism, National Identity, and the Politics of Land, 1880–1914*. Woodbridge, England, and Rochester, N.Y., 2008.

Reshef, Ouriel. *Guerre, Mythes et Caricature: Au berceau d'une mentalité française*. Paris, 1984.

Rosenblatt, Helena. *Liberal Values: Benjamin Constant and the Politics of Religion*. Cambridge, 2008.

Sahlins, Peter. *Boundaries: The Making of France and Spain in the Pyrenees*. Berkeley and Los Angeles, 1989.

Sand, Shlomo. *The Invention of the Jewish People*. Translated by Yael Lotan. London and New York, 2009.

Schlesinger, Stephen C. *Act of Creation: The Founding of the United Nations*. Boulder, Colo., 2003.

Schulze, Hagen. *The Course of German Nationalism: From Frederick the Great to Bismarck, 1763–1867*. Translated by Sarah Hansbury-Tension. Cambridge, 1991.

Scott, Joan Wallach. *Gender and the Politics of History*. Rev. ed. New York, 1999.

———. *Only Paradoxes to Offer: French Feminists and the Rights of Man*. Cambridge, Mass., 1996.

———. *The Politics of the Veil*. Princeton, 2007.

Searle-White, Joshua. *The Psychology of Nationalism.* New York, 2001.

Sheehan, James J. *Where Have All the Soldiers Gone? The Transformation of Modern Europe.* Boston and New York, 2008.

Sherman, Daniel J. *The Construction of Memory in Interwar France.* Chicago, 1999.

Sherman, Daniel J., and Terry Nardin, eds. *Terror, Culture, Politics: Rethinking 9/11.* Bloomington, Ind., 2006.

Smith, Anthony D. *The Antiquity of Nations.* Cambridge, 2004.

———. *Chosen Peoples.* Oxford, 2003.

———. *The Cultural Foundations of Nations: Hierarchy, Covenant, and Republic.* Malden, Mass., and Oxford, 2008.

———. *The Ethnic Origins of Nations.* Oxford, 1986.

———. *National Identity.* London, 1991.

———. *The Nation in History: Historiographical Debates about Ethnicity and Nationalism.* Hanover, N.H., 2000.

Smith, Jay M. *Nobility Reimagined: The Patriotic Nation in Eighteenth-Century France.* Ithaca and London, 2005.

Snyder, Louis L. *The Idea of Racialism: Its Meaning and History.* Princeton, 1962.

Sommer, Doris. *Foundational Fictions: The National Romances of Latin America.* Berkeley, Calif., 1991.

Spencer, Philip, and Howard Wollman. *Nationalism: A Critical Introduction.* Thousand Oaks, Calif., and London, 2002.

Steger, Manfred B. *Gandhi's Dilemma: Nonviolent Principles and Nationalist Power.* New York, 2000.

Stevenson, David. *Cataclysm: The First World War as Political Tragedy.* New York, 2004.

———. *The Outbreak of the First World War: 1914 in Perspective.* Basingstoke, England, and New York, 1997.

Stibbe, Matthew. *Women in the Third Reich.* London, 2003.

Strachan, Hew. *The First World War.* New York, 2004.

———. *The Outbreak of the First World War.* Oxford, 2004.

Suny, Ronald Gregor, and Terry Martin, eds. *A State of Nations: Empire and Nation-Making in the Age of Lenin and Stalin.* Oxford, 2001.

Surkis, Judith. *Sexing the Citizen: Morality and Masculinity in France, 1870–1920.* Ithaca, 2006.

Townson, Michael. *Mother-Tongue and Fatherland: Language and Politics in German.* Manchester, 1992.

Tuveson, Ernest Lee. *Redeemer Nation: The Idea of America's Millennial Role.* Chicago, 1968.

Vaillant, Janet G. *Black, French, and African: A Life of Léopold Sédar Senghor.* Cambridge, Mass., 1990.

Veer, Peter van der, and Hartmut Lehmann, eds. *Nation and Religion: Perspectives on Europe and Asia.* Princeton, 1999.

Vertovec, Steven, and Robin Cohen, eds. *Conceiving Cosmopolitanism: Theory, Context, Practice.* Oxford, 2002.

Waldstreicher, David. *In the Midst of Perpetual Fetes: The Making of American Nationalism, 1776–1820*. Chapel Hill, 1997.

Weber, Eugen. *Peasants into Frenchmen: The Modernization of Rural France, 1870–1914*. Stanford, Calif., 1976.

Weinberg, Gerhard L. *Visions of Victory: The Hopes of Eight World War II Leaders*. Cambridge, 2005.

————. *A World at Arms: A Global History of World War II*. 2nd ed. Cambridge, 2005.

Wells, Audrey. *The Political Thought of Sun Yat-Sen: Development and Impact*. Basingstoke, England, and New York, 2001.

Wiebe, Robert H. *Who We Are: A History of Popular Nationalism*. Princeton, 2002.

Wills, Garry. *Lincoln at Gettysburg: The Words That Remade America*. New York, 1992.

Winter, Jay. *Remembering War: The Great War between Memory and History in the Twentieth Century*. New Haven and London, 2006.

Wood, Gordon S. *The Radicalism of the American Revolution: How a Revolution Transformed a Monarchical Society into a Democratic One Unlike Any That Had Ever Existed*. New York, 1991.

Yuval-Davis, Nira. *Gender and Nation*. London and Thousand Oaks, Calif., 1997.

Zimmer, Oliver. *Nationalism in Europe, 1890–1940*. Basingstoke, England, and New York, 2003.

SCHOLARLY WORKS ON THE HISTORY OF NATIONALISM:
ARTICLES AND BOOK CHAPTERS

Alter, Peter. "Nationalism and Liberalism in Modern German History." In *Nationality, Patriotism and Nationalism in Liberal Democratic Societies*, edited by Roger Michener, pp. 81–106. St. Paul, Minn., 1993.

Anderson, Benedict R. "The Goodness of Nations." In *Nation and Religion: Perspectives on Europe and Asia*, edited by Peter van der Veer and Hartmut Lehmann, pp. 197–203. Princeton, 1999.

Anderson, James D. "How We Learn about Race through History." In *Learning History in America: Schools, Cultures, and Politics*, edited by Lloyd Kramer, Donald Reid, and William L. Barney, pp. 87–106. Minneapolis, 1994.

Armstrong, Nancy. "Captivity and Cultural Capital in the English Novel." In *Revolutionary Histories: Transatlantic Cultural Nationalism, 1775–1815*, edited by W. M. Verhoeven, pp. 104–21. Basingstoke, England, and New York, 2002.

Balibar, Etienne. "The Nation Form: History and Ideology." In *Becoming National*, edited by Geoff Eley and Ronald Grigor Suny, pp. 132–49. New York and Oxford, 1996.

Bell, David A. "Lingua Populi, Lingua Dei: Language, Religion, and the Origins of French Revolutionary Nationalism." *American Historical Review* 100, no. 5 (December 1995): 1403–37.

Bhabha, Homi K. "DissemiNation: Time, Narrative, and the Margins of the Modern Nation." In *Nation and Narration*, edited by Homi K. Bhabha, pp. 291–322. London, 1990.

Blom, Ida. "Gender and Nation in International Comparison." In *Gendered Nations: Nationalisms and Gender Order in the Long Nineteenth Century*, edited by Ida Blom, Karen Hagemann, and Catherine Hall, pp. 3–26. Oxford and New York, 2000.

Dinwiddy, John. "England." In *Nationalism in the Age of the French Revolution*, edited by Otto Dann and John Dinwiddy, pp. 53–70. London, 1988.

Duara, Prasenjit. "Postcolonial History." In *A Companion to Western Historical Thought*, edited by Lloyd Kramer and Sarah Maza, pp. 417–31. Oxford and Malden, Mass., 2002.

Dumont, Franz. "The Rhineland." In *Nationalism in the Age of the French Revolution*, edited by Otto Dann and John Dinwiddy, pp. 157–70. London, 1988.

Elshtain, Jean Bethke. "Sovereignty, Identity, Sacrifice." In *Reimagining the Nation*, edited by Marjorie Ringrose and Adam J. Lerner, pp. 159–75. Buckingham and Philadelphia, 1993.

Frey, Hugo, and Stefan Jordan. "National Historians and the Discourse of the Other: France and Germany." In *The Contested Nation: Ethnicity, Class, Religion and Gender in National Histories*, edited by Stefan Berger and Chris Lorenz, pp. 200–30. Basingstoke, England, and New York, 2008.

Gilroy, Paul. "One Nation under a Groove: The Cultural Politics of 'Race' and Racism in Britain." In *Becoming National*, edited by Geoff Eley and Ronald Grigor Suny, pp. 352–69. New York and Oxford, 1996.

Godechot, Jacques. "The New Concept of the Nation and its Diffusion in Europe." In *Nationalism in the Age of the French Revolution*, edited by Otto Dann and John Dinwiddy, pp. 13–26. London, 1988.

Gosewinkel, Dieter. "Citizenship in Germany and France at the Turn of the Twentieth Century: Some New Observations on an Old Comparison." In *Citizenship and National Identity in Twentieth-Century Germany*, edited by Geoff Eley and Jan Plamowski, pp. 27–39. Stanford, Calif., 2008.

Hall, Stuart. "Cultural Identity and Diaspora." In *Colonial Discourse and Post-Colonial Theory: A Reader*, edited by Patrick Williams and Laura Chrisman, pp. 392–403. New York, 1993.

———. "Ethnicity: Identity and Difference." In *Becoming National*, edited by Geoff Eley and Ronald Grigor Suny, pp. 339–49. New York and Oxford, 1996.

Harris, Ruth. "The 'Child of the Barbarian': Rape, Race and Nationalism in France during the First World War." *Past and Present* 141 (November 1993): 170–206.

Kamenka, Eugene. "Political Nationalism—the Evolution of the Idea." In *Nationalism: The Nature and Evolution of the Idea*, edited by Eugene Kamenka, pp. 2–20. New York, 1976.

Karaim, Reed. "America's Border Fence: Will It Stem the Flow of Illegal Immigrants?" In *Issues in Race, Ethnicity, Gender and Class: Selections from the CQ Researcher*, pp. 141–63. Los Angeles, 2010.

Lerner, Adam J. "The Nineteenth-Century Monument and the Embodiment of National Time." In *Reimagining the Nation*, edited by Marjorie Ringrose and Adam J. Lerner, pp. 176–96. Buckingham and Philadelphia, 1993.

Levinger, Matthew. "The Prussian Reform Movement and the Rise of Enlightened Nationalism." In *The Rise of Prussia, 1700–1830*, edited by Philip G. Dwyer, pp. 259–77. Harlow, England, 2000.

McClintock, Anne. "'No Longer in a Future Heaven': Nationalism, Gender and Race." In *Becoming National*, edited by Geoff Eley and Ronald Grigor Suny, pp. 260–84. New York and Oxford, 1996.

Offen, Karen. "Depopulation, Nationalism, and Feminism in Fin-de-Siècle France." *American Historical Review* 89, no. 3 (June 1984): 648–76.

Pfaff, William. "In Sarkoland." *New York Review of Books* 54 (14 June 2007).

Plamenatz, John. "Two Types of Nationalism." In *Nationalism: The Nature and Evolution of the Idea*, edited by Eugene Kamenka, pp. 22–36. New York, 1976.

Potter, David M. "The Historian's Use of Nationalism and Vice Versa." *American Historical Review* 67, no. 4 (July 1962): 924–50.

Salehyan, Idean. "U.S. Asylum and Refugee Policy towards Muslim Nations since 9/11." In *Immigration Policy and Security: U.S., European, and Commonwealth Perspectives*, edited by Terri E. Givens, Gary P. Preeman, and David L. Leal, pp. 52–65. New York, 2009.

Smith, Anthony D. "The Nation: Invented, Imagined, Reconstructed?" In *Reimagining the Nation*, edited by Marjorie Ringrose and Adam J. Lerner, pp. 9–28. Buckingham and Philadelphia, 1993.

Smith-Rosenberg, Carol. "Captured Subjects/Savage Others: Violently Engendering the New American." *Gender and History* 5, no. 2 (June 1993): 177–95.

Vincent, K. Steven. "National Consciousness, Nationalism, and Exclusion: Reflections on the French Case." *Historical Reflections/Réflexions Historiques* 19, no. 3 (Fall 1993): 433–49.

Williams, Louise Blakney. "Overcoming the 'Contagion of Mimicry': The Cosmopolitan Nationalism and Modernist History of Rabindranath Tagore and W. B. Yeats." *American Historical Review* 112, no. 1 (February 2007): 69–100.

USEFUL WEBSITES FOR THE STUDY OF NATIONALISM

Association for Research on Ethnicity and Nationalism in the Americas. <www.cas.sc.edu/arena/>. 1 October 2010. Website based at the University of South Carolina; it provides links to conferences and books on nationalism and sponsors H-Nationalism, a valuable scholarly Listserv for discussions of nationalism (<www.h-net.org/~national/>).

Association for the Study of Ethnicity and Nationalism (ASEN). <www.lse.ac.uk/collections/ASEN/>. 1 October 2010. Website based at the London School of Economics; it includes links to conferences and information about ASEN's important quarterly journal, *Nations and Nationalism*.

Europa: Gateway to the European Union. <http://europa.eu/index_en.htm>. 1 October 2010. English-language portal to the official website of the European Union; it provides updated information on member nations and EU history.

Internet Modern History Sourcebook: Nationalism. <www.fordham.edu/halsall/ mod/modsbook17.html>. 1 October 2010. Website based at Fordham University; it provides links to original source materials on nineteenth-century cultural and liberal nationalism.

The Nationalism Project. <www.nationalismproject.org/>. 1 October 2010. Website with the most wide-ranging links to recent scholarly work on nationalism, journal articles, information on conferences, and other materials; a reliable scholarly site for locating up-to-date materials for further research.

Stanford Encyclopedia of Philosophy: Nationalism. <http://plato.stanford.edu/ entries/nationalism/>. 1 October 2010. Website based at Stanford University; it provides a good overview of nationalist thought, useful bibliographical listings, and links to other resources on nationalism.

Index

Page numbers in italics indicate illustrations or maps

racist policies and, 165, *166*; as personal immortality, 111–12. *See also* Education

China, 167, 174, 189

Chirac, Jacques, 194, 196

Chosen People, 86–87, 100, 123, 127, 139, 192, 201; Jewish state and, 152–53

Christianity, 88–89, 92; icons and languages of, 89; millennium and, 87; missionaries and, 64; sacrifice and, 94–95, 101, 146; salvation and, 97, 99; symbols of, 90. *See also* Catholicism; God; Judeo-Christian tradition; Protestantism

Churchill, Winston, 168

Church-state alliances, 86, 112

Citizenship: family as educators in, 112–13; French new definition of, 39, 41–42, 48, 196; racist exclusions from, 119

"City on a Hill," 86, 123

Civic nationalism. *See* Political nationalism

Civil service, 188

Civil War, American, 126, 143–46

Clausewitz, Carl von, 51

Cold War, 185; end of, 22–23, 173, 189, 190, 197; nationalist conflicts and, 172

Collective national identity: American construction of, 86, 126–27, 130–31, 137, 138, 142, 191, 193, 196–97; attractions of, 15; belief in distinctive characteristics and, 16, 23, 26, 56, 200; biological conceptions of, 115–21; collision of individual rights with, 56; dangers of, 15–16; diverse cultures and, 181, 183–84, 186, 188; exceptionalism and, 121–24, 192; factors in construction of, 1–5, 57–70, 62, 73–74, 79–80, 191; Fascism and Nazism and, 164, 170; French construction of, 39–40, 42–43, 45–47, 191, 196–97; gender and, 103–15; general will and, 30, 32–33, 34, 40; Jewish state and, 151–53, 181; memory and, 73–74; mission of, 87–88; narratives of, 20–21, 57, 68–69; new historical approaches to, 16, 74–79; new nations and, 173, 176–77, 181–82; personal identity and, 10–11, 15–16, 32–33, 34, 56, 101–2, 182, 202; premodern origins of, 10, 11–12, 13; religion and, 82, 84; representative national leaders and, 76; as response to external threats, 148; twentieth-century continuance of,

148. *See also* Cultural identity; Ethnic identity; Race; Self-determination

Collège de France, 76, 79

Colley, Linda, 104

Colonies. *See* Anticolonialism; Imperialism

Common descent belief, 12

Common Market, 185, 186

Communism, 28, 160, 161

Congress of Vienna map of Europe (1815), 55

Connor, Walker, 12

Conscription, 45, 49, 149, 155, 156, 168

Conservatism, 25, 48, 49, 90; new nationalism and, 56, 162

Constitution, U.S., 90, 143–44

Continental Congress, 35–36

Cooper, James Fenimore, 70; *Leatherstocking Tales*, 69

Corsica, 184

Cosmopolitan nationalism, 182–83

Creole nationalisms, 35

Croatia, 190

Cultural identity, 1–5, 7–28, 202; alternative theories and, 11–13; anticolonial movements and, 175, 177–82; as basis of nationalism, 24, 25, 26, 34, 56, 171; components/constant reconstruction of, 16; cross-cultural borrowings and, 175, 177–78; distinctive national traits and, 68–69, 71, 171, 174, 201; early American emphasis on, 126, 129–30; essentialism vs. differences and, 182; family and gender and, 101–15, 121; French nationalism and, 40, 42; German emphasis on, 51–52, 54, 58, 60–63, 71, 74, 148–49; history and, 17–21, 27, 62, 74–75; Italian nationalism and, 148; lands and, 57–59; language and, 60–68; marginalized groups and, 151–53, 190–91; military images and, 99; minorities' autonomy and, 184; multiple identities and, 13–17; narratives of, 57, 68–69; national symbols and, 11, 17, 19, 42, 45, 46, 56, 89–95, 104, 147, 191; political components of, 26, 56, 67, 180; postcolonial nationalism and, 175–79; race and, 103, 115–21; superiority claims and, 63–64, 103, 122, 177; transnational cooperation vs., 184. *See also* Multiculturalism

Cultural studies, 2, 20–21

Czechoslovakia, 156, 167

Dante Alighieri, 90

Darwin, Charles, *The Origin of Species*, 115

Death: Gettysburg battlefield and, *145*; memorials and monuments to, 45, 56, 81, 93–94, 99, 100; as national sacrifice, 5, 95–99, 111, 135, 143, 164–65, 201, 202; twentieth-century warfare statistics, 147; World War I and, 156, 161, 167. *See also* Immortality

Death camps, 170

Declaration of Independence, American (1776), 35–36, 56, 90, 143

Declaration of the Rights of Man and Citizen, French (1789), 40–41, 48, 56

Decolonization. *See* Anticolonial movements; Postcolonial nationalism

De Gaulle, Charles, 168, 185–86

Degeneration: racial, 119–20; sexual, 113, 114

Democracy, 128, 137–38, 158, 193, 200

Derivative nationalism, 26

Dialects, 62

Diaspora, 16

Difference, influence of, 5, 21–23, 56, 80; anxiety about outsiders and, 191–92; Chosen People image and, 86; Fascism and Nazism and, 163–64; German nationalism and, 17, 52, 54, 74; imagined community and, 56, 181; national narratives and, 200; nation building and, 182; race and, 142–43, 150–51

Dissent, 32; repression of, 43

Divine guidance, 139

Divine mission. *See* Chosen People; Mission, national

Divine right, 29, 30, 32, 34, 59

Division of labor, 12–13, 110–11

Documents, national, 90–91, 100, 143–44

Dreyfus Affair, 151

DuBois, W. E. B., 153, 160; "The Conservation of the Races," 153

Dumont, Louis, 32

Eastern Europe, 24, 26, 188

Economic development, 12–13, 32; American freedoms and, 134, 135, 136, 138, 139; education and, 66; German World War I defeat and, 163, 165; global competition and, 148, 149; globalization and, 173, 182, 188; national rivalries and, 79; Soviet model of, 161; transnational cooperation and, 184, 185–86, 188. *See also* Capitalism

Education, 80, 121, 147; French Revolution influence on, 39, 64, 65; modern standardization and, 12–13; national histories and, 79; as nationalization tool, 5, 64–66, 68, 91, 112–13, 149, 151, 177, 201; women's role and, 110, 112

Elite hierarchy, 29, 30, 39, 41, 75–76, 129; American system vs., 129, 133, 134, 137

Emerson, Ralph Waldo, 68, 72–73, 104, 106; "The American Scholar," 68; "English Traits," 118

Emotional messages, 4, 5, 7, 12, 13, 200; components of, 17, 81–82; French Revolution and, 45. *See also* Sacrifice, national

Empire. *See* Imperialism

Enemies, national coherence when facing, 21, 22, 56, 151

England. *See* British nationalism

English language, 60, 118, 123, 142–43

Enlightenment ideas, 28, 30, 31–32, 116–17; conservative critiques of, 48, 49, 51, 52, 54, 56; romantic literary critique of, 69

Equality, 30, 35, 40–42; American claims of, 128, 129, 133, 134, 137, 142; French and American distinctions and, 41–42, 46, 54, 56

Ethnic cleansing, 15–16, 24, 190

Ethnic identity, 2, 5, 11–12, 13, 101, 147, 199, 201; Balkans and, 149, 154, 156, 158, 189–90; conflicts and violence and, 11, 15–16, 21, 190; critics of, 183, 188; minorities and, 21–22, 148; as nationalism basis, 24, 25, 26, 56; new nation rivalries and, 182; postcolonial cultural hybridity and, 178; self-determination and, 148–49, 156, 158, 161, 167; transnational cooperation vs., 184. *See also* Multiculturalism

Ethnohistory, 11–13, 20; recent cultural/multicultural approach and, 16–17

Euro (currency), 186

Eurocentrism, 35

Europe: American cultural break from, 68, 126, 127, 128, 130; balance of power and, 151; hostility toward immigrants in, 190–91; international alliances and, 150; map of states after Congress of Vienna, 55; map

of states in 1914, *152*; map of states after
1918, *159*; multiculturalism and, 173, 184,
188–89; Protestant national churches and,
86; transnational cooperation and, 4, 5,
184, 185, 188–90, 197. *See also* Napoleonic
wars and empire; New World–Old World
dichotomy; World War I; World War II
European Coal and Steel Community, 185
European nationalism, 2–3, 27, 28; adverse
consequences of, 147; American similarities with, 3–4, 5, 8, 10–11, 28, 35, 38, 124,
143, 193, 199; political sovereignty and,
31–32; post-1945 changes in, 184–89;
themes of, 31–32, 56. *See also* British
nationalism; French nationalism; German nationalism; Italian nationalism
European Union, 4, 5, 184, 185, 188, 189, 197
European University Institute, 186
Exceptionalism, 121–24, 192. *See also*
American exceptionalism

Family, 3, 101–15, 147; biological/cultural
reproductive role of, 111–13, 201; concept
of nation as, 2, 99, 103, 106–7, 108, 110,
121, 125, 201; gendered division of labor
and, 110–11; Nazi ideal of, *166*; sacrifice
for nation by, 99, 140; virtuous traits of,
14, 113, 201–2; womanhood-nationhood
linkage and, 104, 108
Fanon, Frantz, 179–80; *The Wretched of the
Earth*, 179, 180
Fascism, 163–64, 167
Fatherland, 58, 84–85, 86, 99, 103
Ferdinand II, king of Spain, 21
Festivals. *See* Celebrations and holidays
Fichte, Johann Gottlieb, 7–8, 17, 68, 72,
80, 123, 148, 179, 188; *Addresses to the
German Nation*, 7–8, 28, 52, 58–59, 65,
96–97, 116; German history studies
and, 74–75; German philosophy and,
71, 74–75; on immortality of deceased
patriots, 96–97; on immortality through
bearing children, 111–12; land and,
58–59; language and, 60, 61, 62, 63,
71, 116; on Luther, 92; on resistance to
Napoleon, 74–75, 122, 168, 178, 179–80;
on significance of writers, 67, 180
Flags, 81–82, 89–90, *91*, 99, 100, 196; des-
ecrations of, 81–82, 90; symbolism of, 90

Flint, Timothy, 130
Forgetting and national history, 73–74
Founding Fathers, 73, 92, 103, 132, 133, 137
Fourteen Points (Wilson), 156, 158, 184
Fourth of July celebrations, 38, 90, 190
France. *See* French nationalism; French
Revolution; Napoleonic wars and empire
Franco-Prussian War, 148
Franklin, Benjamin, 133
Franz Ferdinand, archduke of Austria, 154
"Fraternity," 46, 48
Frederick II, king of Prussia, 76
Freedom, 138–41, 146, 192–94
French Enlightenment. *See* Enlightenment
ideas
French Indochina. *See* Vietnam
French language, 40, 45, 60; German cri-
tique of, 61, 62; republican standardiza-
tion of, 62–63, 64
French nationalism, 24, 25; anticolonial
nationalism and, 159–60, 179–80; belief
in distinctive culture of, 40, 42; continuance of themes of, 194, 196; cultural
minorities and, 184; Declaration of the
Rights of Man and Citizen and, 40–41,
48, 56; declining birth rate and, 113–14;
education reforms and, 39, 64–66;
exceptionalism and, 122–23, 192; family
roles and, 103, 110–11; flag symbolism
and, 90, *91*, 196; gendered symbol of, 45,
104, *105*, 108; German historical enmity
and, 52, 54, 69, 122, 123, 148–49, 154–55,
184; German post-1945 collaboration
with, 184–86, *187*, 188; historians and,
76–79; hostility toward immigrants and,
190, 191, 194, 196; human rights distinctions and, 41–42, 54, 56; language and,
40, 45, 60–64, 66; literature and, 70, 90;
memorial monuments and, 94, *162*, 186;
military sacrifice and, 7–8, *98*; mission
of, 194, 196; national anthem and, 8, *27*,
28, 46, 99, 196; old regime and, 21, 26,
34, 39–41, 56, 62; political emphasis of,
191; racist theory and, 116, 119–21; World
War I and, 150, 154, 156, 161, *162*; World
War II and, 167–68. *See also* Michelet,
Jules; Napoleonic wars and empire
French Revolution, 39–56, 168, 202; American nationalists and, 38–39; calendar

and, 42; critiques of, 48–52, 54, 56, 62, 117, 119; "de-Christianization" and, 100; democratic themes of, 158; emergence of nationalism and, 5, 19, 28, 29–30, 34, 39–40, 196, 197; festivals of, 45, 46, 47; as imagined utopian community, 77; language standardization and, 62–63, 64, 66; Marianne symbol of, 45, 104, *105*, 108; national identity and, 76–77; nationalist political legacy of, 54, 56, 196, 200–201; new rituals and symbols of, 42–43, 45, 46; political significance of, 25, 26, 32–33, 45

French revolutionary wars, 7–8, 42–43, 48, 49, 52, 100, 104, 128. *See also* Napoleonic wars and empire

Freneau, Philip, 36, 38–39, 126, 131–36, 143; background and early career of, 131–32; eulogy for Washington of, 132–34; on Native American displacement, 135–36; prediction of 1940 life in New York by, 136; on superiority of American institutions, 134–36; works of, 131

Gandhi, Mohandas, 174–76, 179
Gelber, Harry, 172
Gellner, Ernest, 12–13
Gender, 3, 101–15, 151, 154, 182; family and, 108, 110–11; inequalities and, 40, 41, 46, 56, 110, 151; nationalist stereotypes of, 103–4, 107–8, 110, 121, 124, 125; national symbols and, 45, 99, 104, *105*, 108, *109*, 154, 197; Nazi racist policy and, 165, *166*. *See also* Manliness; Women
General will, 30, 32–33, 34, 40
Genocide, 116, 170
Gentz, Friedrich von, 51–52
Georgin, François, *Napoleon at Arcis-sur-Aube*, 22
Germania (symbol), 104, 108, *109*
German nationalism, 7–8, 24, 25, 34; critics of, 69; critique of French Revolution and, 48, 51–52, 54, 62; as cultural/ethnic, 26, 51–52, 54, 58, 60–63, 71, 74, 148–49; cultural superiority claims of, 63; education and, 65; empire of, 148, 149, 150, 154; exceptionalism and, 122; female symbol of, 104, 108, *109*; flag symbolism and, 90; French enmity and, 58, 61, 122, 123, 149,

154, 184; French post-1946 collaboration and, 184–86, *187*, 188; historians and, 74–76, 79; hostility toward immigrants and, 190; immortality of deceased patriots and, 96–97; influence after 1870 of, 148–49; linguistic identity and, 54, 58, 60–62, 70, 74, 116; memorial monument and, 94; military immortality and, 96–97, 100; Napoleonic expansion and, 74–75, 122, 168, 177, 178; Nazism and, 24, 116, 119, 163, 164–68, 170; philosophy and, 71, 74–75; political unification and, 148; racist theory and, 116, 165, *166*, 167; religion and, 86, 89, 92, 112; romanticism and, 69, 71–73, 74; sanctified texts and, 90–91; Versailles Treaty and, 158–59; World War I and, 150, 154–56, 165–66; World War I defeat effects on, 158, 173–74; World War II and, 167–68, *169*. *See also* Fichte, Johann Gottlieb

Gettysburg Address (1863), 143, 144–46, 194; text of, 144, 146
Ghana, 181
Global competition, 148, 149
Globalization, 173, 182, 188
Gobineau, Arthur de, 104, 119–21, 124, 150, 165, 184; *Essay on the Inequality of the Human Races*, 119–21
God, 82–85, 88, 93, 100; divine guidance by, 139; fusion with country of, 82, 85, 89; national metaphors and, 85; transcendence of, 83–84. *See also* Chosen People
Goethe, Johann Wolfgang von, 51
Görres, Joseph, 52, 54
Government. *See* Political nationalism; Sovereign rights
Great Britain. *See* British nationalism
Great War. *See* World War I
Greenfeld, Liah, 10, 14–15
Grégoire, Abbé Baptiste Henri, 63, 64
Grenadier on Elba Island (Vernet), *98*
Grimm, Jacob, 70
Grosby, Steven, 12, 13

Hale, Nathan, 7, 8, *9*, 17, 28
Hall, Stuart, 16
Hayes, Carlton J. H., 82–83, 89–90; "Nationalism as a Religion," 82–83
Hazlitt, William, 70

Hegel, Georg Wilhelm Friedrich, 51

Hercules, 45

Herder, Johann Gottfried von, 51, 52, 58, 59; language theory and, 60–61; philosophy and, 74; *Reflections on the Philosophy of the History of Mankind*, 58

Heretics, national traitors as, 92–93

Heroes, 58, 62, 69–70, 73, 91, 92–94, 103, 125, 131–33, 135, 137; monuments and memorials to, 93–94, 100, 161, *162*

Herzl, Theodor, 151–52, 160; *The Jewish State*, 152

Hinduism, 201

Historicism, 74, 75

History, 16, 74–79, 80, 99, 125, 201; Bancroft narrative of American past and, 126, 136–43; Chosen People motif and, 86–87; cultural identity and, 17–21, 27, 62, 74–75; divine guidance of, 139; historians and, 75–79; memory and forgetting and, 5, 73–74, 97; modern nationalism and, 2, 3, 9–10, 11, 17–21, 56, 74, 75; national exceptionalism belief and, 122; nationalist rewriting of, 21; premodern nationalist thought and, 10, 11–12; religion and, 82–83; transitions in, 17–18; unique eras theory of, 74, 75

Hitler, Adolf, 163; *Mein Kampf*, 165, 167

Hobsbawm, Eric, *The Invention of Tradition*, 19–20, 21

Ho Chi Minh, 159–60, 173, 174, 179

Holidays. *See* Celebrations and holidays

Holocaust, 170

Homelands. *See* Lands and boundaries

Homosexuality, 113

Human rights, 1, 2, 24, 25, 30–34, 38–42, 146, 197; anticolonial nationalism and, 159–60; distinctions in, 41–42, 54, 56; eighteenth-century revolutions and, 54, 56; Enlightenment and, 31–32, 49; Napoleonic France and, 48; nationalism and, 32–34, 39, 42, 44, 45, 51, 56, 201; repression for national interest of, 170; wartime protection of, 170

Humboldt, Wilhelm von, 51

Hungary, 149, 156

Hunt, Lynn, 40

Hybridity. *See* Multiculturalism

"Hymn to Liberty" (anthem), 46

Identities: biological conceptions of, 115–21; multiplicity of, 13–17; nationalist movements and, 151–54, 175–76; as relational, 21–23. *See also* Collective national identity; Cultural identity; Personal identity; Race

Identity crisis, 14–15

Imagined community, 56, 181

Immigrants, 26, 130, 139, 173, 193; "melting pot" concept and, 183; nationalist hostility toward, 148, 190–91, 194, 196; race and culture and, 142, 143

Immortality: from bearing children, 111–12, 201; from national sacrifice, 95–97, 99–101, 135, 140, 161

Imperialism, 29, 34, 35, 48, 147; America and, 123, 124; Britain and, 34, 153, 173–74, 175; collapse of, 173, 197; cultural critique of, 178–80, 182–83; France and, 48, 58, 149, 159–60, 167, 173–74, 179–80; Germany and, 148, 149, 150, 154; global competition and, 149–51; racist theories and, 123; self-determination and, 148–49, 173–74; World War I effects on, 159–61, 173–74. *See also* Anticolonial nationalism; Napoleonic wars and empire

Independence movements, 57, 79, 171; documents of, 35–36, 40–41, 48, 56, 90; India and, 174–76. *See also* American Revolution; Anticolonial nationalism; Self-determination

India, 174–76, 181, 183, 188

Individual identity. *See* Personal identity

Individualism, 32–34, 68; Fascist discounting of, 164

Individual rights. *See* Human rights

Industrialization, 12–13, 151

Integral nationalism, 24

Intellectuals, 15, 51, 201; anti-Western imperialism and, 174, 179–80; Enlightenment critique and, 51, 52, 56; French Revolution and, 48; German nationalism and, 52, 54, 69. *See also* Narrative, national; Writing

Internationalism. *See* Transnational cooperation

Iran, 82

Iraq war, 193

Martyrs, 7, 8, 45, 91, 140

Marx, Anthony W., 21

Marxism, 160

Mass media, 66, 147, 163, 201

Mazzini, Giuseppe, 80, 97, 124, 148, 179; *The Duties of Man*, 59, 65; national family concept of, 106–7, 111, 113; religious nationalism of, 85, 87–88, 89, 93

Medieval woman image, 108, *109*

Meinecke, Friedrich, 116

Melville, Herman, *White-Jacket*, 127

Memorials and monuments, 45, 56, 81, 93–94, 99, 100, 149; Bancroft oration and, 143; Gettysburg Address and, 143, 144–46, 194; international reconciliation rituals and, 186; September 11 terrorist attacks and, 193; World War I and, 161, *162*

Memory, 3, 5, 16, 73, 96; immortality of deceased patriots and, 97; political use of, 191; selective forgetting and, 73–74; violence and, 190

Merkel, Angela, 186

Messianic mission, 78–79, 86–87, 88–89, 94–95, 201

Metternich, Prince, 90

Mexican immigrants, 190, 191

Michelet, Jules, 76–78, 80, 84–85, 153–54, 201; on family and reproduction, 112, 113–14; French exceptionalism and, 122–23, 192; nationalist gender stereotypes and, 110; *The People*, 77–78, 84, 110, 123

Mickiewicz, Adam, 63–64, 71–72, 79, 80, 124, 153–54, 179, 192; on "Eastern" vs. "Western" nations, 176–77; on family-nation connection, 108, 110, 112; messianic nationalism of, 86–87, 88–89; self-determination and, 149

Middle-class mores, 107

Middle East, 147, 149; immigrants from, 190; League of Nations mandates in, 173–74, 182; nationalism and, 153, 171, 200; Palestine and, 152, 181–82

Military occupations, 148

Military service. *See* Conscription; Sacrifice, national; Warfare

Millennialism, 87

Minorities, 148; autonomy and, 184; persecution of, 15–16, 21–22, 24, 190, 191. *See also* Immigrants

Mission, national, 123–28, 130, 139–40, 172; American leaders and, 193–94; decolonization and, 174, 175, 177; French republicanism and, 194, 196; as messianic, 78–79, 86–87, 88–89, 94–95, 201; as unique, 4, 200

Mitterrand, François, 186, *187*

Modernity, nationalism linked with, 9–15, 18–19, 34, 56, 83–84

Molière (Jean Baptiste Poquelin), 70, 90

Monarchy, 40, 45, 59, 96; American values vs., 128; French restoration of, 90; people's sovereignty vs., 29, 30, 32, 34, 40, 42, 56; Prussian leadership and, 76

Montesquieu, Charles de, 30

Moors, 21

Morality, 14, 100, 101, 107, 201; American new society and, 127, 128; decline in, 93, 113, 114; Gandhi's nationalism and 175; women as guardians of, 110

Mosse, George, 107–8

Mother country, 99, 103

Motherhood, 110, 111, 201; Nazi cult of, 165, *166*

Mother tongue, 103

Mount Vernon, 94

Multiculturalism, 4, 5, 15–17, 147–48, 173, 182–98, 197, 200; American model for, 183–84, 189, 193; cultural borrowing and, 175, 177–78; late twentieth-century Europe and, 186, 188; new nations and, 181, 184; reactions against, 189–98

Muslims. *See* Islam

Mussolini, Benito, 163, 164

Napoleon Bonaparte, 48, *50*, 117, 167, 179; tomb of, 94, *95*

Napoleonic Code, 103

Napoleonic wars and empire, 7–8, 22, 49, 52, *67*, 100, 104, 128, 151, 197; impact on German nationalism of, 61, 74–75, 89, 92, 122, 123, 168, 178; map of Europe, *53*; military defeat and, 54, 90; resistance to, 74–75, 122, 168, 172, 177, 178, 179–80; World War II compared with, 168, 170

Narratives, national, 11, 16, 17, 20–21, 28, 57, 68–69, 80, 149; American identity development and, 36–39, 68, 126, 130–36, 194; Britain and, 49; components of, 200;

documents and, 90–91, 100, 143–44;
French Revolution and, 44–46; on gender and family, 101–15; German "blood"
and, 164; memory and resentments
and, 190; military casualties and, 161;
nineteenth-century romanticism and, 62;
physical displays of, 56; religious history
and, 87–88, 93, 140; sacrifice and, 97. *See
also* History; Writing

National anthems, 7–8, 27, 28, 46, 90, 99

National Assembly (France), 40, 41, 43

National coherence, 15, 21

National Front (France), 194, 196

National Gazette (Philadelphia newspaper),
131

National identity. *See* Collective national
identity

Nationalism: appeal of, 2; basic themes of,
5, 125, 182; central assumption of, 10–11;
changing contexts of, 28; characteristic
political patterns of, 34–35; coining
of term, 30, 39; comparisons and, 25;
contemporary challenges to, 4, 5, 15–17;
continuities/similarities in, 3, 5, 198,
199–201; contrasting models of, 24–25;
dynamic continuance of, 197–98; emergence of, 5, 9–13, 27, 83–84; emotional
attraction of, 13, 81–82; evolutions in,
200; identity and, 14–15, 21–23, 56;
influential works on history of, 18–21;
legacy of, 172; liberal vs. conservative
distinctions and, 56; modernizing effect
of, 9–15, 18–19, 34, 56, 83–84; patriotism vs., 11; premodern heritage of, 20;
radicalization of, 170; recurring themes
of, 56, 200; religious themes and, 82–101;
transatlantic similarities and, 3–4, 5,
8, 10–11, 28, 35, 38, 124, 143, 193, 199;
varieties of, 23–28. *See also* Collective
national identity; Cultural identity;
Political nationalism; Race; Racist theories; *specific countries*

Nationalism, long nineteenth-century
(1789–1914), 2–3, 48–52, 101–24; American nationalism and, 125–46; cultural
identity emphasis of, 61–62; economic
development and, 12–13; emergence
from late eighteenth-century revolutions of, 5; European boundaries and, 55

(map); family and, 101–15, 103; gender
and, 104–15; historical importance
of, 27; historical studies and, 74–76;
land and, 57–59; language and, 60–68;
national exceptionalism and, 121–24;
optimism of, 121, 136; race and, 103,
114–21; religious components of, 83–101,
127; romanticism and, 57–58, 69, 71–73,
74, 158, 178; sexual morality and, 107;
twentieth-century replications of, 27, 151,
153, 156, 173, 174, 179–80, 197

Nationalism, twentieth-century (1870–
1945), 3–5, 11, 147–71; basic nationalist
themes and, 56, 125, 147, 151, 179–80;
continued influence of, 5; emotional
messages of, 4; factors in reformulation
and expansion of, 160–61; Fascism and
Nazism and, 163–68; national identity
movements and, 151–54; period prior to
World War I and, 148–54; racist theories
and, 115–21, 150, 165, 184; self-determination and, 148–63. *See also* World War I;
World War II

Nationalism, twentieth-century (post-
1945), 172–98; decolonization and,
173–82; multicultural diversity and,
147–48, 182–84, 200; post–Cold War
resurgence of, 189–98; repetition of
nationalist themes and, 191–94, 196,
197; transnational cooperation and, 148,
184–92, 200

National movements: vulnerable social
groups and, 151–54

National sovereignty. *See* Sovereign rights

Nation-state, 10; Anderson definition of, 19,
21; consolidation of, 21–22; Fascist pri-
macy of, 163, 164; internal consolidation
of, 149; language distinction and, 60–68;
modern belief in, 54, 85, 147–71; "old"
and "new" distinction, 26, 176; open vs.
closed, 24; polarities and, 21, 22, 24. *See
also* New nations

Native Americans, 54; land and, 58, 126,
129–30, 135–36, 138–39, 153; racist view
of, 115, 118–19, 126, 138, 142, 143

NATO, 190

Natural rights, 30, 32, 45, 49. *See also*
Human rights

Nature, 57–58

Nazism, 24, 163, 164–68; racist nationalism and, 116, 119, 165, 166, *167*, 170, 200; reaction against, 182. *See also* World War II

Negritude concept, 179

Nehru, Jawaharlal, 176

Neufchâteau, François de, "Hymn to Liberty," 46

New nations, 26, 173, 176–78, 180–82, 189–98, 200; cultural borrowing and, 175, 177–78, 184; ethnic rivalries and, 182; map of (1945–75), *181*

Newspapers, 66, 79, 80, 149, 151, 201; Freneau and, 131

New World–Old World dichotomy, 68, 126, 127, 128; Bancroft's view of, 137, 138–39; Freneau's view of, 133–35

Nigeria, 181

Nobility, 39, 41

Normans, 117

North Africa, 156, 190, 194

Novels, 69–70, 79, 127

Obama, Barack, 193–94, *195*

Old regimes, 21, 26, 34–35, 39–41, 56, 62, 176

Oral tradition, 11

Oratory, 90, 91

O'Sullivan, John, 127, 129, 130

O'Sullivan, Timothy H., *Incidents of the War, 145*

Other, unifying influence of, 21–23, 56, 163

Ottoman Empire, 149, 150, 153, 155, 156, 158, 179; breakup of, 173–74

Paine, Thomas, 38, 39, 194; *Common Sense,* 36–37; *Rights of Man,* 48

Pakistan, 181

Palestine, 152, 181–82

Palestinians, 181

Parades, 99

Patriotism, 39; nationalism vs., 11

Pearl Harbor attack (1941), 192, 193

"People," the: as Freneau's national heroes, 135; historians of, 76–78, 137; idealized family and, 110–11; national writing about, 69, 76, 77–78, 110, 123; sovereignty of, 25–26, 29, 30–31, 137, 138, 201–23

Personal identity, 2, 4, 7, 13–16, 19, 32–33, 34, 101–2, 182, 202; general will and, 30; multiple identities and, 13–14, 17;

national ideal as component of, 8, 10–11; national soul and, 84

Philippines, 123, 124, 181

Philology, 70, 79

Philosophy, 70–71, 73, 74–75, 76, 79, 80

Pietism, 86

Pilgrimages, 94

Pils, Isidore, *Rouget de Lisle Singing "La Marseillaise," 27*

Poetry, 46, 70, 71–73, 76, 79, 80, 91; Freneau and, 38–39, 126, 131–36

Polish nationalism, 63–64, 71–72, 79, 192; family superiority and, 108, 110, 112; flag and, *91*; messianic claims and, 86–87, 88–89; self-determination and, 149, 156, 158; World War II and, 167. *See also* Mickiewicz, Adam

Political nationalism, 2, 4, 5, 10, 19, 24, 25, 29–56, 188, 190, 199, 200; American early emphasis on, 126, 128, 129, 131–32, 134, 137–38, 141–42, 191; canonical works of, 90–91; cultural components of, 26, 56, 67, 180; elites and, 75–76; French and American inequalities and, 41–42, 48; narratives and, 57; racist nationalism vs., 116; religion and, 86; superiority claims and, 122; themes of eighteenth-century revolutions and, 30, 35–36, 40, 45, 54; twentieth century and, 147, 151

Popular sovereignty. *See* Sovereign rights

Postcolonial nationalism, 4, 25, 173–82, 200; cultural hybridity and, 175, 177–78, 184; Gandhi's moral aims and, 175; major challenges to, 182; map of new nations, *181*; population of new nations, 180–81; transnational collaboration and, 180

Poststructuralist theories, 20

Potter, David, 14

Premodern discourses, 10, 11–12, 13, 20

Progress, 40, 127

Propaganda, 81, *157*, 161; Nazi, 116, *166*

Protestantism, 21, 29, 82, 92, 94, 183; American nationalism and, 82, 86, 94, 127, 139; Chosen People theme and, 86; Germany and, 86, 89, 92, 112; sublimated sexuality and, 107

Protestant Reformation, 32

Prussia, 43, 51, 76. *See also* German nationalism

Publishing industry, 19, 40, 66; national identity and, 68, 69–70, 79–80, 131. *See also* Newspapers; Writing

Puritanism, 86, 127, 139

Qaeda, Al-, 191

Race, 3, 12, 101, 103, 147, 183; American nationalism and, 32, 41, 54, 58, 115, 117–19, 123, 126, 129–30, 142–43, 153–54; biological meaning of, 102, 103, 115–21, 124; gender traits and, 104; integral nationalism and, 24, 56, 101, 150–51; multicultural themes and, 178; scapegoating and, 21, 165, 167, 170. *See also* Ethnic identity

Racine, Jean, 90

Racist theories, 25, 26, 27, 114–21; Bancroft and, 118–19, 142–43; discrediting of, 182, 184, 200; genocide and, 116, 170; as imperial rationale, 123; inherent traits and hierarchies and, 115, 117, 118, 120, 122, 165; mixed-race fears and, 114–15, 119–20, 165; as nationhood basis, 150–51, 201; Nazi racial purity ideology and, 164–68

Radical Reconstruction, 143

Ramsey, David, 36, 38; "Oration on American Independence," 37

Ranger, Terence, 19–20

Ranke, Leopold von, 75–76

Realpolitik, 151

Réattu, Jacques, *The Triumph of Liberty*, 33

Regionalism, 184

Religion, 3, 4, 5, 11, 14, 32, 34, 82–101, 122, 182; American nationalism and, 126–27, 128, 130–31, 139–42, 192; Chosen People theme and, 86–87, 122, 123, 124, 130, 139, 201; collective nationalism and, 15, 28, 46, 79, 82–101, 183, 190, 201; French secularism and, 45, 100, 196; nationalist fusion with, 99–101, 111, 125, 154; national symbol analogues with, 89–95; persecution of minorities and, 21–22, 190, 191. *See also specific religions*

Renan, Ernest, 73, 74, 148–49, 150, 189

Repression, 15–16, 170

Republicanism, 38, 42, 45, 52, 133–35, 194, 196; French "virtues" of, 40

Respectability, 107

Resurrection images, 96, 97

Revolutions, age of (1775–1850), 5, 19, 25, 26, 199; conservative reaction against, 56; key political themes of, 54–56, 191; nationalism and, 28, 29–30, 32, 33, 34, 39, 44–45; religion and, 82. *See also* American Revolution; French Revolution

Rhineland, 52, 167

Rights, 30, 45, 49, 58; conflicts between individual and national, 32–34; linkage of national with individual, 1–2; self-determination and, 161. *See also* Human rights; Sovereign rights

Romantic nationalism, 28, 57–58, 62, 151, 197; divine power and, 85; themes of, 69, 71–73, 74, 158, 178

Rome, ancient, 75, 85, 88

Roosevelt, Franklin, 168, 192, 193, 194

Rosenberg, Alfred, 164, 165; *The Myth of the Twentieth Century*, 164

Rouget de Lisle, Claude Joseph, 7–8, 17; "La Marseillaise," 8, 27, 28, 46, 99

Rousseau, Jean-Jacques, 34, 49; *The Social Contract*, 30, 31, 32–33, 45

Russia, 72, 114, 150, 189; World War I and, 154, 155, 156, 158. *See also* Soviet Union

Russian Revolution (1917), 158, 160–61

Sacrifice, national, 4, 5, 7, 8, 14, 45, 74, 81, 91, 94–99, 111, 143, 192; as Fascist and Nazi theme, 164–65; Gettysburg Address on, 145–46; messianic mission and, 78–79, 86–87, 88–89, 94–95, 201; nationalistic wars and, 44, 94, 96–97, 135, 140, 156, 161, 162–63, 202; theological justification for, 94, 99, 100, 101; World War II and, 168

Sacrilege, 90

Sahlins, Peter, 21

Sainte-Beuve, Charles Augustin, 70

Salt March (India), 176

Salvation, national, 83–89, 84, 88, 97, 99, 123

Sarkozy, Nikolas, 186, 196

Saxons, 117, 118, 183. *See also* Anglo-Saxons

Scapegoating, 21, 165, 167, 170

Schliermacher, Friedrich, 86

Scholarship, 70, 75

Schuman, Robert, 185

Scotland, 184

Uncle Sam (symbol), 104
Uniforms, 99
United Nations, 4, 170
United States. *See* American nationalism
United States Magazine and Democratic Review, 127
Unknown soldiers, tombs of, 161, *162*
Urbanization, 114

Veit, Philipp, *Germania*, *109*
Verdun commemoration (1984), 186, *187*
Vernet, Horace, *Grenadier on Elba Island*, *98*
Versailles Treaty (1919), 158, 159–61, 167
Vietnam, 159–60, 181
Violence, 15–16, 26, 27, 28, 197; of French Terror, 46, 48; of 1990s Balkan conflicts, 190; of twentieth-century total wars, 170, 171, 172
Virgin Mary, 45
Volk, 52
Volksgeist, 74
Voltaire, 30, 49, 90

Wales, 184
Walhalla (Germany), 94
Warfare: alliance system and, 150; conflicting national interests and, 27, 147, 150; conscription and, 45, 49, 149, 155, 156, 168; contemporary changes in, 197; Gettysburg Address themes and, 144–46; individual sacrifice and, 7–8, 14, 81, 95–101, 135, 140, 161; international arms race and, 149; memorials to, 93–94, 111, 161, *162*, 186, *187*; modern costs of, 171; as modern crusades, 96; national centralization and, 155–56; nationalist cultural images and, 99; nationalist justifications for, 5, 43–44, 79, 97, 99, 147, 190, 192, 193–94, 202; racist beliefs and, 114–15, 120, 151; transnational prevention of, 185, 186, 188; twentieth-century death statistics and, 147; twentieth-century violence and, 170, 171, 172; violation of women and, 114–15. *See also* Revolutions, age of; Total wars; *specific wars*

War of 1812, 128, 129
Washington, George, 92, 94, *132*, 136, *141*; adulation of, 131–33, 137; as symbol, 45
"What Is the Third Estate?" (Sieyès), 41, 42
Wilhelm I, emperor of Germany, 148
Wilson, Woodrow, 158–61, 167, 173, 174, 192, 193; Fourteen Points, 156, 158, 184
Women: national duties of, 107–8, 110, 111, 112; as national symbols, 45, 104, *105*, 108, *109*, 154; political exclusion of, 41, 46, 56; racial nationalism and, 114–15, 165, *166*; reproductive role of, 110, 111, 165, *166*, 201; symbolism of, 108, *109*; wartime violation of, 114–15
World War I, 4, 27, 82, 148, 151, 154–62, 170, 197, 202; alliances and, 150, 154; casualties of, 156, 161; catalyst for, 154–55, 190; contributing factors to, 151; French-German national hatreds and, 123, 154–55; German defeat and, 163, 164, 165–66; memorials and, 161, *162*, 186, *187*; nationalist identity movements and, 151–54; results of, 150, 151–53, 158, 159–61, 167; Wilson's Fourteen Points and, 156, 158, 184. *See also* Self-determination
World War II, 4, 27, 148, 167–71, 197, 202; nationalist themes and, 167–68, 192, 193
Writing, 11, 32, 46, 57, 66–67; American captivity narratives and, 115; American nationalism and, 36–39, 126, 127, 131–36; colonial alienation and, 179–80; national identity formation and, 18–21, 61–64, 67, 68–73, 79–80, 131, 180, 201; political identity and, 29, 36–40; romanticism and, 69; sanctified texts and, 90–93. *See also* Narratives, national

Yeats, W. B., 183
Yorktown, battle of (1782), 38
Yugoslavia, 189

Zeitgeist, 74
Zionism, 151–53, 181